# Ultimate Bitbucket for Automating Workflows

*Master Git, Automate Git Workflows, Secure Code Quality, and Supercharge CI/CD with Bitbucket Cloud and Smart Custom App Extensibility*

**Orange Editorial Board**



www.orangeava.com

**First Published:** June 2025

**Published By:** Orange Education Pvt Ltd, AVA®

**Address:** 9, Daryaganj, Delhi, 110002, India

275 New North Road Islington Suite 1314 London,
N1 7AA, United Kingdom

**ISBN (PBK):** 978-93-49887-69-5
**ISBN (E-BOOK):** 978-93-49887-42-8

**Scan the QR code to explore our entire catalogue**

www.orangeava.com

# Technical Review Partner

**Thinknyx® Technologies** is a team of professionals with years of experience in IT technology. Their expertise spans software development, IT infrastructure management, cloud solutions, automation, container management, web and app development, security, and professional services. Recognized as a reputable brand, Thinknyx® Technologies provides IT consulting and comprehensive training in both information technology and soft skills. Additionally, they offer talent acquisition and recruitment solutions to diverse organizations worldwide.

**Mr. Kulbhushan Mayer**, the Co-Founder of Thinknyx® Technologies, is a certified expert in DevOps, SRE, Cloud, and Containerisation, with over 17 years of IT experience. He has expertise in technologies such as Public/Private Cloud, Containers, Automation tools, Continuous Integration/Deployment/Delivery tools, Monitoring and Logging tools, and more. Mr. Mayer is passionate about sharing his technical expertise with a global audience through various forums, conferences, webinars, blogs, and LinkedIn. Furthermore, he has reviewed multiple books on Automation, DevOps, and DevTools, for different vendors.

# Preface

*Ultimate Bitbucket for Automating Workflows* is a comprehensive guide designed to take you from the fundamentals of Git to advanced automation workflows using Bitbucket Cloud. In today's fast-paced digital world, automation is not just a convenience but a necessity. This book is structured into ten chapters covering a wide range of topics:

**Chapter 1** introduces the core principles of Git, detailing its origins, key concepts, and why it is indispensable in modern development.

**Chapter 2** delves into Bitbucket Cloud, guiding you through account setup, workspace management, and understanding various subscription plans.

**Chapter 3** explains the pull request workflow–from creation and review to merging–ensuring efficient collaboration.

**Chapter 4** covers Bitbucket administration and Jira integration, streamlining repository management and cross-team communication.

**Chapter 5** highlights advanced code review features to uphold code quality and security.

**Chapter 6** explores Bitbucket Pipelines and CI/CD integration, automating builds, tests, and deployments.

**Chapter 7** discusses deployment strategies and self-hosted runners for flexible pipeline management.

**Chapter 8** focuses on code quality, security, and integrating third-party tools to enhance development workflows.

**Chapter 9** provides an overview of Bitbucket Cloud APIs for automation and integration.

**Chapter 10** examines the integration of Atlassian Forge for extending and customizing Bitbucket functionalities.

This book is intended for both newcomers who need a solid foundation and experienced professionals aiming to optimize their development workflows. Each chapter builds on the previous ones, offering practical examples and real-world scenarios to empower you to master automation in the software development lifecycle.

# Downloading the code bundles and colored images

Please follow the links or scan the QR codes to download the
***Code Bundles and Images*** of the book:

**https://github.com/ava-orange-education/Ultimate-Bitbucket-for-Automating-Workflows**

The code bundles and images of the book are also hosted on
***https://rebrand.ly/b6623b***

In case there's an update to the code, it will be updated on the existing GitHub repository.

# Errata

We take immense pride in our work at **Orange Education Pvt Ltd,** and follow best practices to ensure the accuracy of our content to provide an indulging reading experience to our subscribers. Our readers are our mirrors, and we use their inputs to reflect and improve upon human errors, if any, that may have occurred during the publishing processes involved. To let us maintain the quality and help us reach out to any readers who might be having difficulties due to any unforeseen errors, please write to us at :

**errata@orangeava.com**

Your support, suggestions, and feedback are highly appreciated.

## DID YOU KNOW

Did you know that Orange Education Pvt Ltd offers eBook versions of every book published, with PDF and ePub files available? You can upgrade to the eBook version at **www.orangeava.com** and as a print book customer, you are entitled to a discount on the eBook copy. Get in touch with us at: **info@orangeava.com** for more details.

At **www.orangeava.com**, you can also read a collection of free technical articles, sign up for a range of free newsletters, and receive exclusive discounts and offers on Print Books and eBooks.

## PIRACY

If you come across any illegal copies of our works in any form on the internet, we would be grateful if you would provide us with the location address or website name. Please contact us at **info@orangeava.com** with a link to the material.

## ARE YOU INTERESTED IN AUTHORING WITH US?

If there is a topic that you have expertise in, and you are interested in either writing or contributing to a book, please write to us at **business@orangeava.com**. We are on a journey to help developers and tech professionals to gain insights on the present technological advancements and innovations happening across the globe and build a community that believes Knowledge is best acquired by sharing and learning with others. Please reach out to us to learn what our audience demands and how you can be part of this educational reform. We also welcome ideas from tech experts and help them build learning and development content for their domains.

## REVIEWS

Please leave a review. Once you have read and used this book, why not leave a review on the site that you purchased it from? Potential readers can then see and use your unbiased opinion to make purchase decisions. We at Orange Education would love to know what you think about our products, and our authors can learn from your feedback. Thank you!

For more information about Orange Education, please visit **www.orangeava.com**.

# Table of Contents

# CHAPTER 1

# Getting Started with Git

## Introduction

In this chapter, we will introduce Git, focusing on its core features, the process of installing and configuring Git, and key commands used for various operations.

By the end of this chapter, you will have a comprehensive understanding of Git. You will learn how to use Git to track changes, maintain a detailed history of your code, and collaborate effectively with your team in a structured and organized way.

## Structure

In this chapter, we will cover the following topics:

- Git: A Definition
    - A Brief History of Git
- Fundamental Git Concepts
- Installing Git
    - Set Up a Local Git Repository
    - Git Configuration (Config)
    - .git folder
    - Git Commit
    - .git Folder Post-Commit
- Git Branch
- Merging in Git
    - Merging Changes
    - Understanding Merge Types

- Git Merge Conflict
- Resolve a Merge Conflict

- Git Rebase

# Git: A Definition

Git is an essential tool in modern software development, offering a robust system for version control and team collaboration. Imagine you are writing a document with a team and everyone is making edits. Git enables you to save various versions of the document, review the changes made, identify who made them, and seamlessly merge necessary updates. If needed, you can effortlessly revert to an earlier version. Think of it as a rewind button for your project, ensuring efficient and well-organized teamwork.

# A Brief History of Git

Git was originally developed by **Linus Torvalds**, the creator of the Linux operating system kernel, in **2005**. At the time, Torvalds and the Linux community were using a proprietary version control system. When this system's licensing terms changed, the Linux community needed a new, free, and open-source version control system that could handle a large number of contributors with ease.

## Let us Get Started!

Before delving into the specifics of Git, it is important to first understand Distributed Version Control Systems (DVCS). A DVCS is a type of version control system where each user maintains a complete copy of the entire repository, including all historical versions of the project. This approach is decentralized, meaning there is no single central server managing the repository. Instead, every participant has their own local copy.

Git is a prominent example of a DVCS. It is designed to handle projects of any size with efficiency and speed. Unlike traditional systems that rely on a central server, Git provides each user with a local copy of the repository. This decentralized setup offers several advantages:

- **Efficiency**: Local operations are executed quickly because they do not depend on a central server.
- **Flexibility**: Users can experiment with changes and create branches without impacting the main project until they are ready.
- **Robustness**: The decentralized nature ensures that the project's history is preserved across multiple locations.

To visualize how a DVCS such as Git works, consider the following simplified diagram:

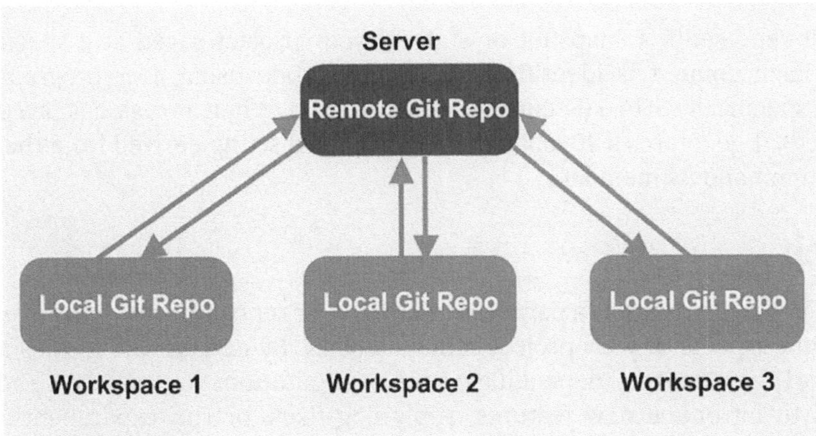


***Figure 1.1:*** *Git DVCS*

In this diagram:

- **Local Git Repository**: Each user, represented by Workspace 1 and Workspace 2, has a complete repository containing the entire project history. This allows users to work independently on their local machines without needing constant access to a central server.
- **Remote Git Repository**: Acts as a central repository where users share their changes. This central hub facilitates collaboration by integrating updates from various local repositories.
- **Bidirectional Arrows**: These arrows demonstrate the flow of changes between the local and remote repositories. They indicate that changes can be fetched from the remote repository to the local repositories and, conversely, pushed from the local repositories to the remote repository.

This distributed approach makes Git a powerful tool for both individual developers and collaborative teams, ensuring robust performance and reliable data management.

# Fundamental Git Concepts

Let us understand some fundamental Git concepts:

## Repository (Repo)

A repository is a storage location for your project, containing all files and their revision history. Each time you edit a document or file, the existing version becomes part of the history, and the new edited version is recorded as the latest version. Repositories can be local (stored on your machine) or remote (hosted on a server).

## Commit

A commit represents a snapshot or state of your project saved at a specific point in time. Each commit is identified by unique code using a cryptographic hash function, specifically SHA-1 (Secure Hash Algorithm 1). When a version is saved (that is, committed), it generates a 40-character hexadecimal string derived from the content of the commit and its metadata.

## Branch

A branch in Git functions as a parallel version of your repository, allowing you to work on different aspects of your project simultaneously. By default, Git creates a branch named "**`main`**" or "**`master`**," depending on the configuration. You can create additional branches to introduce new features, apply bug fixes, or run experiments without affecting the main project. This approach promotes clean, organized development, especially when working in teams.

Branches are often referred to as "**`refs`**" (references), which are pointers to specific commits in your repository. These terms, **`branch`** and **`ref`**, are used interchangeably and will frequently appear in various contexts throughout this book as we explore Git's functionality further.

Branch names can include:

- Letters: A-Z, a-z
- Digits: 0-9
- Special Characters: -, _, ., /

However, branch names cannot contain spaces or certain symbols, such as:

- * (asterisk)
- ? (question mark)

## Clone

Cloning creates a local copy of a remote repository, including all its history and branches. This allows you to work on the project locally while maintaining a complete record of changes.

Here is a diagram illustrating the Repository, Clone, Branch, and a Commit:

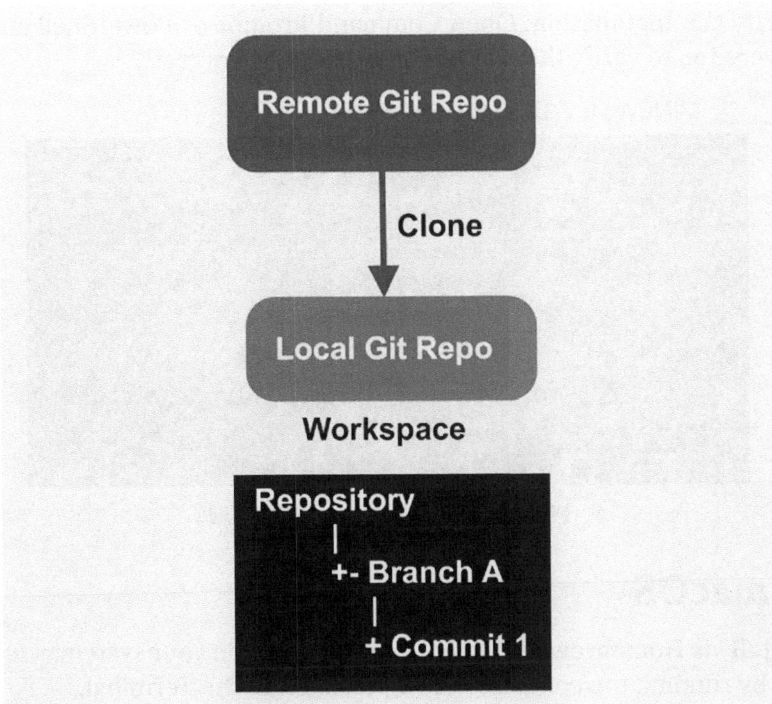


**Figure 1.2:** *Remote and Local Repo*

In this diagram:

- **Repository**: The top-level container.
- **Branch A**: A single branch starting from the repository.
- **Commit 1**: The only commit on Branch A.

# Installing Git

Now that we have explored the core concepts of Git, let us dive into setting up a local Git repository and applying those concepts in practice. Git is supported across various operating systems, and in this section, we will guide you through the steps to install Git on major platforms: Windows, macOS, and Linux.

## Git on Windows

1. **Download the Git Installer**: Go to the official Git website, https://git-scm.com/ and download the Git installer for Windows.
2. **Run the Installer**: Launch the downloaded installer and follow the on-screen instructions. You can proceed with the default settings or customize the installation according to your preferences.

3. **Verify the Installation**: Open Command Prompt or PowerShell and type **`git --version`** to verify that Git has been installed correctly.

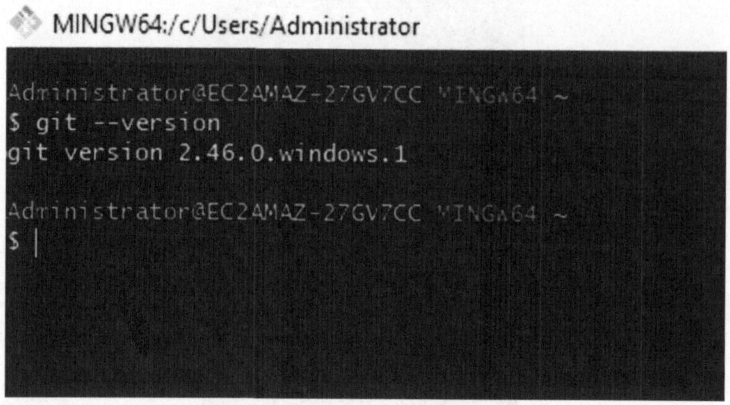


***Figure 1.3****: Git Bash on a Windows*

## Git on macOS

1. **Install via Homebrew**: If Homebrew is installed on your system, you can install Git by running the command brew install git in the Terminal.
2. **Alternative Method**: If you prefer, you can also download the Git installer directly from the official Git website, https://git-scm.com/ and follow the provided installation instructions.
3. **Verify the Installation**: Open Terminal and type **`git --version`** to confirm that Git is installed.

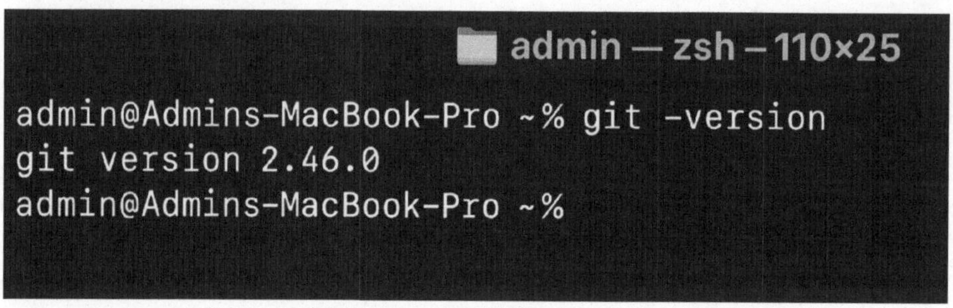


***Figure 1.4****: Git on a Mac Terminal*

## Git on Linux

**Using Package Manager:**

For Debian-based distributions (for example, Ubuntu), **`install git`** by running:

```
sudo apt-get install git
```

For Red Hat-based distributions (for example, Fedora), use:

```
sudo yum install git
```

**Verify the Installation:**

- Open a terminal and type **`git --version`** to ensure that Git is installed properly.

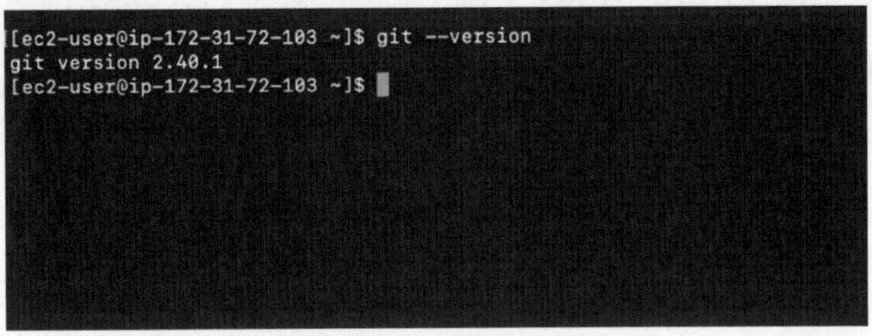


***Figure 1.5***: *Git on a Linux Terminal*

# Set Up a Local Git Repository

With Git now installed, let us begin by setting up a local Git repository. This will also give us the opportunity to explore fundamental Git concepts we already discussed, such as **`branch`** and **`commit`**.

## Create a Local Git Repository

We will start by creating a directory for your project and initializing it as a Git repository. In this example, we will create a directory called bitbucket-book on a macOS terminal and initialize a new Git repository within it.

1. **Create a new directory**: In the Terminal, run the following commands:

   ```
   mkdir bitbucket-book
   cd bitbucket-book
   git init
   ```

2. **Initialize the repository**: After running the **`git init`** command, you should see a message as follows:

   ```
   Initialized empty Git repository in /Users/suhassundar/Desktop/
   bitbucket-book/.git/
   ```

   This message confirms that an empty Git repository has been created in the specified directory.

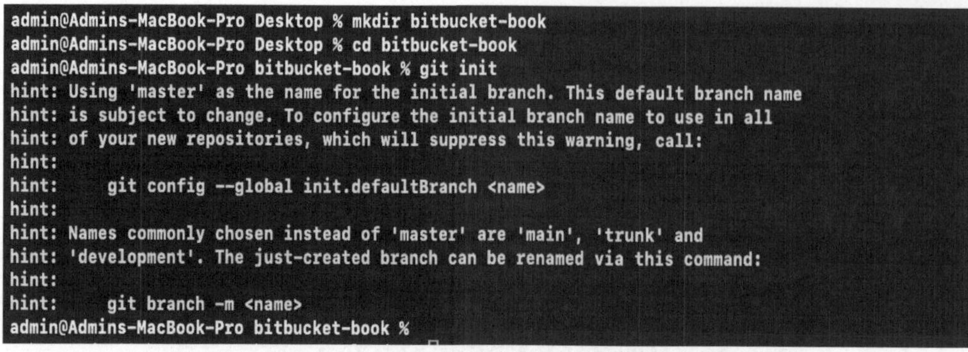


***Figure 1.6:*** *Git Repo Init*

### Setting the Default Branch

Upon initializing the repository, you might notice a warning about the default branch name:

```
hint: Using 'master' as the name for the initial branch. This
default branch name
hint: is subject to change. To configure the initial branch name
to use in all
hint: of your new repositories, which will suppress this warning,
call:
hint:
hint:  git config --global init.defaultBranch <name>
hint:
hint: Names commonly chosen instead of 'master' are 'main',
'trunk', and 'development'.
```

Git is informing you that the default branch name is master, but this can be configured based on the naming convention your team follows. Common alternatives include **`main`**, **`trunk`**, or **`development`**. For this example, we will stick with the master branch as the default.

# Git Configuration (Config)

The `git config` command allows you to configure Git settings and preferences on your system. These settings determine how Git behaves, as well as storing user information such as your name and email, which are used to tag commits.

### Common Usage of `git config`

- **Set your name**: The following command sets your name in Git:

  ```
  git config --global user.name "Your Name"
  ```

- **Set your email address**: This sets the email associated with your Git commits:

  ```
  git config --global user.email "youremail@example.com"
  ```

These settings ensure that all your commits are tagged with your name and email.

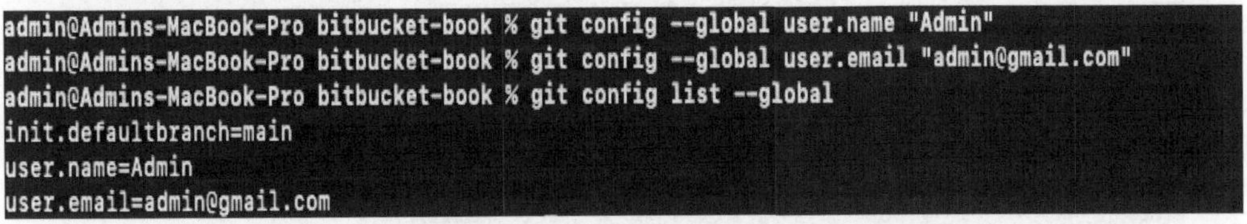


**Figure 1.7**: *Git Configuration*

# Types of Git Configuration

Git allows configuration at different levels, each affecting a different scope:

- **System-wide configuration** (`--system`): Applies to all users on the system and every repository on the machine. These settings are typically stored in **`/etc/gitconfig`**.

  ```
  git config --system
  ```

- **Global configuration (`--global`)**: Applies to all repositories for the current user. These settings are stored in **`~/.gitconfig`** or **`~/.config/git/config`**.

  ```
  git config --global
  ```

- **Local configuration (default)**: Applies only to the specific repository where the command is run. These settings are stored in **`.git/config`** inside the repository folder.

  ```
  git config
  ```

# `.git` Folder

Now that we have successfully created a Git repository, let us explore the contents of this repository. Since we have not added any data yet, you might wonder what an empty repository contains. When you initialize a repository with **`git init`**, a **`.git`** directory is created, which is hidden by default. This folder contains all the essential files Git needs to manage the version history of your project.

# Listing the Working Directory Contents

You can list the contents of the repository directory, including hidden files, by running the following commands: **`ls -la`**

```
ls -la .git
```

```
admin@Admins-MacBook-Pro bitbucket-book % ls -la
total 0
drwxr-xr-x   3 admin  staff   96 Sep 14 18:20 .
drwx------@ 12 admin  staff  384 Sep 14 18:35 ..
drwxr-xr-x   9 admin  staff  288 Sep 14 18:26 .git
admin@Admins-MacBook-Pro bitbucket-book % ls -la .git
total 24
drwxr-xr-x  9 admin  staff  288 Sep 14 18:26 .
drwxr-xr-x  3 admin  staff   96 Sep 14 18:20 ..
-rw-r--r--  1 admin  staff   23 Sep 14 18:26 HEAD
-rw-r--r--  1 admin  staff  137 Sep 14 18:26 config
-rw-r--r--  1 admin  staff   73 Sep 14 18:26 description
drwxr-xr-x 16 admin  staff  512 Sep 14 18:20 hooks
drwxr-xr-x  3 admin  staff   96 Sep 14 18:20 info
drwxr-xr-x  3 admin  staff   96 Sep 14 18:20 objects
drwxr-xr-x  4 admin  staff  128 Sep 14 18:20 refs
```

**Figure 1.8:** *.git directory contents*

You will notice that the .git folder is present, containing various files and subdirectories. These elements are crucial for managing the internal workings of Git. Let us break down the contents of the .git directory and understand the role each file or folder plays.

## Understanding the Contents of the `.git` Directory

- **`HEAD` (File)**: This file points to the current branch or commit that you are referencing. It essentially tells Git which commit you are "**`on`**."

  *Example: we are on default branch:* `ref: refs/heads/main`

- **`config` (File)**: The config file contains settings specific to the **`Git`** repository. These settings can include user information, repository-specific configurations, and references to remote repositories.

  *Example content:*

  ```
  [core]
  repositoryformatversion = 0
  filemode = true
  ```

- **`description` (File)**: This file is typically used by Git web interfaces (such as **`Gitweb`**) to describe the repository. It does not impact the operation of Git itself and is often left with a default message in personal repositories.

- **`hooks/` (Folder)**: The hooks folder contains sample scripts that can automate tasks at various stages of the Git workflow, such as before a commit or after a merge. While these hooks are inactive by default, you can enable them by renaming and customizing them as needed.

  *Example hook files:* `pre-commit.sample`, `post-commit.sample`

- **`info/` (Folder)**: Inside the info folder, you will find a file named exclude, which allows you to define files or patterns to be ignored by Git in this repository. This is similar to **`.gitignore`**, but the exclude file is specific to the local repository and is not shared with others.

  *Example content in **`info/`**exclude:*

  ```
  *.log
  ```

- **`objects/` (Folder)**: The objects folder is where Git stores all your objects, such as commits, files (blobs), and directories (trees). Each object is stored with a name derived from its SHA-1 hash, and the folder structure helps Git efficiently manage these objects.

  *Example directory structure:*

  ```
  objects/
  9f/
  3abc52...  # This file contains a blob/tree object
  ```

- **`refs/` (Folder)**: The **`refs`** directory stores references to commits. These references are organized into subdirectories, such as **`heads/`** (for branches), **`tags/`** (for version tags), and **`remotes/`** (for tracking branches from remote repositories).

  *Example structure:*

  ```
  refs/
    heads/
      main  # Points to the latest commit in the 'main' branch
    tags/
      v1.0  # Points to a tagged version
  ```

# Git Commit

Having discussed the contents of an empty Git repository, let us proceed by creating a commit and observing how these actions affect the .git folder. This will help us understand how Git manages project history.

# Creating and Committing a File

1. **Create a File**

   First, let us add a new file to our repository and make our first commit. In the working directory (the directory on your local filesystem where you work with project files), create a file named bitbucket.txt with the content "**`hello`**":

   ```
   echo "hello" > bitbucket.txt
   ```

   This command creates the file bitbucket.txt and writes "**`hello`**" into it.

2. **Check the Status**

   Use git status to see the current state of your repository:

   ```
   git status
   ```

   Output:

   ```
   On branch master

   No commits yet

   Untracked files:
   ```

   (use "**git add <file>...**" to include in what will be committed.)

   **bitbucket.txt**

   If nothing is added to commit but untracked files are present, use "**git add**" to track.

   This output indicates that bitbucket.txt is an untracked file, meaning Git is not yet monitoring it. You need to add the file to the staging area before committing.

3. **Add the File to Staging**

   Add **bitbucket.txt** to the staging area with:

   ```
   git add bitbucket.txt
   ```

   Run **git status** again to check the staging area:

   ```
   git status
   ```

   Output:

   ```
   On branch master

   No commits yet

   Changes to be committed:
   ```

   (use "**git rm --cached <file>...**" to unstage)

   new file: **bitbucket.txt**

   Now **bitbucket.txt** is staged for commit, meaning it is prepared to be included in the next commit.

4. **Commit the Changes**

   Commit the changes with a message:

   ```
   git commit -m "first commit"
   ```

Output:

```
[master (root-commit) b17872a] first commit
 1 file changed, 1 insertion(+)
 create mode 100644 bitbucket.txt
```

This command creates the first commit, recording the state of the repository at this point. The output shows the commit hash (b17872a), which is a unique identifier for this commit.

5. **Check the Status Again**

   Run git status to confirm that the working directory is clean:

   ```
   git status
   ```

   Output:

   ```
   On branch master
   nothing to commit, working tree clean
   ```

   The working tree is now clean, meaning there are no uncommitted changes.

6. **View Commit History**

   Use **`git log`** to view the commit history:

   ```
   git log
   ```

   Output:

   ```
   commit b17872af155bb9d616850be0228cd03e4b5def0d (HEAD -> master)
   Author: Suhas S <sundararajurama@gmail.com>
   Date:   Sat Sep 14 19:58:09 2024 +0530
       first commit
   ```

   The **`git log`** command shows details about the commit, including the commit hash, author, date, and commit message. **HEAD** indicates that this is the latest commit on the master branch.

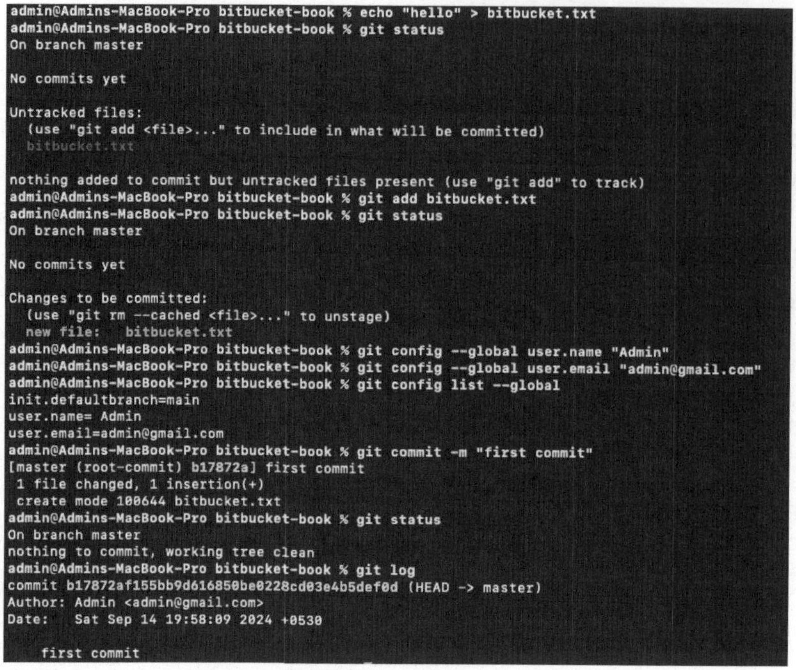


**Figure 1.9:** *Git Commit*

**Visualize Git commit workflow using a diagram:**

- **Working Directory**: The directory where you make changes to files before staging and committing them.
- **Staging Area (Index)**: A temporary area where changes are gathered before committing them to the repository.
- **Commit**: A snapshot of your repository at a particular point in time, saved with a unique identifier.

**Figure 1.10:** *Git Version Control Process*

# .git Folder Post-Commit

After making a commit, Git structures and stores the commit information as objects within the .git directory. This section explores how Git manages these objects and how they are organized in the repository.

## Exploring the .git/objects Folder

When you commit a file, Git stores different types of objects–such as commits, blobs (file contents), and trees (directory structures)–in the .git/objects directory. The directory is organized into subdirectories named after the first two characters of the SHA-1 hash of each object, with the remaining characters used as the filename.

Here is how the **`.git/objects`** folder appears after a commit:

```
— objects
│    ├── 3a
│    │   └── 45e6ec9f78af5bd36766a94d50124b75bf3725
│    ├── b1
│    │   └── 7872af155bb9d616850be0228cd03e4b5def0d
│    ├── ce
│    │   └── 013625030ba8dba906f756967f9e9ca394464a
```

- **`3a/45e6ec9f78af5bd36766a94d50124b75bf3725`**: Tree object
- **`b1/7872af155bb9d616850be0228cd03e4b5def0d`**: Commit object
- **`ce/013625030ba8dba906f756967f9e9ca394464a`**: Blob object

**Object Types and Their Content**

1. **Commit Object (`b17872af155bb9d616850be0228cd03e4b5def0d`)**

   A commit object records a snapshot of the repository at a specific point in time, including the reference to the tree object that represents the directory structure.

   Check the type of the object:

   ```
   git cat-file -t b17872af155bb9d616850be0228cd03e4b5def0d
   ```

   Output:

   ```
   commit
   ```

   View the content of the commit object:

   ```
   git cat-file commit b17872af155bb9d616850be0228cd03e4b5def0d
   ```

   Output:

   ```
   tree 3a45e6ec9f78af5bd36766a94d50124b75bf3725
   author Suhas S <sundararajurama@gmail.com> 1726324089 +0530
   committer Suhas S <sundararajurama@gmail.com> 1726324089 +0530
   ```

first commit

The commit object contains:

- tree 3a45e6ec9f78af5bd36766a94d50124b75bf3725: Reference to the tree object.
- author and committer: Metadata about who made the commit and when.
- Commit message: Describes the purpose of the commit.

2. **Tree Object (`3a45e6ec9f78af5bd36766a94d50124b75bf3725`)**

   A tree object represents a snapshot of the directory structure and file references at the time of the commit.

   Check the type of the object:

   ```
   git cat-file -t 3a45e6ec9f78af5bd36766a94d50124b75bf3725
   ```

   Output:

   ```
   tree
   ```

   View the content of the tree object:

   ```
   git ls-tree 3a45e6ec9f78af5bd36766a94d50124b75bf3725
   ```

   Output:

   ```
   100644 blob ce013625030ba8dba906f756967f9e9ca394464a    bitbuck-
   et.txt
   ```

   The tree object maps file names to blob objects. It shows that bitbucket.txt is a regular file (blob) with content referenced by the hash `ce013625030ba8dba906f756967f9e9ca394464a`.

3. **Blob Object (`ce013625030ba8dba906f756967f9e9ca394464a`)**

   A blob object stores the content of a file but not its metadata.

   Check the type of the object:

   ```
   git cat-file -t ce013625030ba8dba906f756967f9e9ca394464a
   ```

   Output:

   ```
   blob
   ```

   View the content of the blob object:

   ```
   git cat-file blob ce013625030ba8dba906f756967f9e9ca394464a
   ```

   Output:

   ```
   hello
   ```

   The blob object contains the raw content of the file bitbucket.txt.

**Summary**

After committing a file, Git stores the file contents (blobs), directory structures (trees), and commits metadata in the .git/objects directory. This organization allows Git to efficiently track changes, manage project history, and provide robust version control. The commit object references the tree object, which, in turn, references the blob objects containing file contents.

# Git Branch

In the previous example, we committed changes to the default branch master and explored how Git tracks different objects in the `.git` folder. Now, we will create a new branch called develop and explore the internal Git structure when switching between branches and committing changes.

## Create and Switch Branches

1. **Create a New Branch:**

   To create a branch named develop, run:

   ```
   git branch develop
   ```

2. **List All Branches:**

   To list all branches (local and remote):

   ```
   git branch -a
   ```

   Output:

   ```
     develop
   * master
   ```

   The asterisk (*) shows that master is the current active branch.

3. **Switch to the** develop Branch:

   To switch to the newly created develop branch:

   ```
   git checkout develop
   ```

   Output:

   ```
   Switched to branch 'develop'
   If you run git branch -a again:
   * develop
     master
   ```

   The asterisk now indicates that you are on the develop branch.

## Exploring Changes in the `.git` Folder

- **Check the `HEAD` File:**

  After switching to develop, the **`.git/HEAD`** file updates to point to the new branch:

  ```
  cat .git/HEAD
  ```

  Output:

  ```
  ref: refs/heads/develop
  ```

- **Git Logs After Branch Creation:**

  When a new branch is created, the log folder reflects the branches:

  ```
  ├── logs
  │   ├── HEAD
  │   └── refs
  │       └── heads
  │           ├── develop
  │      │        └── master
  ```

- **No Changes in the Objects Folder Yet:**

  Since no new changes have been committed on the develop branch yet, the **`.git/objects/`** folder remains the same as it shares the same **`HEAD`** commit as the master branch.

## Commit Changes on the `develop` Branch

1. **Modify the File:**

   Append new content to bitbucket.txt:

   ```
   echo "world" >> bitbucket.txt
   ```

2. **Add and Commit the Changes:**

   ```
   git add bitbucket.txt
   git commit -m "first commit on develop branch"
   ```

## Check for New Objects in `.git/objects`

After committing the changes, new objects are created to represent the modified state. Listing the **`.git/objects/`** folder after the commit:

```
— objects
│    ├── 3a
│    │   └── 45e6ec9f78af5bd36766a94d50124b75bf3725
│    ├── 58
│    │   └── b1d1ac731969a1360673b81f031e336ba78793
```

```
│       ├── 84
│       │   └── 24bff4cd26e646857da52076e40be4f16b210a
│       ├── 94
│       │   └── 954abda49de8615a048f8d2e64b5de848e27a1
│       ├── b1
│       │   └── 7872af155bb9d616850be0228cd03e4b5def0d
│       ├── ce
│       │   └── 013625030ba8dba906f756967f9e9ca394464a
```

New objects have been created:

- **58b1d1ac731969a1360673b81f031e336ba78793**: Commit object
- **8424bff4cd26e646857da52076e40be4f16b210a**: Tree object
- **94954abda49de8615a048f8d2e64b5de848e27a1**: Blob object

## Verifying the New Objects

- **Commit Object:**

  ```
  git cat-file -t 58b1d1ac731969a1360673b81f031e336ba78793
  ```

  Output:

  ```
  Commit
  ```

- **Tree Object:**

  ```
  git cat-file -t 8424bff4cd26e646857da52076e40be4f16b210a
  ```

  Output:

  ```
  Tree
  ```

- **Blob Object (New File Content):**

  ```
  git cat-file blob 94954abda49de8615a048f8d2e64b5de848e27a1
  ```

  Output:

  ```
  hello
  world
  ```

## List Commits History

```
git log
commit 58b1d1ac731969a1360673b81f031e336ba78793 (HEAD -> develop)
Author: Suhas S <sundararajurama@gmail.com>
Date:   Sat Sep 14 22:49:34 2024 +0530
```

first commit on develop branch

```
commit b17872af155bb9d616850be0228cd03e4b5def0d (master)
Author: Suhas S <sundararajurama@gmail.com>
Date:   Sat Sep 14 19:58:09 2024 +0530
```

first commit

**Summary**

When we modified the file bitbucket.txt and committed it on the develop branch, Git created:

- A **blob** object to store the updated file's content (hello world).
- A **tree** object to represent the updated directory structure.
- A **commit** object to record the changes and point to the updated tree.

Each change in Git results in new immutable objects, allowing it to maintain a full history of every modification made in the repository.

# Merging in Git

In this section, we will cover how to merge changes from one branch to another in Git, specifically focusing on merging changes from the develop branch into the master branch. We will also discuss different merge strategies and their implications.

## Merging Changes

To merge changes from the develop branch into the master branch, follow these steps:

1. **Switch to the** master Branch

   First, ensure you are on the master branch by running:

   ```
   git checkout master
   ```

2. **Merge the** develop Branch

   Now, merge the changes from the develop branch:

   ```
   git merge develop
   ```

   After executing the **merge** command, you might see output similar to:

   ```
   Updating b17872a..58b1d1a
   Fast-forward
    bitbucket.txt | 1 +
    1 file changed, 1 insertion(+)
   ```

   You can check the contents of bitbucket.txt to see that it now includes changes from the develop branch using Fast-forward merge:

   ```
   cat bitbucket.txt
   ```

   Output:

   ```
   hello
   world
   ```

## Understanding Merge Types

- **Fast-Forward Merge:** A fast-forward merge occurs when the develop branch's history is linear with the master branch. This means no new commits have been made to the master branch since the develop branch was created. In such cases, Git can simply move the pointer of master forward to match develop.
- **ort Merge Strategy (Optimized Recursive Strategy):** The ort strategy, short for Optimized Recursive Tree merge, is the default merge strategy in Git from version 2.33. It is designed to be faster and more efficient by optimizing the recursive merge process.

  To see ort in action, consider the following example where we add new files to both master and develop branches and then merge develop into master:

  ```
  echo "index" > index.txt
  git add index.txt
  git commit -m "index.txt on master"

  git checkout develop
  echo "tutorials" > tutorials.txt
  git add tutorials.txt
  git commit -m "tutorials.txt on develop"

  git checkout master
  git merge develop
  The merge might output:
  Merge branch 'develop'
  Merge made by the 'ort' strategy.
   tutorials.txt | 1 +
   1 file changed, 1 insertion(+)
  ```
- **Squash Merge:** A squash merge combines all commits from the source branch into a single commit on the target branch. This strategy simplifies the commit history by not retaining the original commit structure from the source branch.

  For example, suppose you have made multiple commits on the develop branch:

  ```
  git checkout develop

  echo "squash-1" >> bitbucket.txt
  git add bitbucket.txt
  git commit -m "added squash-1 to bitbucket.txt"


  echo "squash-2" >> bitbucket.txt
  git add bitbucket.txt
  git commit -m "added squash-2 to bitbucket.txt"
  ```

```
git log -2 --oneline

a5b3070 (HEAD -> develop) added squash-2 to bitbucket.txt
ef00edc added squash-1 to bitbucket.txt
```

To perform a squash merge:

```
git checkout master
git merge --squash develop
```

The output will be:

```
Squash commit -- not updating HEAD
Automatic merge went well; stopped before committing as requested
```

This indicates that Git prepared the changes for a single commit but did not automatically commit them. You should review the changes and then create the squash commit manually:

```
git status
git diff --cached
git commit -m "squash merge on master"
```

The resulting commit will consolidate all changes from the develop branch into a single commit on the master branch. The commit history will show:

```
git log -2 --oneline
```

Output:

```
7c655ab (HEAD -> master) squash merge on master
067b572 Merge branch 'develop'
```

By understanding and using these merging strategies, you can better manage your project's commit history and handle changes efficiently.

# Git Merge Conflict

A merge conflict arises when Git encounters differences between branches that it cannot automatically reconcile. This situation typically occurs when two branches have modifications to the same line in a file or when Git is uncertain how to integrate the changes. Resolving merge conflicts requires manual intervention.

# Resolving a Merge Conflict

Let us illustrate a merge conflict with an example:

- **Switch to the** develop Branch
  `git checkout -b develop`

- **Modify a File in the** develop Branch

  ```
  Add a line to bitbucket.txt:
  echo "conflict1" >> bitbucket.txt
  git add bitbucket.txt
  git commit -m "Added conflict1"
  ```
- **Switch Back to the** master Branch

  ```
  git checkout master
  ```
- **Modify the Same File in the** master Branch

  Add a different line to **`bitbucket.txt`**:

  ```
  echo "conflict2" >> bitbucket.txt
  git add bitbucket.txt
  git commit -m "Added conflict2"
  ```

Merging Branches should encounter a Conflict:

1. **Attempt to Merge** develop into master

   ```
   git merge develop
   ```

   This command will result in a merge conflict. Git will mark the conflicting sections in **`bitbucket.txt`** with conflict markers:

   ```
   hello
   world
   squash-1
   squash-2
   <<<<<<< HEAD
   conflict2
   =======
   conflict1
   >>>>>>> develop
   ```

   **What are these Conflict Markers**?

   a. **`<<<<<<< HEAD`**: Indicates the beginning of the conflicting changes from the current branch (master).

   b. **`=======`**: Separates the conflicting changes from the two branches.

   c. **`>>>>>>> develop`**: Marks the end of the conflicting changes from the branch being merged (develop).

Resolving the Merge Conflict:

1. **Open the Conflicted File** (bitbucket.txt)

   Use a text editor to resolve the conflict. You can either combine both changes or choose the appropriate one. For example:

```
hello
world
squash-1
squash-2
conflict1
conflict2
```

2. **Remove Conflict Markers**

   Ensure the file is free of conflict markers (<<<<<<<, =======, >>>>>>>).

3. **Stage the Resolved File**

   ```
   git add bitbucket.txt
   ```

4. **Commit the Merge Resolution**

   ```
   git commit -m "Resolved merge conflict between master and develop"
   ```

Merge conflicts in real-world projects can be diverse and complex, often requiring careful consideration and collaboration to resolve effectively.

# Git Rebase

Git rebase is a powerful tool used to integrate changes from one branch into another by applying commits from one branch on top of another. This process effectively rewrites the commit history, creating a cleaner and more linear progression of commits.

**Working of Git Rebase**

1. **Checkout the Branch**

   To begin the rebase process, switch to the branch that you want to rebase:

   git checkout develop

2. **Rebase onto the Target Branch**

   Apply the commits from your current branch onto the target branch (for example, master):

   git rebase master

   This command will take the commits from develop and reapply them on top of master.

**Rebase versus Merge**

Understanding the difference between rebase and merge is crucial for effective version control:

- **Rebase**: Rewrites the commit history to create a clean, linear progression of commits. It applies commits from one branch on top of another, resulting in a more straightforward history.

- **Merge**: Combines branches while preserving the original commit history and adding a merge commit. It integrates the changes from one branch into another without altering the existing history.

Example of Rebase versus Merge

Consider the following commit history:

- **Master Branch**: `X -- Y -- Z`
- **Develop**: `A -- B -- C`

**Rebase Example**

If you rebase develop onto master, the commit history will look as follows:

```
master: X -- Y -- Z
                   \
develop: A' -- B' -- C'
```

In this scenario:

- **`A'`**, **`B'`**, and **`C'`** are the rebased commits from develop, applied on top of master.
- The history appears linear, as if develop was created from master at the latest commit.

**Merge Example**

If you merge develop into master, the commit history will look as follows:

```
master: X -- Y -- Z -- M
                   \
develop: A -- B -- C
```

In this scenario:

- M is the merge commit that combines develop with master.
- The history retains all individual commits and shows the point at which the branches were merged.

**Summary**

- **Rebase**: Useful for creating a linear history and making a branch up-to-date with the base branch. It simplifies the commit history but rewrites it.
- **Merge**: Useful for combining branches and preserving the complete history of changes. It adds a merge commit and maintains a record of branch integration.

By using rebase and merge appropriately, you can manage your repository's commit history effectively and maintain a clear project history.

# Conclusion

In this chapter, we have covered the fundamentals of Git, including its installation, configuration, and basic usage. By understanding Git's core concepts, setting up your environment, and mastering essential commands, you are now equipped to manage your code effectively and collaborate with others. As you continue to work with Git, you will encounter more advanced features and workflows, but this foundation will serve as a solid base for further learning.

In the next chapter, we will explore topics such as hosting remote repositories in Bitbucket and dive into its cloud features.

CHAPTER 2

# Overview of Bitbucket Cloud

## Introduction

In this chapter, we will explore Bitbucket Cloud, a widely used platform for hosting and managing Git repositories. We will start with an introduction to Bitbucket Cloud and the various subscriptions or plans available, followed by a look at how Atlassian organizations function within the platform. You will also get familiar with navigating the Bitbucket Cloud landing page, creating projects and repositories, and linking local repositories to the cloud. Additionally, we will cover essential topics such as managing large files using Git LFS and ensuring your repositories are efficiently handled in a collaborative environment.

## Structure

In this chapter, we will cover the following topics:

- Introduction to Bitbucket Cloud
- Bitbucket Cloud Account
- Bitbucket Cloud Plans
- Atlassian Organization
- Bitbucket Cloud Landing Page Overview
- Create Project
- Create Repository
- Link Local Repositories to Bitbucket Cloud
- Managing Large Files using Git LFS

# Introduction to Bitbucket Cloud

Bitbucket Cloud is a platform designed to manage source code and foster collaboration through Git repositories. In the previous chapter, we discussed the fundamentals of Git, including how to set it up and create local repositories. While a **local repository** resides on a developer's machine, allowing them to manage changes offline, a **remote repository** is hosted on a server such as Bitbucket Cloud. Remote repositories enable developers to share, synchronize, and collaborate on their code.

A remote repository serves as the central location for collaboration, where team members can **pull updates** and **push changes**, ensuring that all developers have access to the latest version of the code. This process minimizes conflicts, avoids data loss, and provides a reliable backup. Modern platforms such as Bitbucket Cloud go beyond basic repository management by offering advanced features, such as **deployment pipelines** and **release management**, streamlining the development lifecycle.

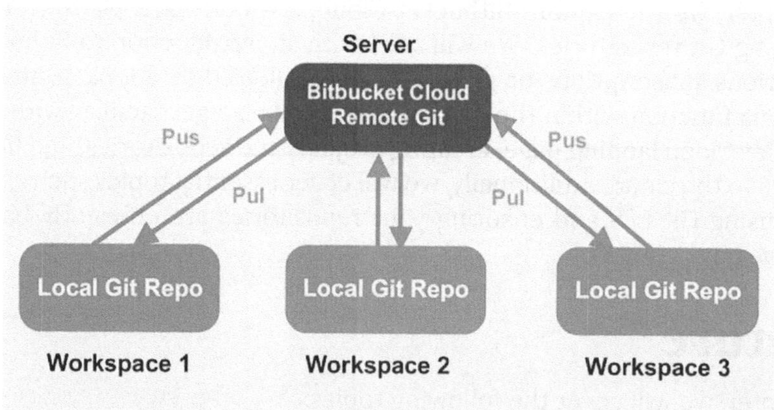


***Figure* 2.1**: *Bitbucket Cloud and Local Repository*

# Bitbucket Cloud Account

The first step in using Bitbucket Cloud is creating an Atlassian cloud account. Since Bitbucket Cloud is part of the Atlassian cloud suite, you need to sign up with an Atlassian Cloud account, which gives you access to Bitbucket Cloud as well as other Atlassian products, such as Jira Cloud and Confluence Cloud.

**Sign Up for an Account**

1. **Visit the Bitbucket Cloud Site**: Go to https://bitbucket.org/account/signup/ .
2. **Create an Account**: You can either use an existing Atlassian Cloud account (if you have one) or register with a new email address. Enter your name, create a password, and follow the on-screen instructions.

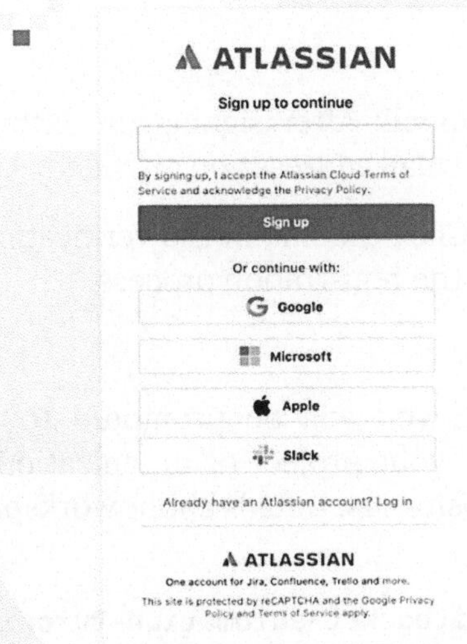


**Figure 2.2**: *Bitbucket Cloud Signup*

If you have already registered with your email, Bitbucket signup page will ask for your password.

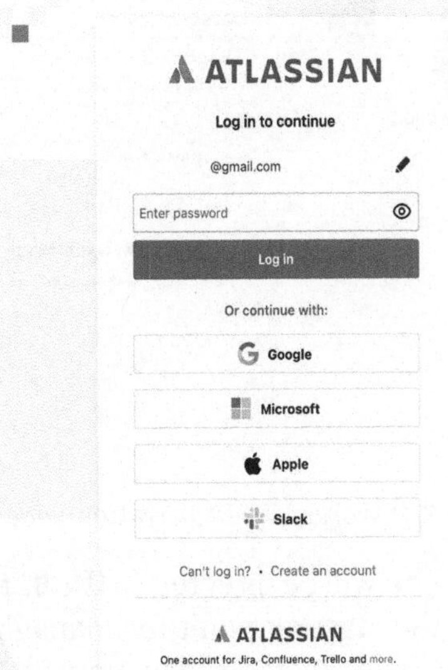


**Figure 2.3**: *Bitbucket Cloud Signup Password Page*

Otherwise, you will receive a passcode via email or a verification link to activate your account.

**Verify Your Email**

1. **Receive Verification Email**: After signing up, Bitbucket Cloud will send a verification link to the email address you provided.
2. **Verify Your Account**: Click the link in the verification email to activate your account and complete the registration process.

**Workspace Setup**

After verifying your account, you will be prompted to create a **workspace**. A workspace is an identifier for your project or organization, where you will create and manage projects and repositories. Details about workspaces will be discussed in later sections of this chapter.

We will create a workspace, "**`bitbucket-automation-tutorial`**".

**Figure 2.4**: *Workspace Registration page*

Once your workspace is set up, you will be directed to the **`Bitbucket Cloud Overview`** or **`Home`** page, which serves as the starting point for managing your repositories and projects. In this example, you see a workspace named **`bitbucket-automation-tutorial`**.

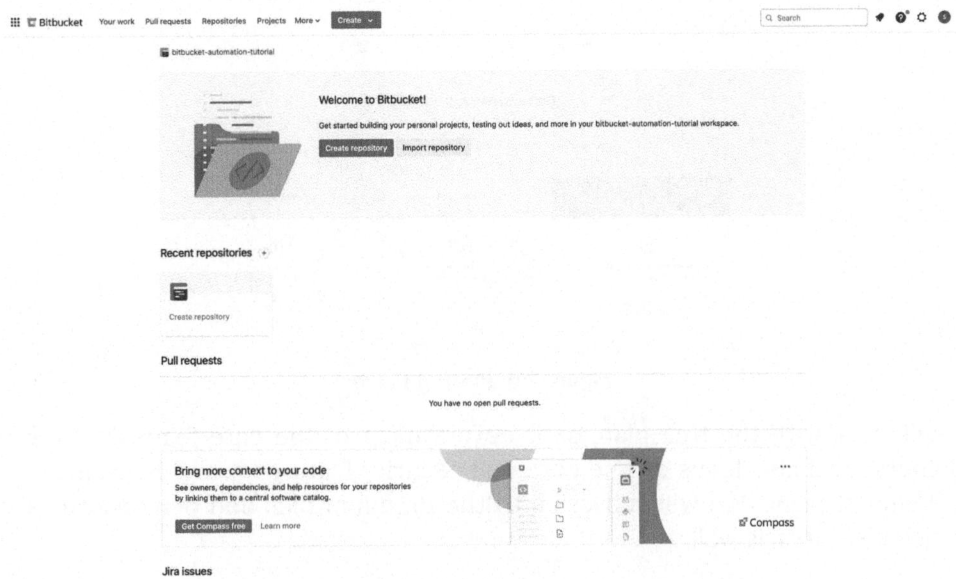


***Figure 2.5***: *Bitbucket Cloud Overview (home) page*

# Bitbucket Cloud Plans

We signed up for a Bitbucket Cloud account on a free plan, which incurs no cost. However, Bitbucket Cloud also offers paid plans, such as Standard and Premium, with additional features.

The page https://www.atlassian.com/software/bitbucket/pricing provides details on the core features offered in the Free, Standard, and Premium plans, as well as the associated pricing.

- **Free Plan:** Ideal for individuals and small teams, offering unlimited public repositories and support for up to five users, with a limited number of build minutes per month.
- **Standard Plan:** Designed for growing teams, including unlimited private repositories, more user slots, and advanced features.
- **Premium Plan:** Suitable for larger teams or organizations, featuring increased build minutes, additional storage, and enhanced support options.

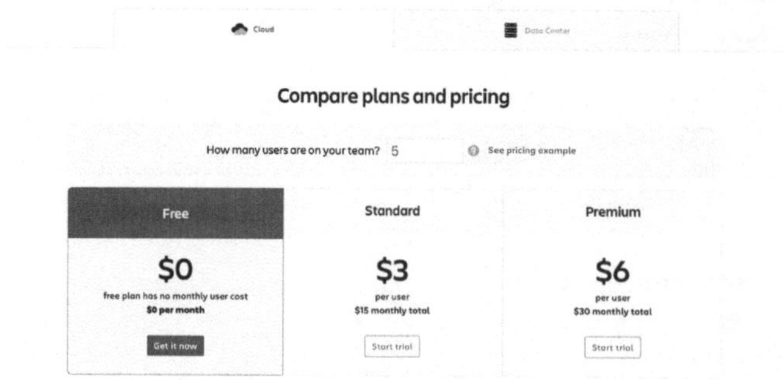


**Figure 2.6**: *Pricing Plans*

We will start with the free plan, as it covers most of the core features. However, this course will also focus on the core and security features available exclusively in the Premium plans. We will subscribe to the Premium plan and demonstrate these advanced features as well.

Core and security features offerings include:

- **Core Features**: These include the number of users, build minutes associated with Bitbucket's CI/CD solution, Jira integration, and the ability to add all request reviewers. These features are available in both free and paid subscriptions. Additional code features such as AI-based pull request descriptions and dynamic CI/CD pipelines are exclusive to the Premium plan.

Core Features

| FEATURE | Free | Standard | Premium |
|---|---|---|---|
| User limit per instance | Up to 5 users | Unlimited | Unlimited |
| Build minutes | 50 minutes per month | 2,500 minutes per month | 3,500 minutes per month |
| Additional build minutes | $10 per 1,000 additional build minutes, per month | $10 per 1,000 additional build minutes, per month | $10 per 1,000 additional build minutes, per month |
| Git LFS (Large File Storage) | 1 GB | 5 GB | 10 GB |
| Code insights | Three integrations | Three integrations | Unlimited |
| Deployment environments | 10 | 100 | 100 |
| Unlimited private repositories | ✓ | ✓ | ✓ |
| Jira integration | ✓ | ✓ | ✓ |
| CI/CD (continuous integration and continuous delivery) | ✓ | ✓ | ✓ |
| Unlimited pull request reviewers | ✓ | ✓ | ✓ |
| Merge checks | ✓ | ✓ | ✓ |
| AI-powered pull request descriptions | | | ✓ |
| AI-enhanced summaries in editor prompts | | | ✓ |
| AI-driven pull request comment creation with custom prompts | | | ✓ |
| AI-enabled spelling, grammar, and tone editing in pull requests | | | ✓ |
| Dynamic CI/CD pipelines | | | ✓ |

**Figure 2.7**: *Pricing Plans Comparison – Core Features*

- **Security and Compliance Features**: Features such as Single Sign-On (SSO) and extended audit logs are available with the "**`Atlassian Guard`**" subscription, which is an enterprise-grade security and administration feature that provides centralized control and enhanced security for managing users across all Atlassian Cloud products. Enforcing merge checks, IP allow-listing, and audit logs are also part of the Bitbucket Cloud Premium subscription.

Security & Compliance

| FEATURE | Free | Standard | Premium |
|---|---|---|---|
| Atlassian Guard (SSO, audit logs) | Requires Atlassian Guard subscription | Requires Atlassian Guard subscription | Requires Atlassian Guard subscription |
| Resource-scoped Access Tokens | Repository level | Repository level | Repository, project, and workspace |
| Encryption in transit and at rest | ✓ | ✓ | ✓ |
| Business continuity and disaster recovery | ✓ | ✓ | ✓ |
| IP allowlisting | | | ✓ |
| Enforced merge checks | | | ✓ |
| Required two-step verification | | | ✓ |
| Scale CI workflows | | | ✓ |
| Deployment permissions | | | ✓ |

***Figure 2.8***: *Pricing Plans Comparison – Security and Compliance*

Paid subscriptions come with dedicated customer support and free subscriptions can avail community-based support.

Support

| FEATURE | Free | Standard | Premium |
|---|---|---|---|
| Support ↗ | Community only | Standard | Premium |
| Guaranteed uptime SLA ↗ | | | 99.9% |

***Figure 2.9***: *Pricing Plans Comparison – Product Support*

Core and security features will be covered in detail in subsequent chapters.

# Atlassian Organization

In the previous section, we created a workspace named "**`bitbucket-automation-tutorial`**." A workspace serves as an identifier for your project or organization, where you can manage projects and repositories. Atlassian offers unified user management across its cloud products, including Bitbucket Cloud. Users, product access, and security features are centrally managed through the admin tool at admin.atlassian.com.

### Hierarchy for Bitbucket Cloud Product

The hierarchy for a Bitbucket cloud as a product is structured as follows:

- **Organization** (top layer)
- **Bitbucket Product Workspace**
- **Projects**
- **Repositories**

An Atlassian Organization helps manage and control access across various Atlassian tools, such as Jira, Confluence, Bitbucket, and Trello. When we created the workspace "**`bitbucket-automation-tutorial`**," an Atlassian Cloud organization with the same name was automatically set up in the admin tool.

# Cloud Admin Tool Overview Page

**Login**: Log in to admin.atlassian.com with your Atlassian Cloud account to access the admin tool overview page.

***Figure 2.10**: Admin tool overview page*

**Admin tool manages cloud products:** Once in the admin tool, you can manage the different products associated with your organization. For example, your Bitbucket workspace can be found under Products tab.

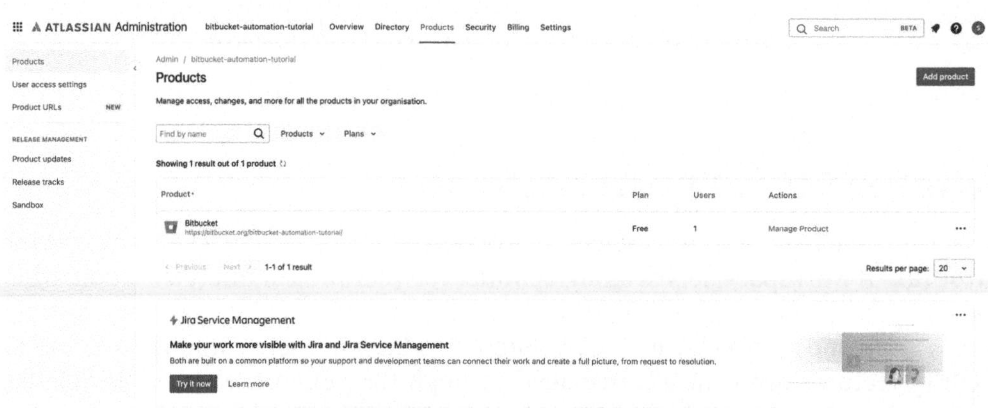


***Figure 2.11**: Admin tool manage products*

The Bitbucket Cloud workspace URL follows the standard format: https://bitbucket.org/workspace-ID/

Example: https://bitbucket.org/bitbucket-automation-tutorial/

## Managing Products

To view and manage the groups associated with your Bitbucket workspace, Click on "`Manage Product`", option is located next to the workspace URL.

- **Groups and Roles**: Groups are logical containers linked to specific roles. Users added to these groups will have access to the products based on their assigned roles. The following are standard groups auto-created during setting up the Bitbucket Cloud workspace.

**Figure 2.12**: *Admin tool manage groups*

- **bitbucket-admins-bitbucket-automation-tutorial**: This group has the "`Product Admin`" role, granting access to all Bitbucket administration features for the "`bitbucket-automation-tutorial`" workspace. This includes managing the workspace, projects, repositories, and other administrative functions.
- **bitbucket-user-access-admins-bitbucket-automation-tutorial**: This group has the "`User Access Admin`" role, which allows users to administer other users and groups for Bitbucket within the "`bitbucket-automation-tutorial`" workspace. Note that this role does not grant product access.
- **bitbucket-users-bitbucket-automation-tutorial**: This group has the "`User`" role, providing access to the Bitbucket workspace but with more limited permissions.

  You can create different groups and assign roles to manage access to the product effectively. Detailed project and repository permissions are configured within the Bitbucket Cloud project and repository settings, which will be covered in later sections of this book.

# Bitbucket Cloud Landing Page Overview

The Bitbucket Cloud landing page, also known as the overview page, offers a centralized view of your repositories and relevant information. Here is a breakdown of the key components and options typically found on this page:

**Navigation Bar**

- **`Bitbucket` Logo**: Clicking the Bitbucket logo usually takes you back to the landing page.
- **`Repositories` Tab**: This tab provides access to all your repositories. You can view repositories you have recently worked on or search for specific ones.
- **`Projects` Tab**: Lists projects within the workspace. Projects help organize your repositories for better management, allowing you to group related repositories and apply permissions and settings at the project level.
- **`Pull Requests`**: View open, merged, and closed pull requests. You can create new pull requests and review existing ones.

**Figure 2.13**: *Bitbucket cloud Overview Page*

- **`Settings` (gear icon)**: Provides access to various settings:

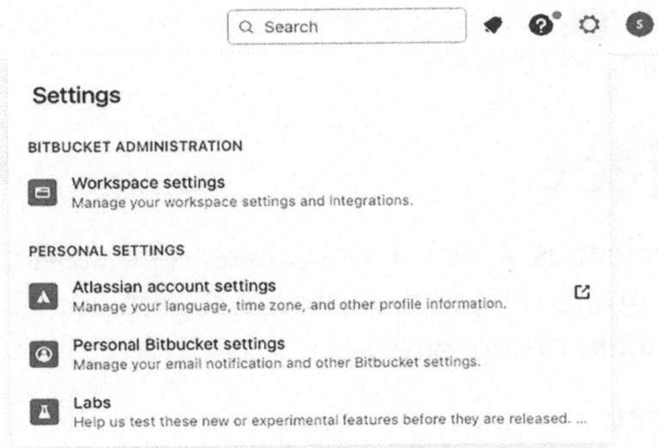


**Figure 2.14**: *Bitbucket cloud Settings*

- **`Atlassian Account Settings`**: Manage overall account details, security, billing, and connected applications.
- **`Workspace Settings`**: Handle workspace-level configurations, including user management, repository settings, integrations, and billing.
- **`Personal Bitbucket Settings`**: Adjust settings specific to your Bitbucket account, such as profile information, notifications, and SSH keys.
- **`Labs`**: Access and provide feedback on experimental features and upcoming functionalities.
- **`Search`**: Use the search bar to find for specific code snippets, functions, variables, or comments within the codebase of your repositories. This is helpful when you need to locate where certain code is used or how it is implemented.

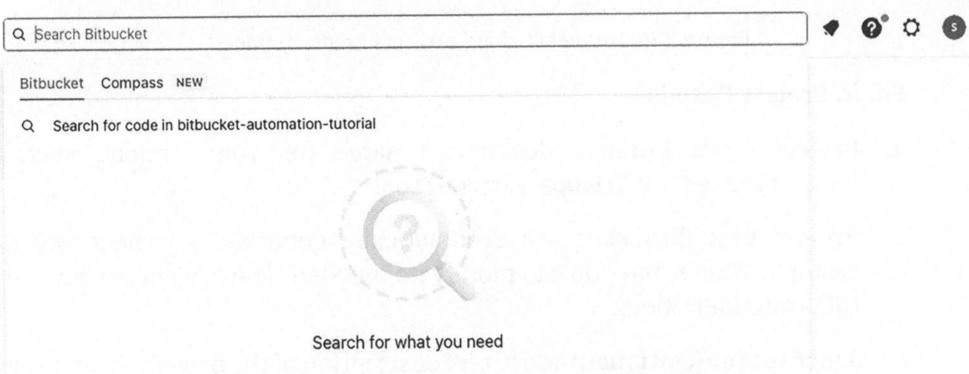


**Figure 2.15**: *Bitbucket cloud Search*

**Dashboard "`Your Work`" Tab:**

- **`Repositories Tab`**: Displays repositories recently accessed from your account.
- **`Pull Requests`**: Shows pull requests you have authored recently.

- **`Jira Issues`**: Displays Jira issues associated with your projects or repositories if Jira keys are linked to them.

# Create Project

A **Bitbucket Cloud project** is a way to organize repositories within a workspace. Projects allow teams to group related repositories together, making it easier to manage and navigate large numbers of repositories.

**Steps to Create a Project:**

1. **Access Projects**:
    a. From the top of the workspace overview page, click on the **`Projects`** tab.
2. **Create a New Project**:
    a. On the Projects page, click the **`Create Project`** button.

***Figure 2.16**: Bitbucket cloud projects creation page*

3. **Fill in Project Details**:
    a. **Project `Name`**: Enter a descriptive name for your project, such as "**`Repositories`**" or "**`DevOps Automation`**."
    b. **Project `Key`**: Bitbucket will automatically generate a project key (for example, REPO), but you can modify it if needed. The project key is used in URLs and identifiers.
    c. **`Description` (Optional)**: Add a brief description of the project for additional context (for example, "*This project contains all automation scripts for CI/ CD pipelines.*").
4. **Set Project Permissions**:
    a. Choose the privacy setting for the project:
        i. **Private**: Only authorized users can view or interact with the project.

ii. **Public**: Anyone can view the project, depending on repository-specific settings.

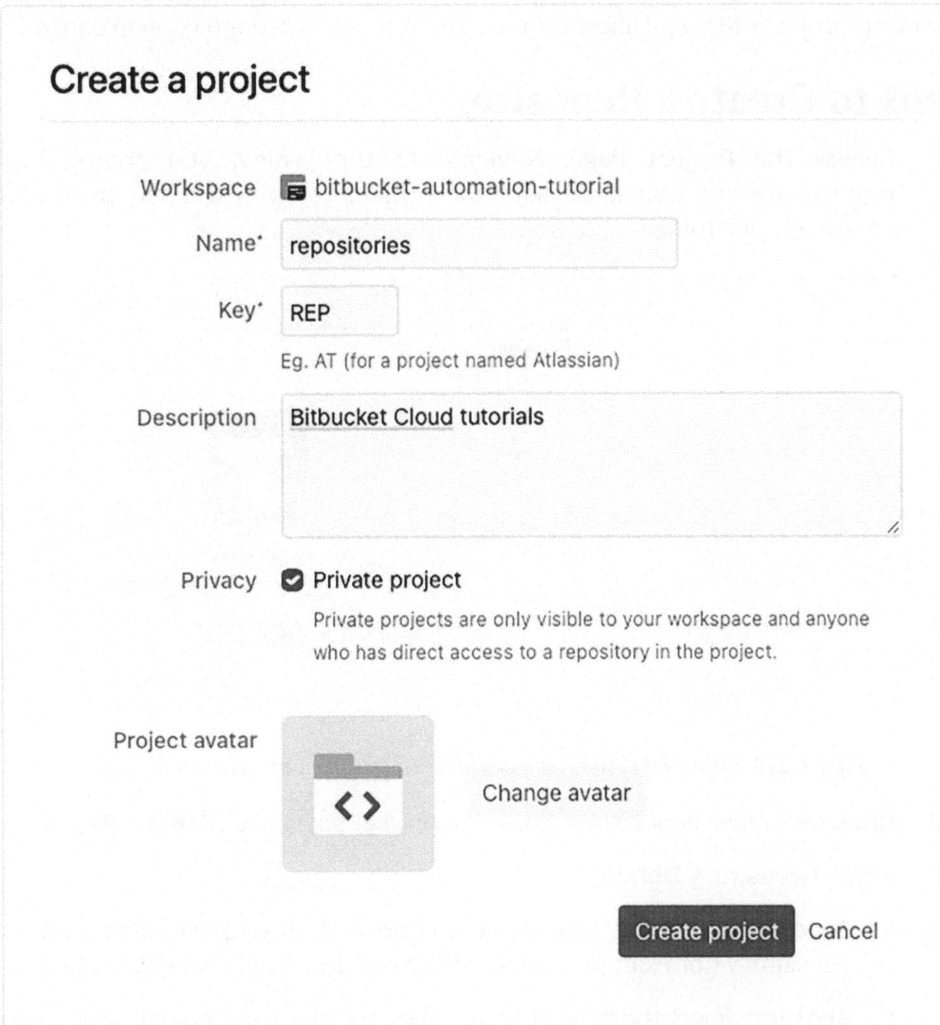


***Figure 2.17**: Bitbucket cloud projects creation form*

5. **Create the Project**: Once all the details are filled in, click the `Create Project` button to finalize.

# Create Repository

Now that you have created a project, you can associate repositories with it. A repository stores your project's files and allows you to track changes through version control, Git.

## Steps to Create a Repository

1. **Access the Project Page**: Navigate to the project you created. If no repositories are associated with the project yet, you will see an option to create a repository.

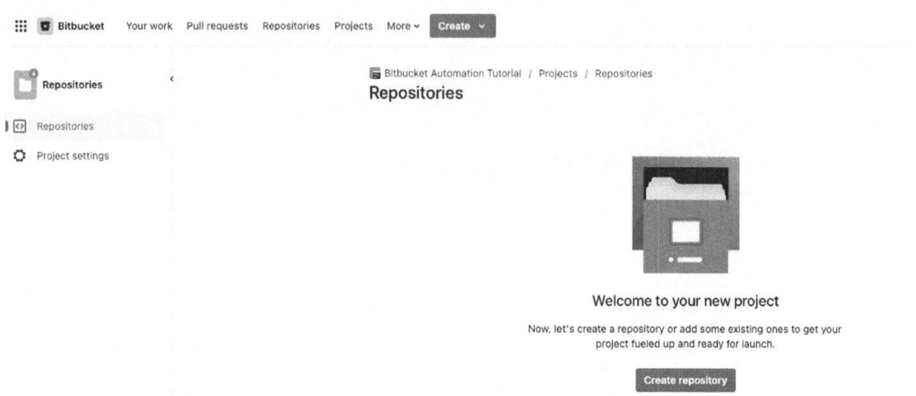


***Figure 2.18***: *Bitbucket cloud repositories creation from projects home page*

2. **Click on Create Repository**: From the project page, click **`Create Repository`**.
3. **Enter Repository Details**:
   a. **`Repository Name`**: Choose a unique and descriptive name for your repository (for example, "**`automation-scripts`**" or "**`frontend-app`**").
   b. **`Project`**: Select the project where the repository will belong. If you do not have any projects, you will need to create one first.
   c. **`Default Branch Name`**: Choose the default branch for your repository (for example, "**`main`**" or "**`master`**").
   d. **`Access Level`**: Select whether your repository will be **`Private`** (inheriting permissions from the project) or **`Public`**.
4. **Optional Features**:
   a. **`Include a README`**: Add a **`README`** file to provide documentation for your repository. This is useful to give a quick overview of your project.

   b. **`Include .gitignore`**: Choose a template for your **`.gitignore`** file to ignore unnecessary files (for example, system files or dependencies) from being tracked by Git.

   c. **`Language`**: Optionally, select the programming language of the repository (for example, Python, Java, or C#). This will optimize repository settings for the language you choose.

5. **Advanced Settings**:

   a. **`Description` (Optional)**: Add a short description for the repository to clarify its purpose.

   b. **`Forking`**: Choose whether to allow other users to fork your repository or not.

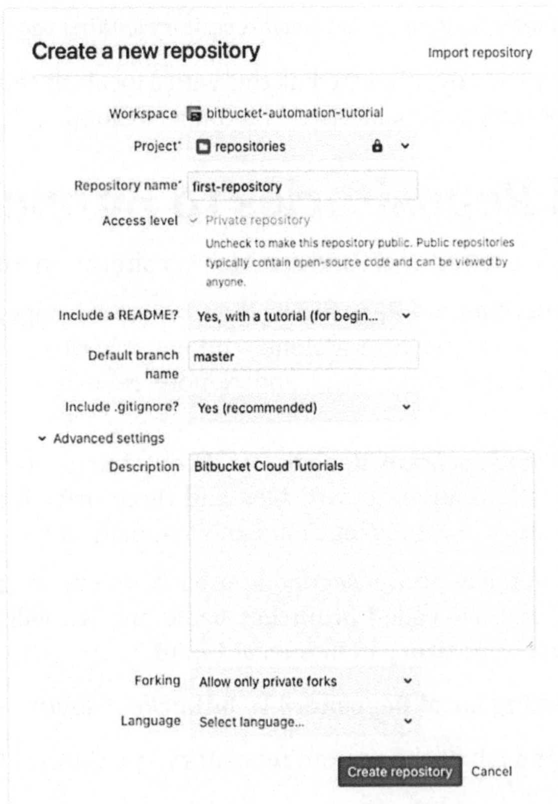


***Figure 2.19**: Bitbucket cloud repository creation page*

After entering all the necessary details, click the **`Create Repository`** button.

Now we have created a remote Bitbucket Cloud repository.

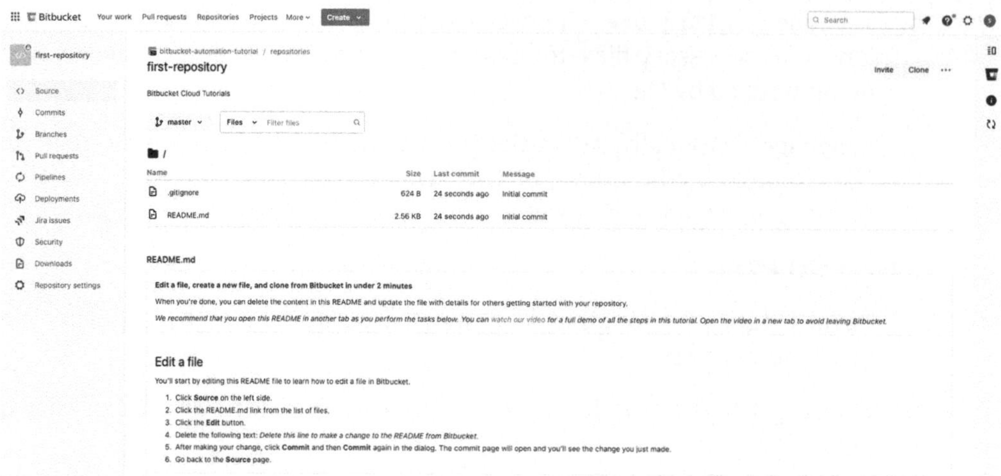


***Figure 2.20**: Bitbucket cloud repository landing page*

In the next section, we will cover how to link this with a local Git repository and explore additional features of remote repositories in Bitbucket Cloud.

# Link Local Repositories to Bitbucket Cloud

There are multiple ways to link local and remote repositories in Bitbucket Cloud.

- **Clone an Empty Remote Repository:** First, create an empty remote repository in Bitbucket Cloud, perform a clone, and start working with this repository locally. When cloning, the local and remote repositories are automatically linked.
- **Link a Pre-Existing Local Repository:** Alternatively, you can create a local repository first, populate it with files and directories (code), then create a remote repository in Bitbucket Cloud and manually link them.

In this section, we will focus on the second approach, where we already have a local Git repository in a directory called **bitbucket-book**, and we will link it to a remote repository named **first-repository** in Bitbucket Cloud.

**Steps to Link an Existing Local Repository to Bitbucket Cloud:**

1. Go to the **`Clone`** tab of the remote repository in Bitbucket Cloud; you will find two types of URLs:

    a. **HTTPS URL**

    ```
    git clone https://bitbucket-automation-tut-admin@bitbucket.
    org/bitbucket-automation-tutorial/first-repository.git
    ```

    This URL requires you to authenticate using your Bitbucket credentials (username/password or an App Password)

b. **SSH URL**

```
git clone git@bitbucket.org:bitbucket-automation-tutorial/
first-repository.git
```

SSH uses SSH keys instead of a **`username/password`** combination.

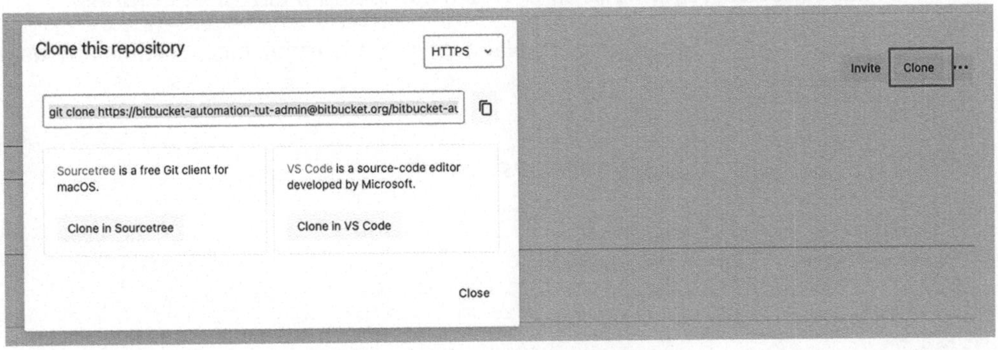


***Figure 2.21****: Bitbucket cloud clone tab*

# Generating SSH Keys and App Passwords

1. **Generate SSH Key**: To generate an SSH key, use the following command in your terminal:

   ```
   ssh-keygen -t rsa -b 4096 -C "your-email@example.com"
   ```

   Follow the prompts to save the key pair **`id_rsa.pub`** and **`id_rsa`**, then add the public key (**`id_rsa.pub`**) to your Bitbucket account under **`Bitbucket Settings`** > **`Personal Bitbucket Settings`** > **`SSH keys`**. Paste the contents of your **`id_rsa.pub`** file into the Key field, then save.

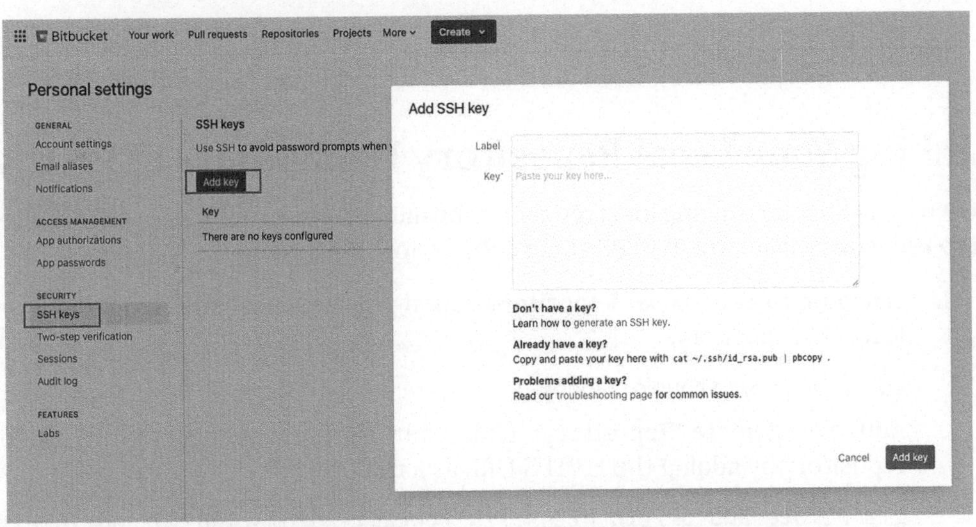


***Figure 2.22****: Bitbucket cloud personal settings – SSH Keys*

2. Generate App Password:

   a. Go to **`Personal settings`** > **`App passwords`** in Bitbucket.

   b. Create a new **`App password`** and select the necessary scopes (for example, repositories: read, write to perform clone and push git operations).

   c. Use this **`App password`** in place of your normal password when using HTTPS.

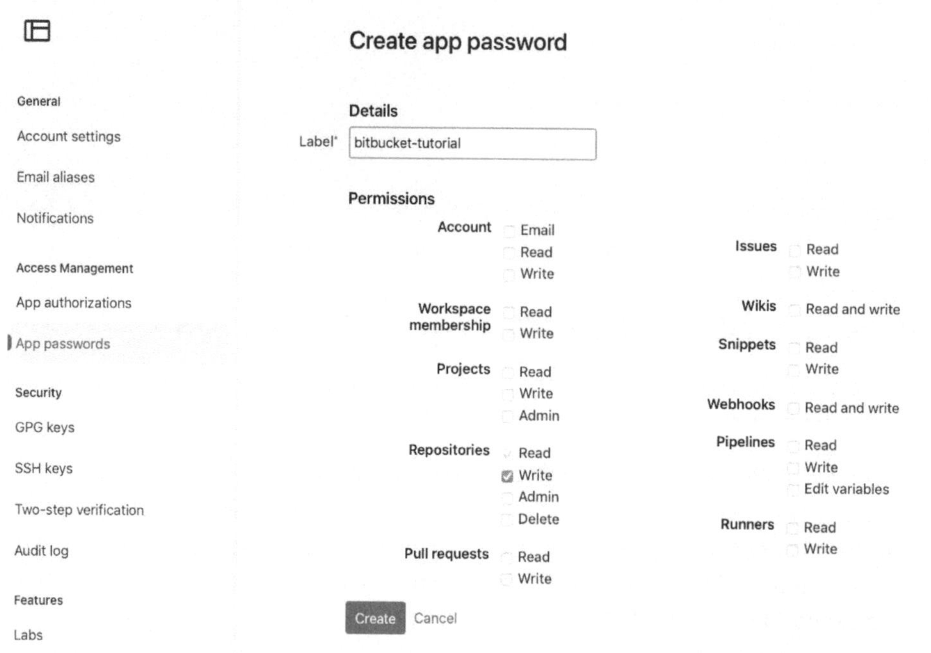


***Figure 2.23**: Bitbucket cloud personal settings – App Password*

## Linking Your Local Repository Using the HTTPS URL

Now we will link the existing local repository **bitbucket-book** to the remote repository **first-repository** using the HTTPS clone URL. Follow these steps:

1. **Navigate to Your Local Repository**: Open your terminal and navigate to your local Git repository:

```
cd /path/to/bitbucket-book
```

2. **Add the Remote Repository**: Link your local repository to the remote repository by adding the HTTPS URL as a remote:

```
git remote add origin https://bitbucket-automation-tut-admin@bit-
bucket.org/bitbucket-automation-tutorial/first-repository.git
```

3. **Push the Local Repository to Bitbucket Cloud**:

   `git push -u origin master`

   The **-u** option sets the main branch in your local repository to track the main branch in the remote repository.

4. **Verify the Remote Link**: Confirm that your local repository is now linked to the remote by running:

   `git remote -v`

**Figure 2.24**: *Linking Your Local Repository Using the HTTPS URL*

The local repository changes have now been synced with the remote repository.

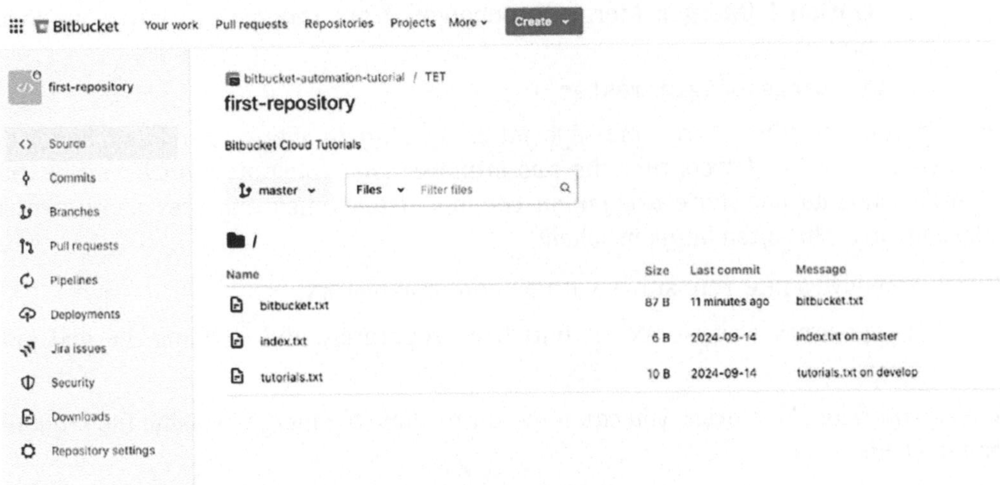


**Figure 2.25**: *Linked Local Repository on remote repository*

In the preceding example, we used the **-f** (force) option with the **git push** command because the commits made locally in the previous chapter (during Git initialization and the initial commit with the **.gitignore** and README.md files) are not the same files and commits made when creating the local remote repository. The **-f** option forces the push from the local repository to overwrite the existing commits on the remote.

However, the **-f** or **force push** should generally be avoided unless absolutely necessary, as it can overwrite important changes on the remote. In normal circumstances, you should first fetch the latest changes from the remote, review any differences, and then merge or rebase the changes before pushing your updates. The following steps explain how to handle this process correctly without force pushing:

## Handling Differences Between Local and Remote Without Force Push

1. **Fetch the Latest Changes from the Remote Repository:**

   ```
   git fetch origin
   ```

2. **Check the Status and Log to Identify Differences:**

   a. Verify if your local branch is behind the remote:

   ```
   git status
   ```

   b. Compare the commits between your local branch and the remote:

   ```
   git log --oneline origin/master..HEAD
   ```

3. Merge or Rebase Remote Changes Locally:

   a. **Option 1 (Merge):** Merge the changes from the remote into your local branch:

   ```
   git merge origin/master
   ```

**Note**: *If you encounter error message fatal: refusing to merge unrelated histories, it is expected as Git detects that the two branches (your current branch master and origin/master) do not share a common commit history, meaning they were created independently. This often happens when:*

- You have a new repository with no common history.
- A repository was cloned or initialized separately and is being merged (our case).

*To merge unrelated histories, you can force Git to allow the merge by using the --allow-unrelated-histories*

```
git merge origin/master --allow-unrelated-histories
```

   b. **Option 2 (Rebase):** Rebase your local changes on top of the remote branch:

   ```
   git rebase origin/master
   ```

4. **Resolve Conflicts (if any):**

   a. If conflicts arise (for example, in the .gitignore file), manually resolve them, then stage the resolved files:

   ```
   git add <conflicted-file>
   ```

b. Continue the merge or rebase process:

```
git merge --continue  # For merging
 git rebase --continue # For rebasing
```

5. **Push Your Local Changes to the Remote:**

   a. After the merge or rebase is completed and conflicts are resolved, push your changes to the remote:

```
git push origin master
```

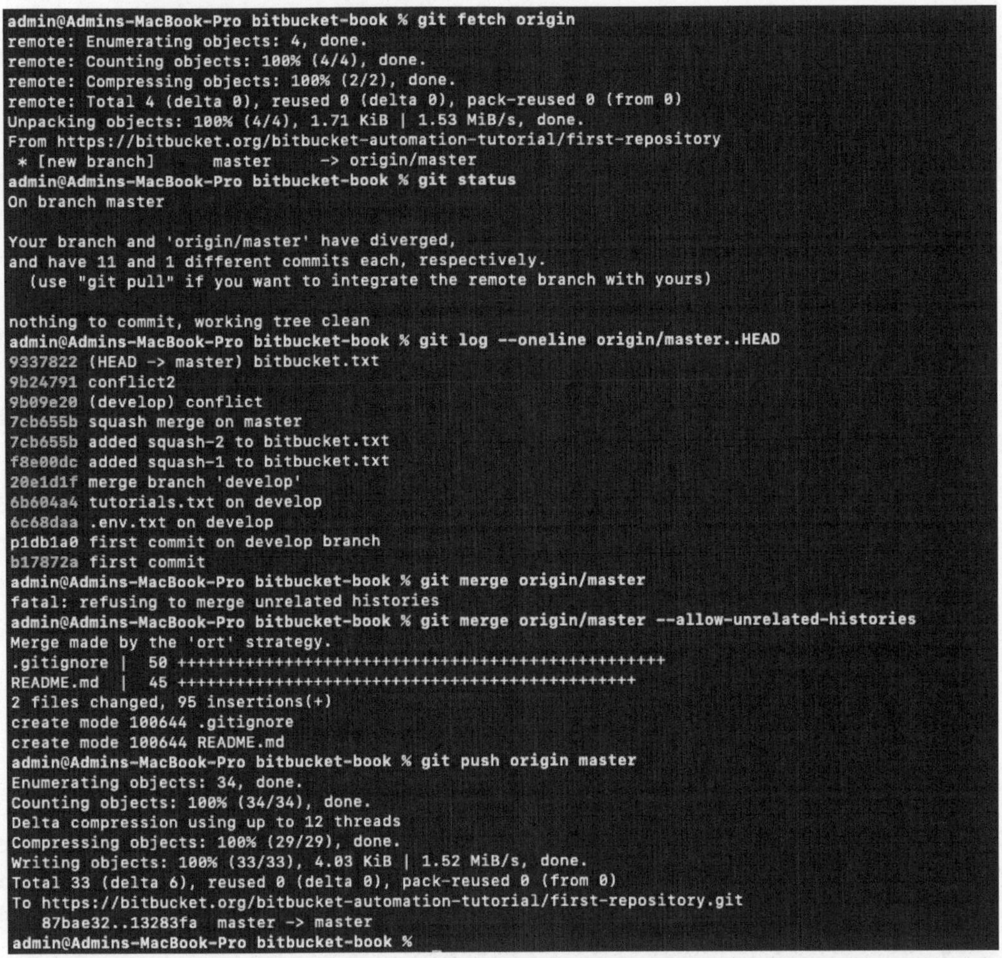


***Figure 2.26***: *Handling Differences Between Local and Remote Without Force Push*

This method ensures that your local changes are safely merged with the remote repository, avoiding accidental overwrites and preserving the integrity of both local and remote commits.

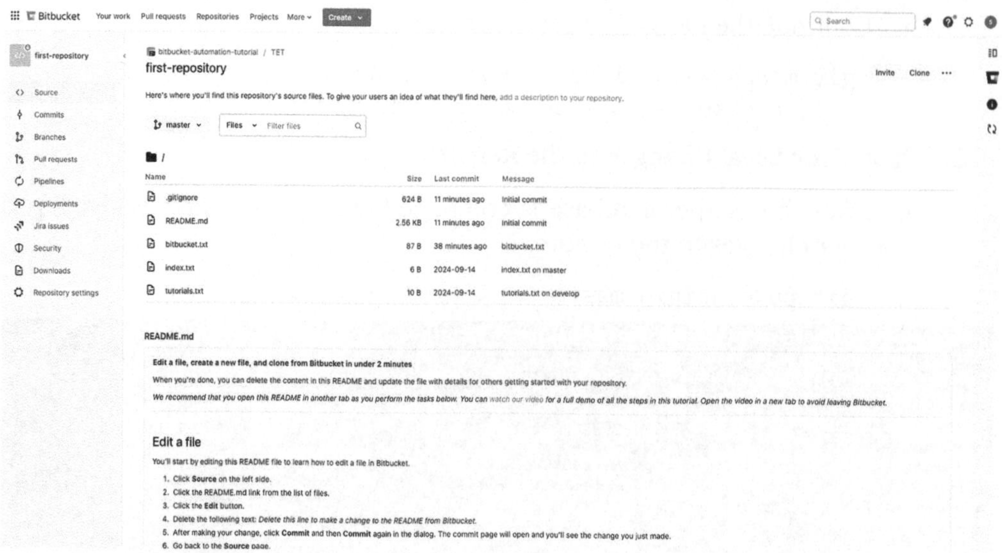


**Figure 2.27**: *Linked Local Repository on remote repository using fetch and push*

After completing these steps, your local repository will be successfully linked to Bitbucket Cloud, allowing you to push, pull changes and collaborate.

Once the local and remote repositories are linked, we can verify the connection by listing both local and remote branches with the following command:

```
git branch -a
```

This will output something like:

```
 develop
* master
  remotes/origin/master
```

- **`develop`** and **`master`** represent the local branches.
- **`remotes/origin/master`** indicates the remote branch in Bitbucket.
- ***** indicates the current local branch, which is master.

The prefix **`remotes/*`** signifies branches in the remote repository (in this case, Bitbucket Cloud), while branches without the remotes/* prefix are local branches. The term **`origin`** is the default name for the remote repository, and we used this when adding the remote URL with the git remote add command.

# Tracking Local and Remote Branches

In the preceding scenario, the local master branch is now **tracking** the remote remotes/origin/master branch because we linked the repositories. Using commands such as git fetch and git merge helped merge the remote changes into the local branch, and subsequently, we pushed the consolidated changes back to the remote master branch.

**`git pull` command**

There is another command called **`git pull`**, which simplifies the process by combining both git fetch and git merge into a single command. It fetches the latest changes from the remote repository and merges them into the current branch in one step.

```
git pull origin master
```

To merge unrelated histories, such as in our case, we need to use: `git pull origin master --allow-unrelated-histories`

This command fetches changes from the remote origin repository's master branch and merges them into the local master branch, even when the histories are unrelated.

To summarize:

- **`git pull`** is a combined command that fetches and merges remote changes into the current branch.
- **`git pull origin master --allow-unrelated-histories`** is useful when linking repositories with unrelated histories.

We can either **`pull`** or **`rebase`** remote changes. Both approaches ensure local and remote branches remain synchronized.

## Bitbucket Cloud 100 MB File Size Push Limit Feature

Bitbucket Cloud has an optional feature of a 100 MB limit on individual file uploads through Git; when enabled, no single file in the repository can exceed this size when pushing to the remote repository.

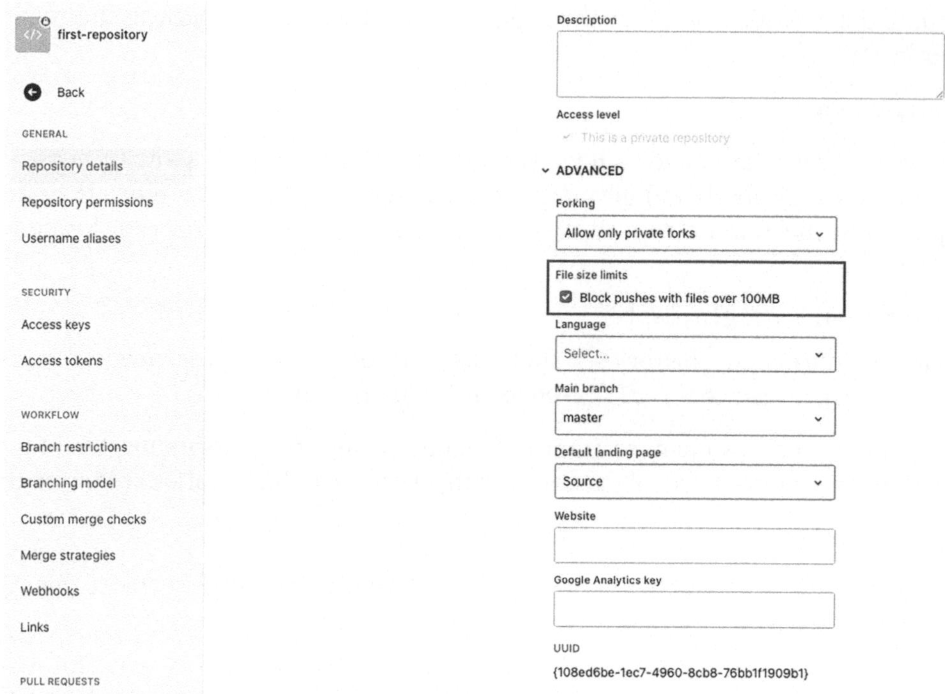


***Figure 2.28**: 100 MB file size push limit feature*

Git was primarily designed for version control of **text files**, such as source code, due to its efficient delta compression, effective merging capabilities, and performance optimizations. It can track small changes and present meaningful diffs, making it ideal for collaborative coding. In contrast, binary files do not benefit from these features, leading to increased storage requirements and performance issues, which is why Git LFS was introduced to manage large binary files separately. Common binary file examples include images (`.jpg`, `.png`, `.gif`), office documents (`.docx`, `.xlsx`), archives (`.zip`, `.rar`), executable files (`.exe`, `.bin`), 3D models (`.obj`, `.fbx`), and fonts (`.ttf`, `.otf`).

For files that are large or equal to 100 MB, it is recommended to use **Git Large File Storage (LFS)**. Storing such files in Git LFS helps manage large files efficiently and keeps your repository's size manageable. Bitbucket Cloud repositories have a hard size limit of 4 GB, and tracking numerous large files can lead to increased repository size, negatively impacting performance and making operations such as cloning and fetching slower.

In the next section, we will cover the steps to enable Git LFS in your repository and how to store large files effectively. By utilizing Git LFS, you can ensure that your repository remains performant and easy to manage, even as you work with larger assets. This approach is essential for developers dealing with media files, datasets, or other large binaries that exceed the typical limits of Git.

# Setting Up Git LFS (Large File Storage) for Bitbucket Cloud

As discussed, Git LFS is useful in managing large files by storing them separately, reducing the repository's size, and maintaining performance while still allowing efficient version control. The following are the steps to install, configure, and use Git LFS:

**Step 1**: Install Git LFS

a. Download and Install Git LFS:

   i. For Windows, macOS, or Linux, download and install Git LFS from the official website https://git-lfs.com

   ii. Alternatively, we can use a package manager:

   - **On macOS**: `brew install git-lfs`
   - **On Ubuntu**: `sudo apt-get install git-lfs`

b. Initialize Git LFS: After installation, run the following command to set up Git LFS in your repository: `git lfs install`

**Step 2**: Configure Git LFS for Your Repository

a. **Track Specific File Types**: Use the git lfs track command to specify which file types should be managed by LFS. For example, to track all **`.mp4`** and **`.zip`** files:

```
git lfs track "*.mp4"
git lfs track "*.zip"
```

b. **Add the `.gitattributes` File**: This command creates or updates a **`.gitattributes`** file in your repository to include the tracked patterns. Make sure to commit this file:

```
git add .gitattributes
git commit -m "Track large files with Git LFS"
```

**Step 3**: Push to Bitbucket Cloud

Now you can add your large files to the repository as you normally would:

```
git add <large-file>
git commit -m "Add large file"
git push origin <branch>
```

```
admin@Admins-MacBook-Pro bitbucket-book % git lfs install
Updated Git hooks.
Git LFS initialized.
admin@Admins-MacBook-Pro bitbucket-book % ls -l 200mb.zip
-rw-r--r--@ 1 admin  staff  18035474 Sep 28 23:04 200mb.zip
admin@Admins-MacBook-Pro bitbucket-book % git lfs track "*.zip"
Tracking "*.zip"
admin@Admins-MacBook-Pro bitbucket-book % git add .gitattributes
admin@Admins-MacBook-Pro bitbucket-book % git commit -m "Track large files with Git LFS"
[master 8650039] Track large files with Git LFS
 1 file changed, 1 insertion(+)
 create mode 100644 .gitattributes
admin@Admins-MacBook-Pro bitbucket-book % git add 200mb.zip
admin@Admins-MacBook-Pro bitbucket-book % git commit -m "Add large file"
[master fe785fd] Add large file
 1 file changed, 3 insertions(+)
 create mode 100644 200mb.zip
admin@Admins-MacBook-Pro bitbucket-book % git push origin master
Uploading LFS objects: 100% (1/1), 18 MB | 3.8 MB/s, done.
Enumerating objects: 7, done.
Counting objects: 100% (7/7), done.
Delta compression using up to 12 threads
Compressing objects: 100% (5/5), done.
Writing objects: 100% (6/6), 668 bytes | 668.00 KiB/s, done.
Total 6 (delta 2), reused 0 (delta 0), pack-reused 0 (from 0)
To https://bitbucket.org/bitbucket-automation-tutorial/first-repository.git
   13283fa..fe785fd  master -> master
admin@Admins-MacBook-Pro bitbucket-book %
```

***Figure 2.29**: git LFS*

After you push large files to Bitbucket using LFS, the storage fees are tracked under LFS storage, but the files are still visible under your Git repository. For example, in the following image, the file "**200mb.zip**" is part of the repository pointing to the "**taste**" branch. When we click on it, it shows the Git LFS level, and we can download the file by clicking on it.

***Figure 2.30**: git LFS in bitbucket cloud user interface*

# Conclusion

In this chapter, you have learned how to create a Bitbucket Cloud account, set up organizations and workspaces, and manage repositories. You now understand how to create projects, repositories, link local and remote repositories, and handle large files using LFS in Bitbucket Cloud. These skills will help you to manage code and collaborate effectively. The next chapter will delve into pull requests.

# CHAPTER 3
# Comprehensive Guide to Pull Requests

## Introduction

In the previous chapters, we explored how to create a remote repository, link a local repository, commit changes to the main or master branch, and touched upon basic Git operations, such as push, pull, and merge. A core feature of distributed version control systems is to provide a collaborative environment for developers to manage, share, and work on code together.

In any software development project, **code versioning** plays a crucial role, where every minor update is tracked and versioned through commits. However, additional considerations must be addressed:

- Are the committed changes properly formatted, syntactically correct, and logically sound?
- Have the committed changes passed all necessary tests?
- Are all the required features included before the code is ready for release?
- How can distributed teams ensure their code changes are merged correctly and reviewed by others?

These challenges are addressed through the use of **pull requests (PR)**. Pull requests provide a feature-rich process that allows teams to review, have checks for tests and builds, and merge code changes. In this chapter, we will delve into how to create a basic pull request to ensure code changes are reviewed and merged successfully. Additionally, we will cover the role of branching in facilitating collaborative code development.

# Structure

In this chapter, we will cover the following topics:

- Create and Merge Pull Requests
- Pull Requests Descriptions and Templates
- Merge Strategies
- Assigning Reviewers
- Pull Request Diff and Activity Tab
- Resolving Pull Request Merge Conflicts

# Create and Merge Pull Requests

In this section, we will review the process of creating and merging pull requests using our Bitbucket Cloud repository named "**`first-repository`**," which contains a master branch. Pull requests allow us to review code before merging changes into the master branch.

We will create a branch named develop, make changes to this branch, commit the changes, and push them to the remote repository. Finally, we will create a pull request to review and merge the changes from develop to master.

## Creating the Develop Branch

There are two methods to create the develop branch:

1. Create a Branch Locally and Push to Remote
    a. Create and switch to the develop branch from master:
    ```
    git checkout -b develop master
    ```
    b. Push the develop branch to the remote repository:
    ```
    git push origin develop
    ```
2. Create a Branch in Bitbucket Cloud UI
    a. Go to your repository.
    b. Navigate to **`Branches`** > **`Create branch`**.
    c. Select **`master`** as the source, Type be a default selection "**`other`**", name the new branch **`develop`**, and click **`Create`** branch.

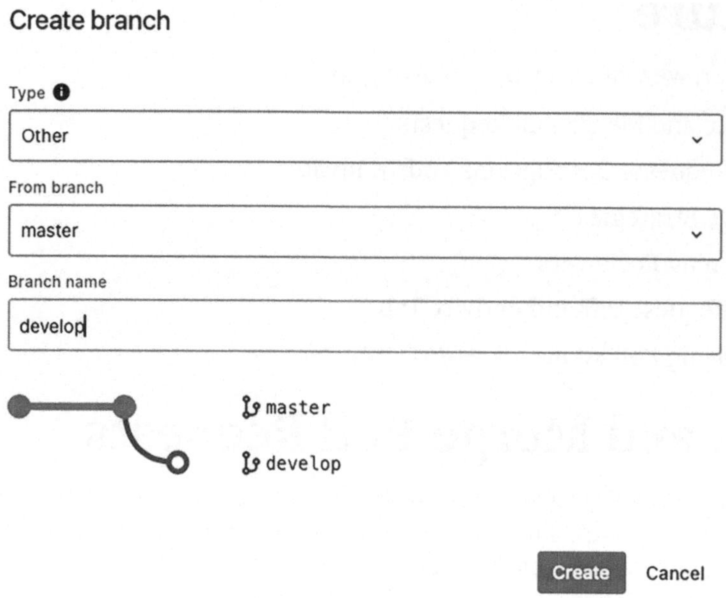


***Figure 3.1**: Create Branch page*

## Creating a Pull Request

Now that the develop branch is created, both develop and master point to the same snapshot of the code. A pull request is essentially merging changes from one branch to another. Let us add new changes to the develop branch.

1. **Edit Files and Commit Changes:** Edit **`tutorials.txt`** to add a new line and push changes to remote develop branch

   ```
   echo "pull-request" >> tutorials.txt
   git add tutorials.txt
   git commit -m "pull request tutorials"
   git push
   ```

2. **Create the Pull Request**

   a. Navigate to the **`Pull Requests`** tab in Bitbucket.

   b. Click **`Create Pull Request`**.

   c. Set **`develop`** as the **`Source Branch`** and **`master`** as the **`Destination`**.

   d. Add a **`Title`** and **`Description`** (optional).

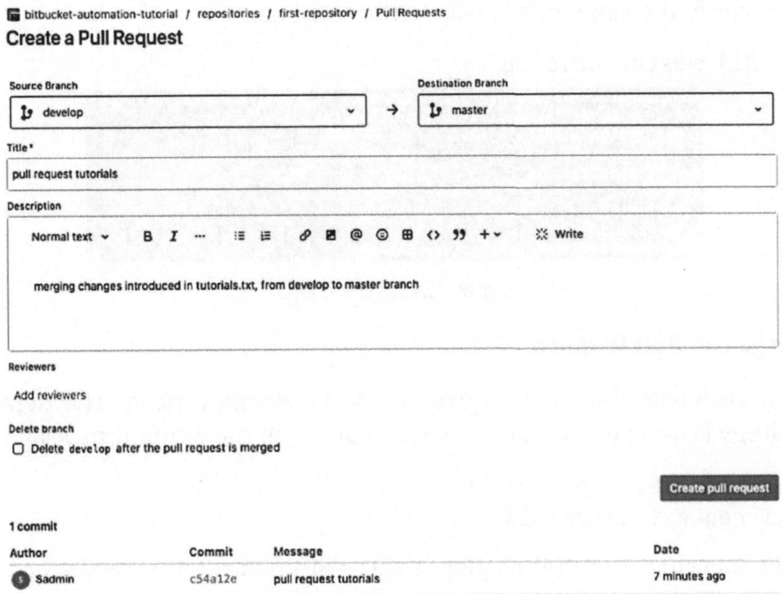


***Figure 3.2**: Create Pull Request page*

On the pull request page, you will see a file diff summary at the bottom; a green background indicates the changes made (for example, **`+pull-request`** in **`tutorials.txt`**).

On the right-side panel, you can see the files and how many lines have been added or removed.

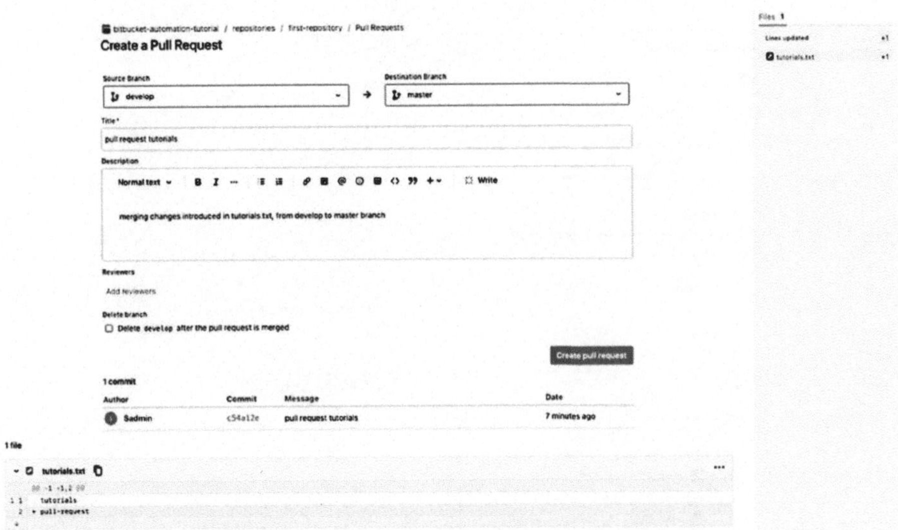


***Figure 3.3**: Create Pull Request page with Files Diff*

You can also verify the same diff locally in the terminal:

```
git diff master develop
```

**Figure 3.4**: *Branch Diff*

3. **Merge the Pull Request**

   After reviewing the pull request, click the **`Merge`** button. The default merge strategy is "**`merge commit`**," which will auto-fill the commit message:

   ```
   Merged in develop (pull request #1)
   pull request tutorials
   ```

   After merging, the pull request page will update with details of the merge, including:

   a. The person who merged the PR.

   b. The merge message in green banner:

   ```
   Merged pull request
   Merged in develop (pull request #1)
   a0f8c65 Author: Suhas Closed by: Suhas
   ```

   The commit **`a0f8c65`** is the **`merge`** commit.

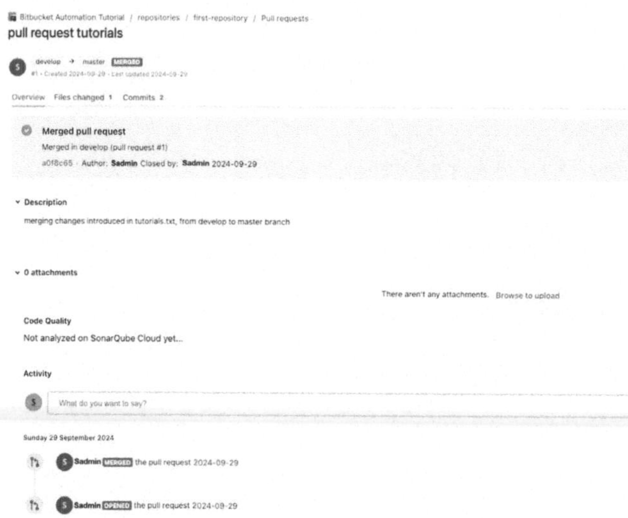


**Figure 3.5**: *Merged Pull Request page*

# Pull Requests Descriptions and Templates

When creating a pull request (PR), the PR site automatically fills in the title and description based on the commits included. If there is a single commit, the commit message will be used as the PR title, and the description will remain empty. However, if multiple commits are introduced in the pull request, the title will be filled with the source branch name, while the description will be auto-filled with the commit messages.

For example, in the following image, you can observe that the source branch name is included in the PR title, and the description is populated with the commit messages. This automation helps streamline the PR creation process and ensures that all relevant information is readily available for reviewers.

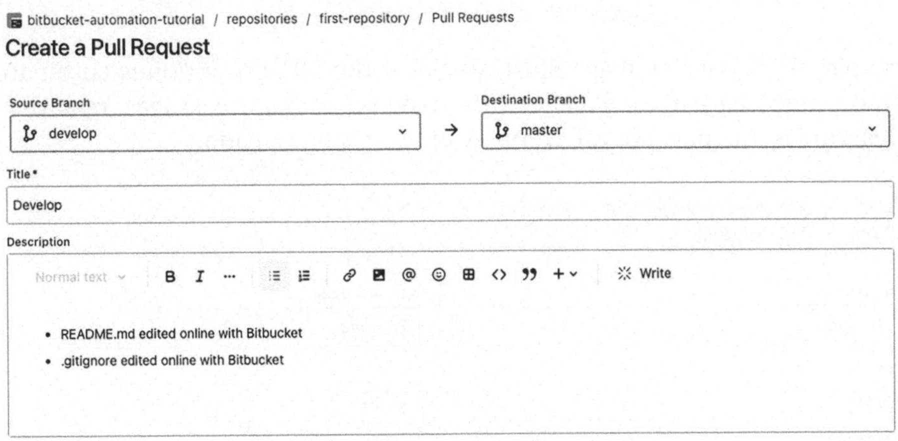


**Figure 3.6**: *Pull Request title and description*

In addition to the automatic generation of titles and descriptions based on commits, there is an option to set a default pull request description in the repository settings. By defining a default description, this text will preload each time a new pull request is created, providing a consistent starting point for contributors. This feature streamlines the PR creation process, ensuring that essential information or guidelines are always included, which can help maintain clarity and uniformity across all pull requests.

We discussed templates and automatic pull request (PR) descriptions generated from commit messages. While commit messages are generally short and meaningful, PR descriptions often require more detailed explanations. Atlassian Intelligence can be leveraged to generate comprehensive descriptions based on commit messages, ensuring clarity and coherence. Atlassian Intelligence can be enabled under workspace settings, Atlassian integrations.

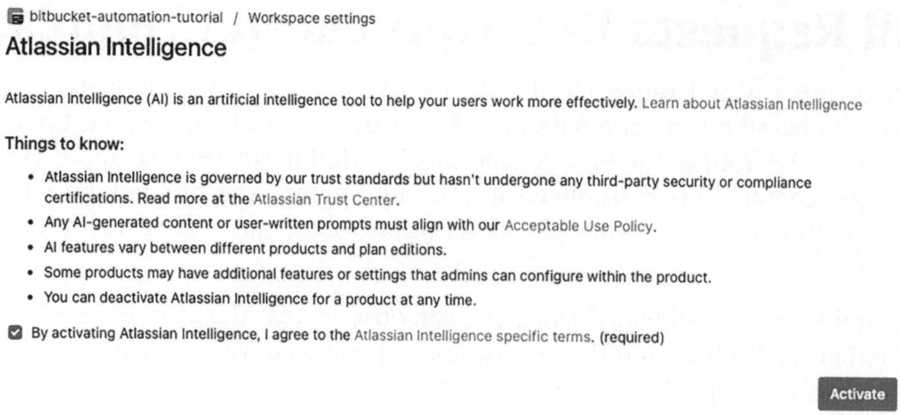


***Figure 3.7**: Atlassian Intelligence (AI)*

For example, the following image illustrates how the PR description is automatically generated using Atlassian Intelligence (AI) based on commit messages, resulting in a more descriptive and meaningful overview of the changes made.

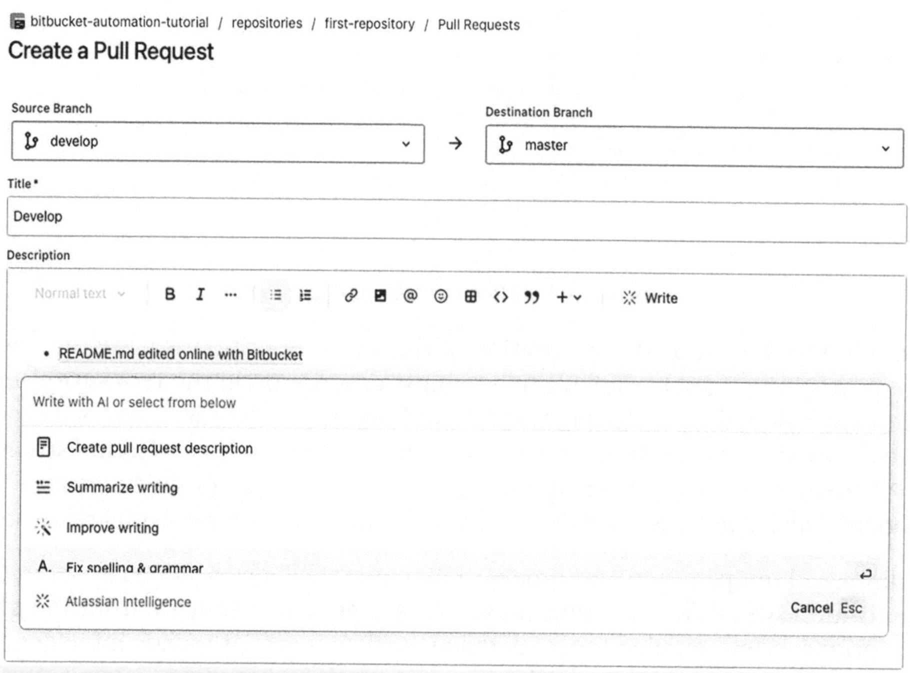


***Figure 3.8**: Pull Request title and description using AI (a)*

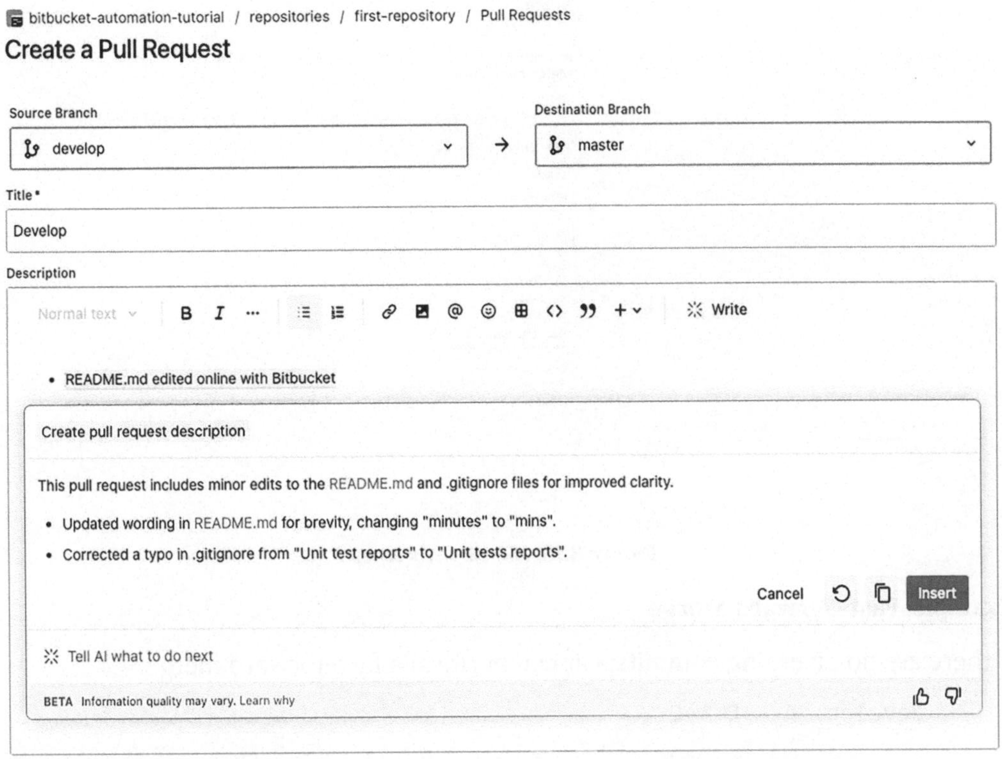


***Figure 3.9***: *Pull Request title and description using AI (b)*

# Merge Strategies

In the repository settings under **`Workflow > Merge Strategies`**, you can select different merge options:

- **`Merge Commit`**: This creates a **`merge`** commit with **`--no-ff`** (no fast forward).
- **`Squash Merge`**: Combines all changes into a single commit with --squash.
- **`Fast-Forward Merge`**: Uses **`--ff-only`**, moving the branch pointer forward without creating a **`merge`** commit if there is no divergence in history.

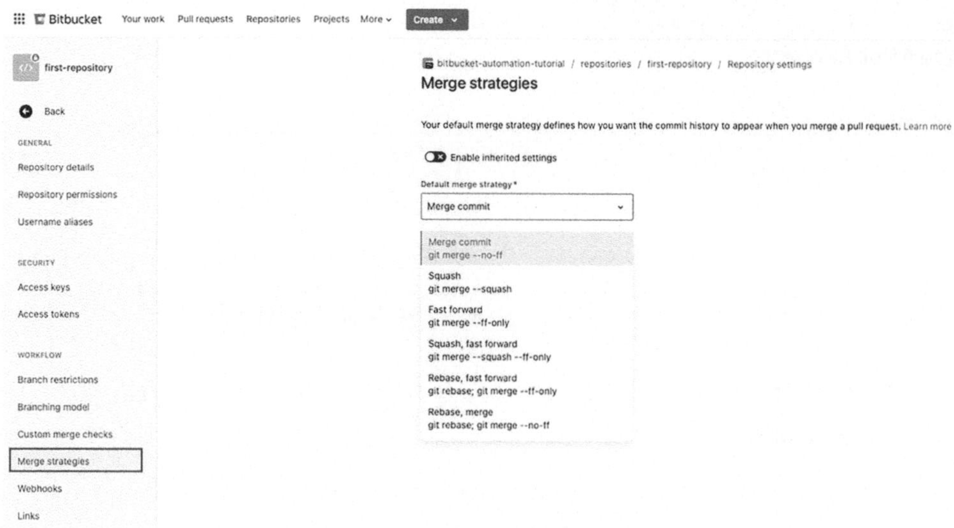


***Figure 3.10**: Merge Strategies*

**Example: Fast-Forward Merge**

If there are no diverging commits, Git can perform a fast-forward merge:

```
develop: A---B---C
                  \
master:            D---E
```

Merges into:

```
master: A---B---C---D---E
```

**Example: Merge Commit**

With a **merge** commit, the history diverges:

```
develop: A---B---C
                  \
master:            D---E
```

Merges into:

```
master: A---B---C---M
                /   \
develop:        D---E
```

In this case, **M** represents the merge commit a0f8c65. The commits **E** and **C** represent the heads of the source and destination branches of the pull request.

- **E (c54a12e)**: This is the head commit of the develop branch, which is the source branch in the pull request.

- **`C (fe785fd)`**: This is the head commit of the master branch before the merge, representing the state of the branch prior to incorporating the changes from develop.

When the merge is completed:

- The merge commit **`M (a0f8c65)`** has two parent commits:
  - **`fe785fd`**: The previous head of master before the merge.
  - **`c54a12e`**: The **`head`** commit of the **`develop`** branch, which contains the changes being merged.

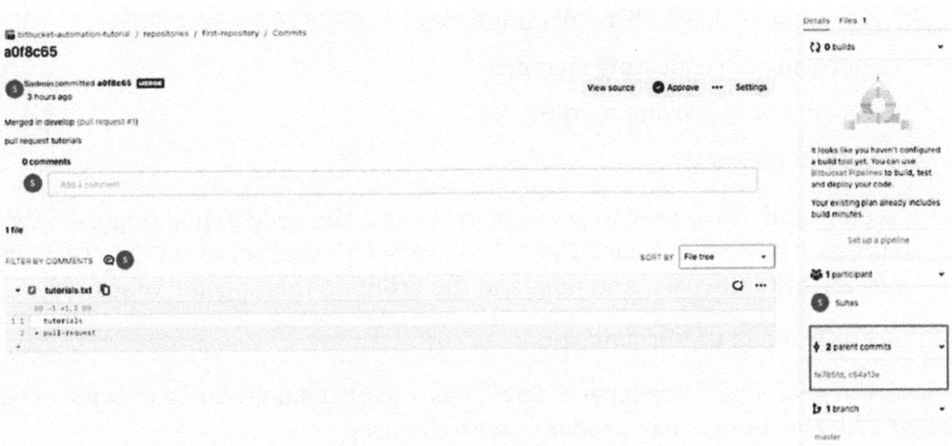


***Figure 3.11***: *Merge Commit Page*

**Comparison between Merge Commit and Fast-Forward Merge**

| **Criteria** | **Merge Commit** | **Fast-Forward Merge** |
|---|---|---|
| **History** | Divergent history, requires a new merge commit | Linear history, no new commit is created |
| **Use case** | When branches have diverged and need to be combined | When branches have not diverged |
| **Collaboration** | Best for larger teams with multiple contributors | Good for single-developer workflows or small projects |

***Table 3.1***: *Merge Commit versus Fast-Forward Merge*

Understanding these strategies helps ensure you use the best one for your team's workflow.

# Assigning Reviewers

We have already self-reviewed and merged a pull request. In typical software development, self-reviewing is not performed; code reviews are conducted by individuals who have relevant expertise and experience in the codebase, such as leads or subject matter experts (SMEs).

They are responsible for reviewing code changes, providing feedback, requesting modifications, and ultimately approving or declining a pull request. The review process ensures that code adheres to the repository's standards and that changes are vetted before being merged into the main branch.

**Key Responsibilities of a Reviewer Include:**

- Examining code changes
- Providing feedback through comments
- Approving or requesting changes
- Blocking or approving merges

**Steps to Add Reviewers:**

Let us add a new user who will be reviewing the code in pull requests. We will create a new group called Code Reviewers with user access at the organization level, invite the user, and then add the group to this specific repository.

To Create a Group in the Organization:

Click on the gear icon > **`Workspace Settings`** > **`User Management`** > **`Groups`** > **`Create Group`** > **`add the user`** > **`add products`** with the user.

***Figure 3.12**: Code Reviewers Groups with Bitbucket Cloud User Access*

We will add the group under **`Repository Settings`** > **`Repository Permissions`** > **`Add Users`** or **`Group`** > with write access.

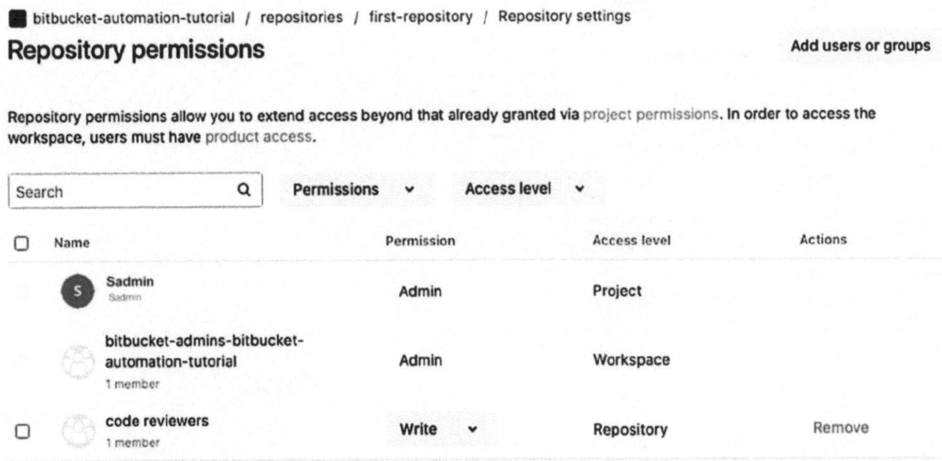


**Figure 3.13**: *Code Reviewers Groups added with Repository Write Access*

Under Repository Settings > Pull Requests, you will find Default Reviewers. Default Reviewers in Bitbucket Cloud are users who are automatically added as reviewers to pull requests (PRs) in a repository. This feature helps streamline the code review process by ensuring that specific individuals or teams are always assigned to review code changes, particularly for critical branches such as master or develop.

Let us add the user as a default reviewer.

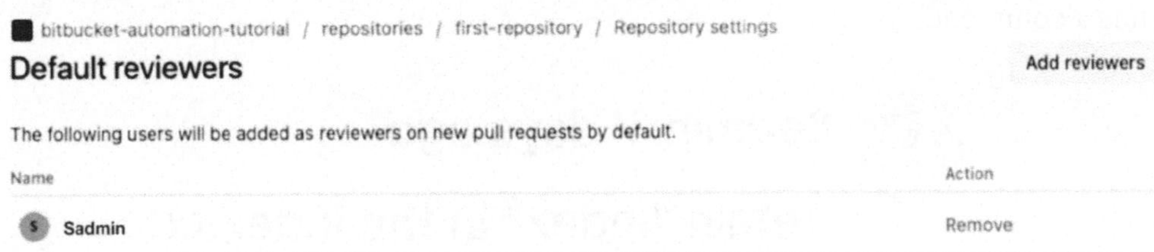


**Figure 3.14**: *Default Reviewers*

Now, we will add more changes in the develop branch and create a pull request to the master branch. On the pull request creation page, you will see the user added as a default reviewer.

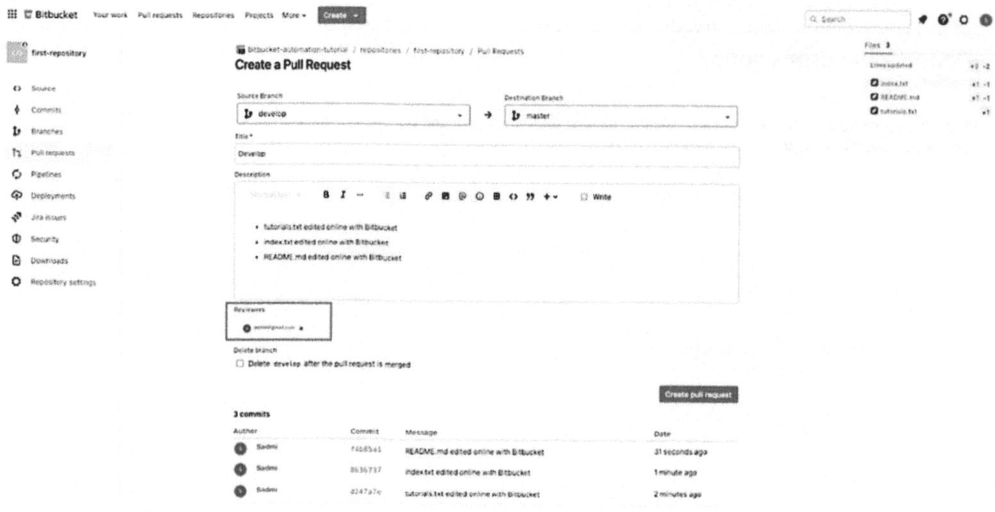


***Figure 3.15**: Default Reviewers in PR creation Page*

You can also manually search for and add reviewers, depending on how many sets of eyes you want on the code apart from the default reviewers.

Create the Pull Request

Now, we will log in with the other user's default account to review and approve the pull request. As the reviewer, we will request changes to revert the modification by adding a comment.

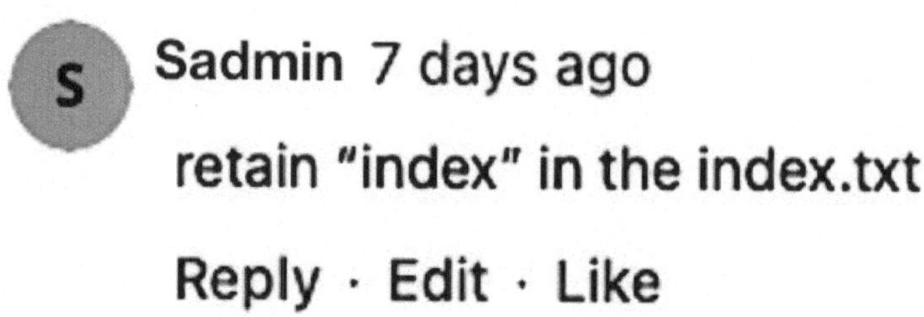


***Figure 3.16**: Default Reviewer PR Comment*

Here, the reviewer and author are both named "**Suhas**," but they are distinguished by their avatars. The reviewer's avatar has an orange background with the letter "**S**," while the author's avatar has a red background with the same letter. This visual difference will help us easily identify the reviewer and the author in the following steps of the review and merge process.

Now, the PR author will make the necessary changes requested by the reviewer and comment as "**done**."

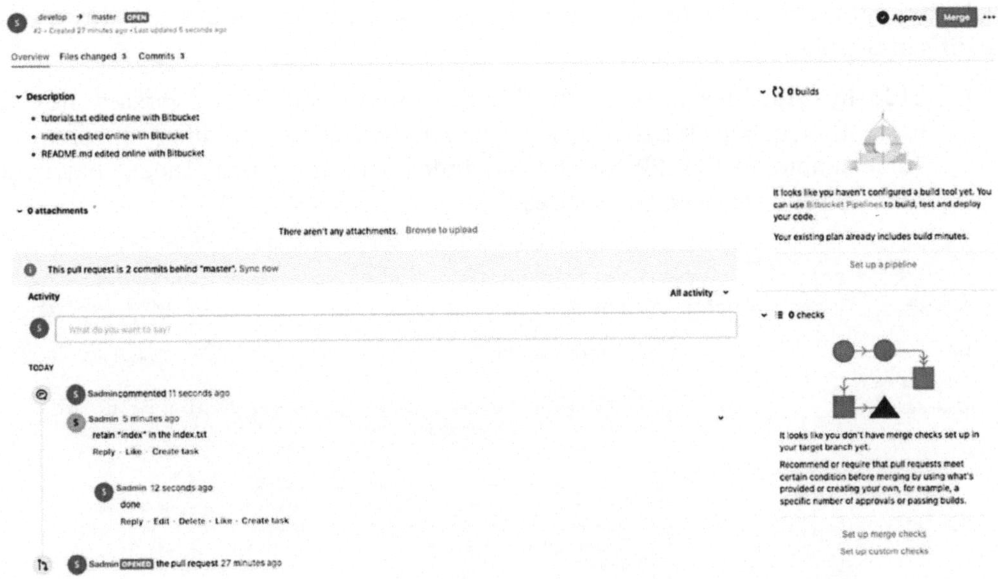


***Figure 3.17***: *PR comments*

Following this, the reviewer will check to ensure that **`index.txt`** is no longer in the diff since the changes were reverted, and they will approve and merge the pull request.

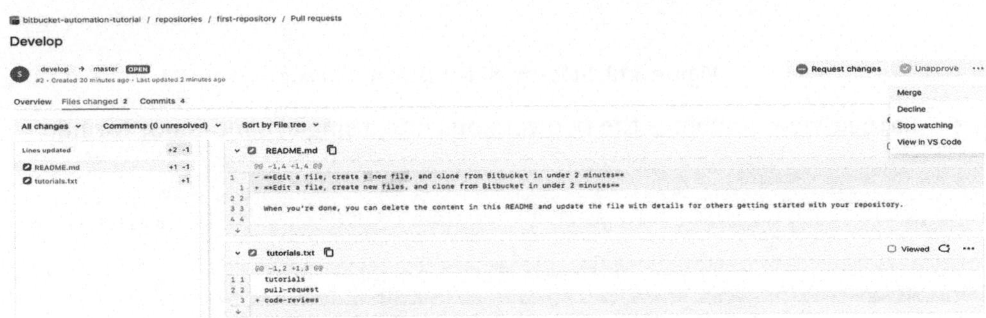


***Figure 3.18***: *PR Approve and Merge*

# Pull Request Diff and Activity Tab

In the previous section, we noted that the reviewer ensures that **`index.txt`** is no longer included in the **`diff`**. Additionally, the reviewer examines the differences in other files, such as **`README.md`**. In this case, deletions are highlighted with a light red background, while additions appear with a green background. This representation is known as the unified view of the diff, allowing reviewers to see both added and removed lines in a single view. Moving forward, we will discuss various types of pull request diffs and the pull request activity tab to gain deeper insights into the review process.

Click on the three dots on the file to select **Side-by-Side** View or **Unified View** to see the diffs in the files.

- **Side-by-Side** View presents the differences between the two versions next to each other, making it easier to see what has been added, modified, or removed. For example, in this PR for the file **index.txt**, the word "**index**" has been removed and replaced by "**indexes**."

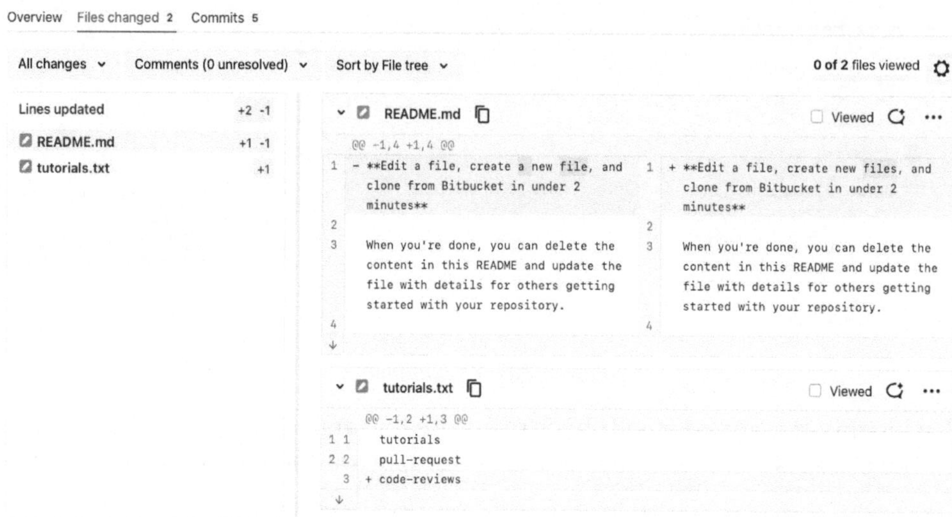

**Figure 3.19**: *Side-by-Side View in PR page*

- **Unified** View combines the two versions into a single, continuous format.

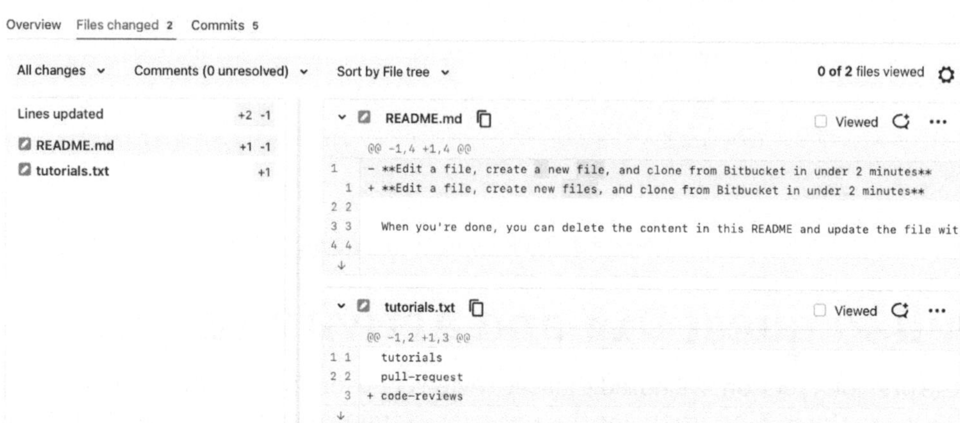

**Figure 3.20**: *Unified View in PR page*

- The Collapse View option will collapse the diff view.

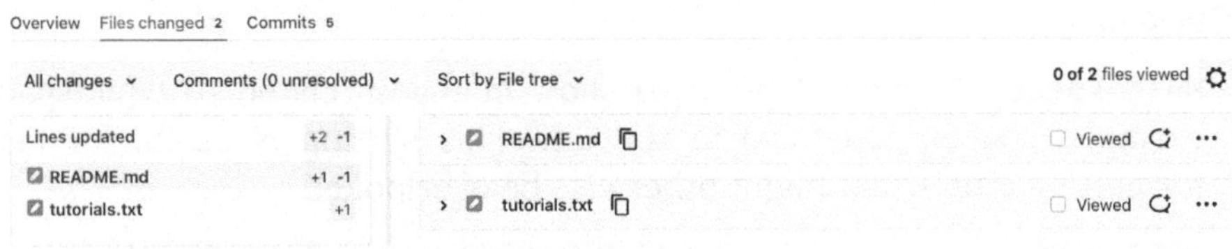


***Figure 3.21**: Collapse View in PR page*

You can access all these options using the gear icon > **`Global View Settings`**. The **`diff view settings`** allow users to customize how they view changes between different versions of files in pull requests for the entire **`diff`** instead of individual files.

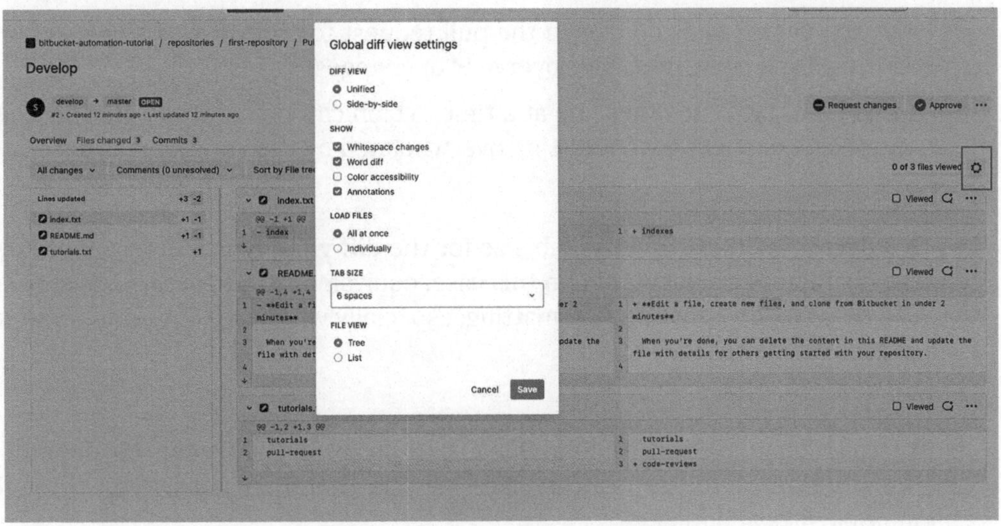


***Figure 3.22**: Global View Settings*

**`DIFF VIEW` Types:**

- **`Unified View`**: Displays changes in a single-column format, with additions and deletions highlighted in different colors. Context lines are included to provide surrounding information.
- **`Side-by-Side View`**: Presents the original and modified versions of the file next to each other in two columns. This format allows for easy visual comparison of changes.
- **`Gobble Diff`**: A specialized view that collapses multiple consecutive unchanged lines into a single line for a cleaner view, focusing on the actual changes and making it easier to see what has been modified without distraction.

**`SHOW` Options:**

- **`Whitespace Changes`**: Option to show changes related to whitespace (for example, spaces and tabs) in the diff. This setting is useful for catching formatting issues that might otherwise be overlooked.
- **`Word Diff`**: Highlights changes at the word level rather than the line level, showing specific words that have been added, removed, or modified. This option is particularly useful for reviewing documentation or text files where precise wording is crucial.
- **`Color Accessibility`**: Settings that adjust color contrasts for better visibility, ensuring that the diff is accessible for users with color vision deficiencies.
- **`Annotations`**: This feature allows users to add comments or notes directly in the diff view, facilitating discussions about specific changes or lines of code.

**`LOAD FILES`**:

- **`All at Once`**: Loads all files in the pull request for review in a single action, allowing for a comprehensive overview of changes.
- **`Individually`**: Loads files one at a time, which can be beneficial for focusing on specific changes without being overwhelmed by the entire diff at once.

**`TAB SIZE`**:

- **`6 Spaces`**: Users can set the tab size for the diff view, which determines how tab characters are displayed (in this case, equivalent to 6 spaces). This setting can help ensure consistent formatting, especially when working with different coding standards.

**`FILE VIEW`**:

- **`Tree`**: Displays files in a hierarchical tree structure, showing the directory organization of the repository. This view is useful for navigating through multiple files and folders.
- **`List`**: Presents files in a flat list format, making it easier to see all files at once without the hierarchical structure. This can be helpful when reviewing changes across many files quickly.

The **`Pull Request Activity` section under `Overview`** tab in PR is an overview of all the actions and changes related to a specific pull request. It shows a chronological list of actions taken on the pull request, such as:

a. The creation of the pull request.

b. Commits added to the pull request.

c. Comments added to the pull request.

d. Changes made to the pull request description or title.

e. Approval or requests for changes from reviewers.

f. Merges or declines of the pull request.

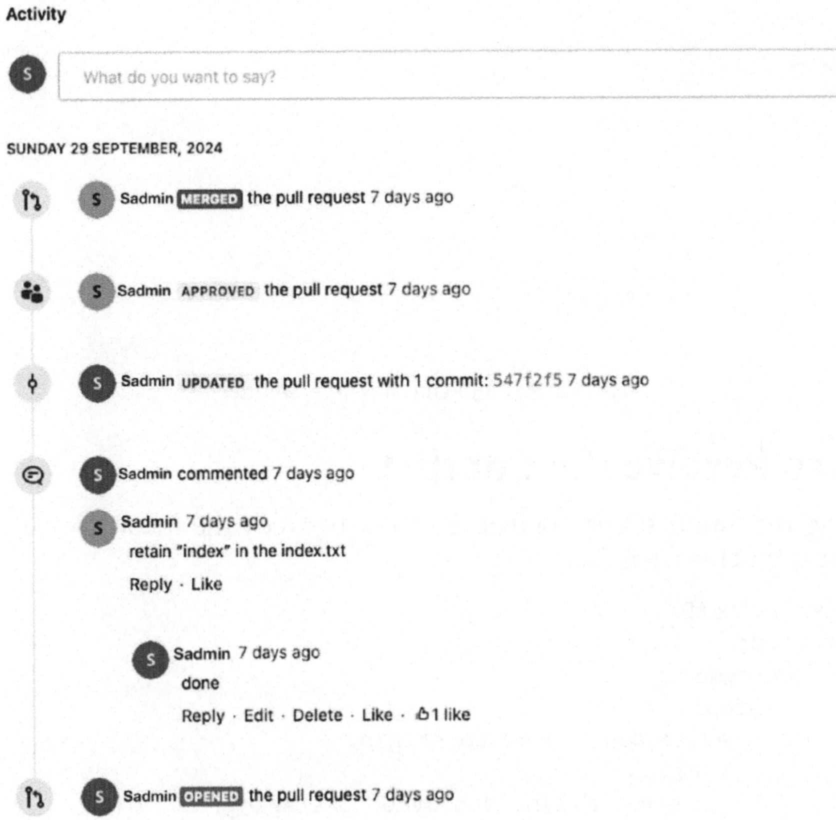


***Figure 3.23***: *Pull Request Activity Section*

# Resolving Pull Requests Merge Conflicts

A merge conflict arises when Git encounters differences between branches that it cannot automatically reconcile. This situation typically occurs when two branches have modifications to the same line in a file or when Git is uncertain how to integrate the changes. Resolving merge conflicts requires manual intervention.

In the following example, where both the **`master`** and **`develop`** branches have the same line changes, the conflict occurs, preventing a merge in Bitbucket Cloud. In such cases, an explanation symbol is displayed on the merge button, indicating that the merge cannot proceed due to conflicts.

**Figure 3.24**: *Pull Request Merge Conflict*

## Steps to Resolve the Conflict

**Identifying the Conflict**: The conflict is shown between the following lines in the **`bitbucket-pipelines.yml`** file:

```
<<<<<<< HEAD
 custom:
   deployment:
   -  step:
        name: deployment to staging
        script:
          - echo "Hello, deployed to staging!"
=======
 default:
   -  step:
        script:
         -  echo "api pipeline trigger"
>>>>>>> fad5ddcc1c78d89c0e26c1cf58f751be85b57d41
```

1. The conflicting lines refer to:

   a. **Develop branch**:

```
custom:
deployment:
   - step:
       name: deployment to staging
       script:
           - echo "Hello, deployed to staging!"
```

b. **Master branch**:

```
default:
    - step:
        script:
            - echo "api pipeline trigger"
```

2. This occurs when both branches have modified the same part of the file, and the conflict needs to be manually resolved.

3. **Manually Resolving the Conflict**: The steps to manually resolve the conflict follow the same pattern as previously discussed in *Chapter 1, Getting Started with Git*. To do this:

   Check out the **`develop`** branch.

   Pull changes from **`master`**:

   ```
   git pull origin master
   ```

4. This will create conflict markers in the file.

5. **Choose How to Resolve**:

   You can **keep the change from the `develop` branch** by editing the file to show:

   ```
   custom:
      deployment:
          - step:
              name: deployment to staging
              script:
                  - echo "Hello, deployed to staging!"
   ```

   **You can keep the change from the master branch:**

   ```
   default:
     - step:
         script:
           - echo "api pipeline trigger"
   ```

   Or you can **combine both, shown as follows:**

   ```
   default:
     - step:
         script:
           - echo "api pipeline trigger"
           - echo "Hello, deployed to staging!"
   ```

6. **Remove the Conflict Markers**: After selecting how you want to resolve the conflict, ensure to delete the conflict markers (**`<<<<<<< HEAD`**, **`=======`**, and **`>>>>>>>`**).

7. **Stage, Commit, and Complete the Merge**:

```
git add bitbucket-pipelines.yml
git commit -m "Resolved merge conflict in bitbucket-pipelines.yml"
```

   Push the resolved changes to the **develop** branch:

```
git push origin develop
```

8. **Review and Merge the Pull Request**: After the conflict is resolved and changes are pushed, you can proceed to review and merge the pull request successfully.

This process ensures that merge conflicts are addressed and the pull request can be finalized without further issues.

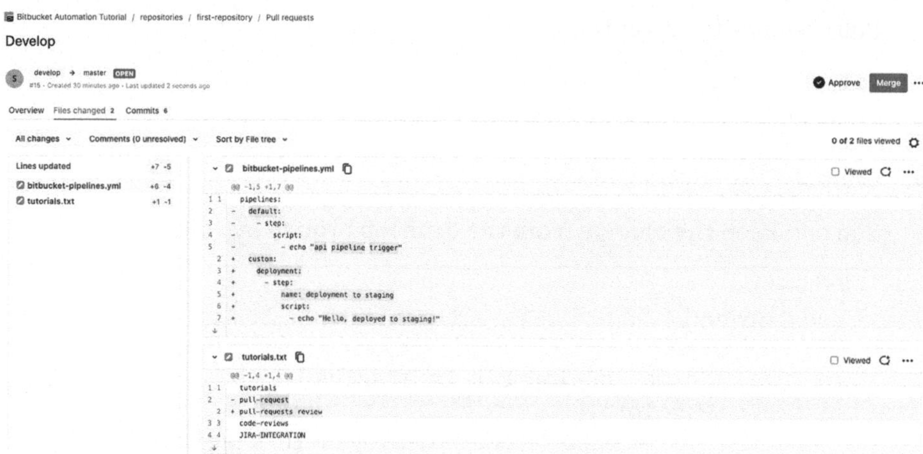

***Figure* 3.25**: *Pull Request Resolved Merge Conflict*

# Conclusion

We discussed several key practices and processes related to managing pull requests effectively in software development. The conversation covered the importance of creating and merging pull requests, ensuring clear descriptions and templates to communicate changes, and selecting appropriate merge strategies to maintain a clean code history. We also highlighted the significance of assigning reviewers with relevant expertise to enhance code quality. Additionally, we explored the pull request diff and activity tab for thorough examination and discussion of changes, as well as strategies for resolving merge conflicts to ensure smooth integration of code contributions. Overall, these practices aim to foster collaboration and streamline the development workflow.

The next chapter will delve into Bitbucket workspace administration and app integrations.

# CHAPTER 4
# Bitbucket Administration and Jira Integration

## Introduction

In this chapter, we will explore the various product settings required to manage Bitbucket workspaces, projects, and repositories effectively. This includes user management, advanced security features, app integrations, and premium features needed to secure your code, perform advanced code reviews, and integrate with Atlassian tools such as Jira to track code changes. These capabilities are crucial for maintaining an efficient and secure development environment. After covering the administration, security, and integration topics, we will delve into advanced pull request automation and CI/CD in Bitbucket Cloud in the upcoming chapters.

## Structure

In this chapter, we will cover the following topics:

- Managing Bitbucket Cloud Access
- Overview of Atlassian Integrations
- Advanced Security Features
- Audit Logs

## Managing Bitbucket Cloud Access

In software development, managing different permissions is essential for ensuring security, controlling access, and defining roles within a project. The following are some common types of permissions that might be required in different areas of a project:

**Repository Permissions (Bitbucket)**

- **Admin:** Full access, including adding collaborators, changing settings, and managing all resources.
- **Developer/Contributor:** Can create and merge pull requests, push to branches, and update code.
- **Read-Only:** Can only view the code and repository contents without the ability to modify.

**Note:** *These are preliminary; actual permissions and roles will be covered in subsequent sections.*

Now, let us delve into creating user groups and adding users for Bitbucket Cloud account. From the workspace settings in the top corner (gear icon), select `User Management.`

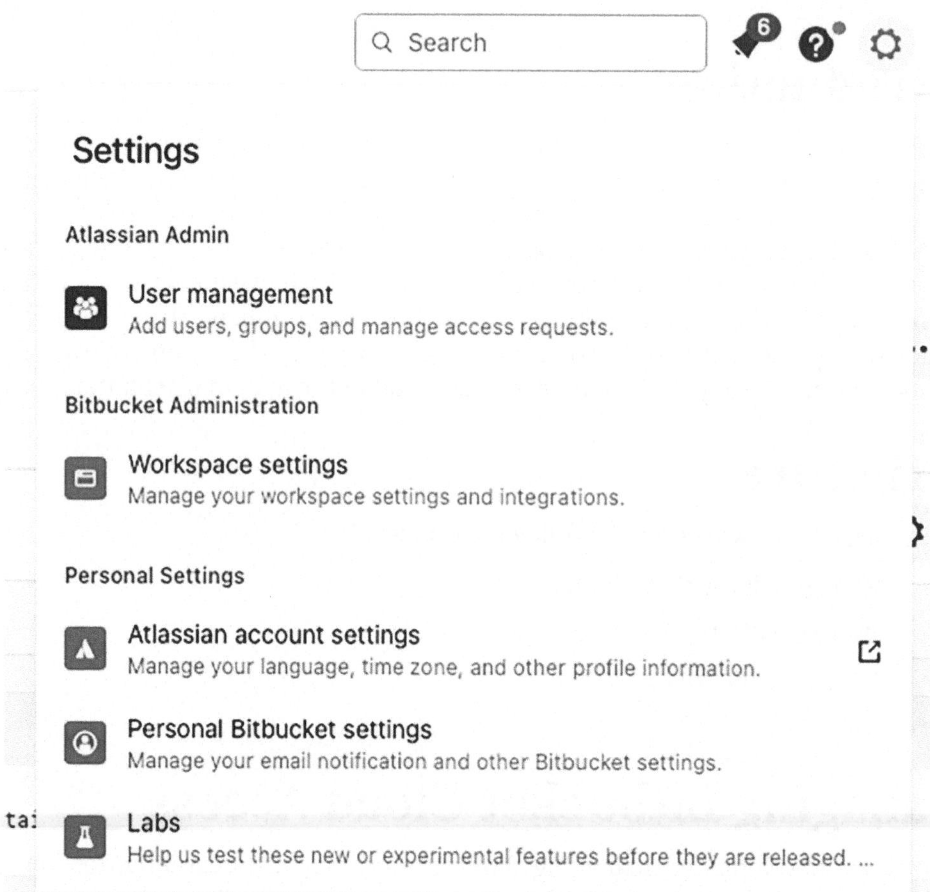


**Figure 4.1**: *Workspace Settings – User Management*

It will take us to the **`Atlassian Admin`** page.

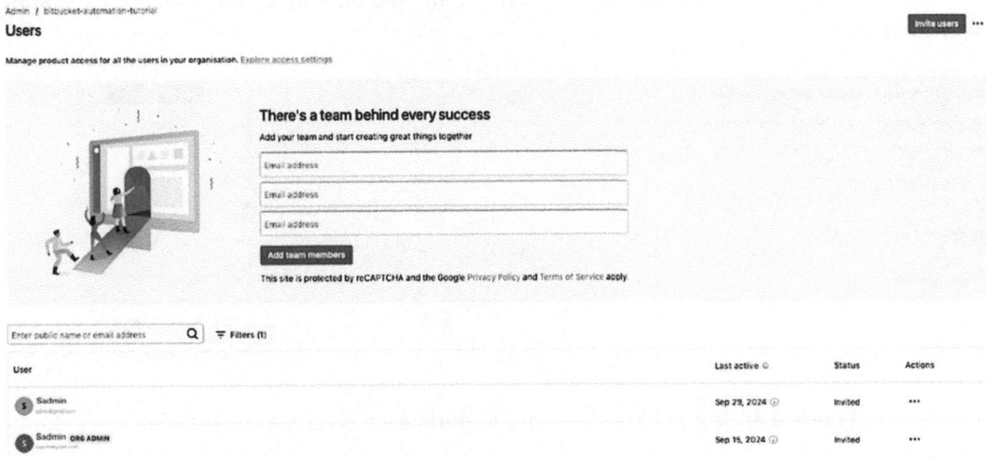


***Figure 4.2***: *Atlassian Admin - User Management*

You will notice that two users have already been invited: one is the **`Org Admin`**, and the other is a PR approver, which was used in the previous chapter on pull requests.

Under the **`Groups`** page, we have the following:

- **Group: `bitbucket-admins-bitbucket-automation-tutorial`**
- **Group: `bitbucket-user-access-admins-bitbucket-automation-tutorial`**
- **Group: `bitbucket-users-bitbucket-automation-tutorial`**
- **Group: `org-admins`**
- **Group: `code-reviewers`**

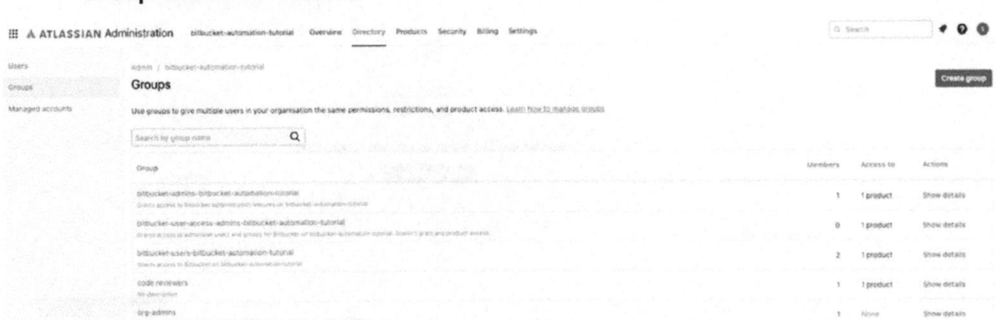


***Figure 4.3***: *Atlassian Admin – Groups Page*

- **Group: `bitbucket-admins-bitbucket-automation-tutorial`**
  With the product role "**`Product Admin`**." All users added here will be granted Bitbucket workspace administration (or product administration). They will be

able to create projects and repositories and add/remove groups and users under projects and repositories. They will also be able to administer workspace features.

**Figure 4.4**: *Group: bitbucket-admins-bitbucket-automation-tutorial*

- **Group: `bitbucket-user-access-admins-bitbucket-automation-tutorial`**

  This group has been created with the Bitbucket product role "**`User Access Admin`**." Users added here will be able to administer users and groups from Atlassian Administration (create groups, invite users) for bitbucket product, but they will not have product access.

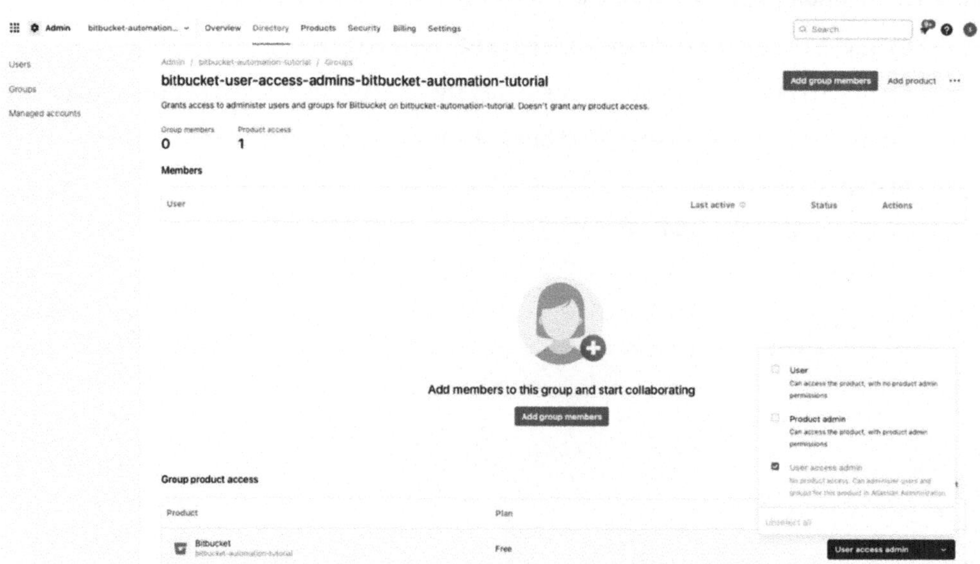

**Figure 4.5**: *Group: bitbucket-user-access-admins-bitbucket-automation-tutorial*

- **`Group: org-admins`**

  Grants access to administer organization-level settings, users, and groups, and to view billing. This is used to administer users in Atlassian Administration, including cloud products such as Jira Cloud and Confluence Cloud. One example is extended audit logs for Bitbucket Cloud, which is managed outside of the Bitbucket Cloud product and will be covered in upcoming sections.

The preceding default groups are created when Bitbucket Cloud is added under an organization.

- **`Group: bitbucket-users-bitbucket-automation-tutorial`**

  This group was created by us with the product role "**`User`**." This is where we add users who need **`read/write`** access to projects and repositories (granular permissions will be defined within Bitbucket Cloud). We can also add users to this group who would need project and repository admin permissions, which can be granted at the project and repository settings in Bitbucket Cloud.

***Figure 4.6***: *Group: bitbucket-users-bitbucket-automation-tutorial*

- **`Group: code-reviewers`**

  A group we created to grant user permissions to the Bitbucket product. We can later add granular permissions to this group at the project and repository level, which can be used for code review and branching permissions.

Now let us delve into the **`Users and User Groups`** view under workspace, projects, and repositories in Bitbucket Cloud.

Under **`Workspace Settings`**, we find **`Workspace Permissions`**, where we can add the user groups created in the **`Atlassian Admin`** page.

The Bitbucket **`Product Admin`** role assigned to groups in Atlassian Admin will be listed here with default admin permissions. For example, the group **`bitbucket-admins-bitbucket-automation-tutorial`** will have admin permissions inherited.

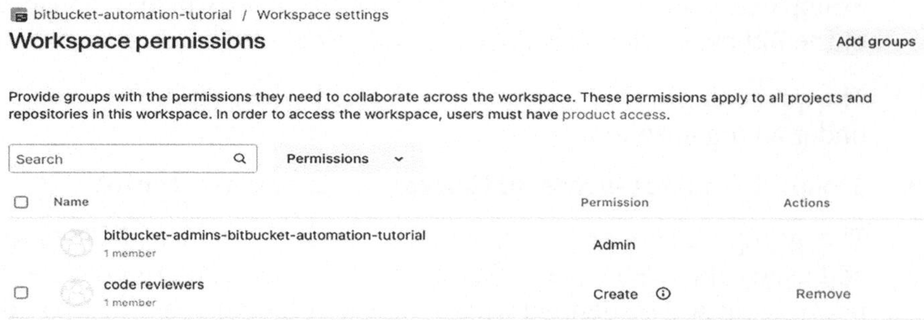


**Figure 4.7**: *Workspace permissions*

The group **code-reviewers**, with the user role "**`Create`**," has also been added here. The main difference is that admin permissions allow users to manage workspace settings and features, while the "**`Create`**" role allows users to create and manage projects. As explained in *Chapter 2, Overview of Bitbucket Cloud*, the hierarchy of permissions is organized at the levels of organization, workspace, projects, and repository.

Let us now click on **`Projects`**, select the **`Repositories`** project, and go to **`Project Settings`** > **`Project Permissions`**. Here, you will notice that the group **`bitbucket-admins-bitbucket-automation-tutorial`** has inherited admin permissions from the workspace. At this level, we can add a user or group and grant access at the project level. Let us add **`bitbucket-users-bitbucket-automation-tutorial`**.

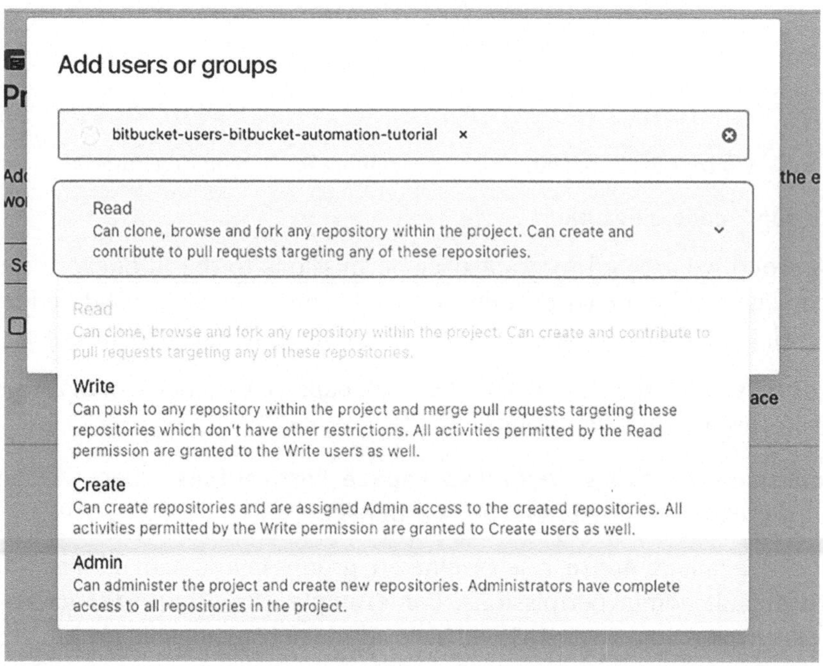


**Figure 4.8**: *Project permissions*

At the project level, there are three roles: **Write**, **Create**, and **Admin**.

- **Create** allows users to create repositories within the project and manage them.
- **Admin** allows users to manage repositories and project settings (for example, project-level branch restrictions, branching model, and tags).
- **Write** grants users read and write permissions, including the ability to merge pull requests across all repositories under the project. Let us grant **Admin** permissions to the group and add it.

Now, proceed to the **Project Home Page** and select the **first-repository** that we worked on in previous chapters, which is associated with the **Repositories** project. Go to **Repository Settings** > **Repository permissions**.

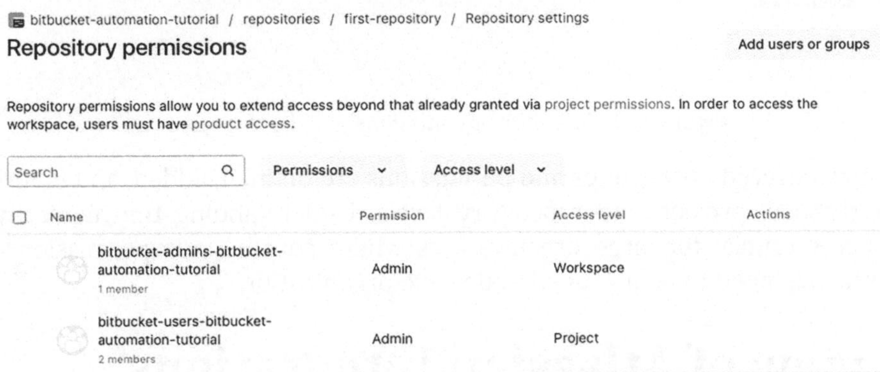


***Figure 4.9**: Repository permissions*

The groups **bitbucket-admins-bitbucket-automation-tutorial** and **bitbucket-users-bitbucket-automation-tutorial** have been added by default with admin permissions, inherited from the workspace and project, respectively.

The **code-reviewers** group has **Create** permissions at the workspace level but did not inherit permissions since it is not the owner of the **Repositories** project. However, we can still add this group with repository-specific permissions—let us say, **Write**.

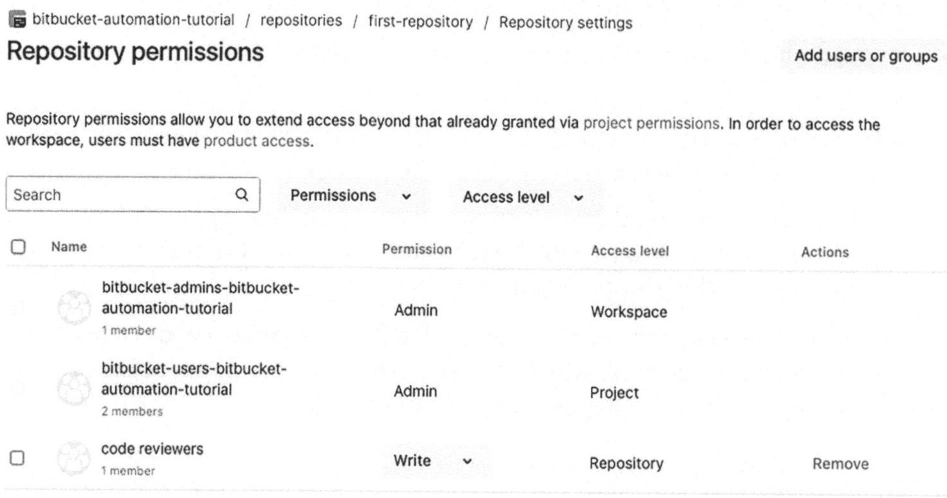


***Figure 4.10**: Repository permissions – add groups*

We have now covered how groups and permissions are defined, added, and inherited at the workspace, project, and repository levels. Understanding the hierarchy of permissions is crucial for large organizations where source code permissions for multiple projects need to be managed under one organization.

# Overview of Atlassian Integrations

Atlassian offers a range of integrations that enhance collaboration, productivity, and visibility across teams and projects. These integrations, powered by Atlassian Integrations, enable smarter and more efficient workflows within the Atlassian ecosystem.

# Key Atlassian Integrations

**Jira** is a powerful project management tool that helps teams plan, track, and manage their work, particularly for software development projects. It offers customizable workflows, issue tracking, and reporting to streamline project delivery.

**Atlassian Intelligence** in Bitbucket allows you to generate AI-assisted pull request descriptions, which we briefly covered in *Chapter 3, Comprehensive Guide to Pull Requests*.

Now, let us delve into Jira software integration, one of the most commonly used integrations in the software development lifecycle.

## Setting Up Jira Integration

Before we start the integration, let us subscribe to Jira Software. Go to Atlassian Admin at https://admin.atlassian.com, select **`Products`**, and choose Jira.

The default name suggestion based on our email will appear for the site, but let us use "**`bitbucket-automation-tutorials`**" as the site name.

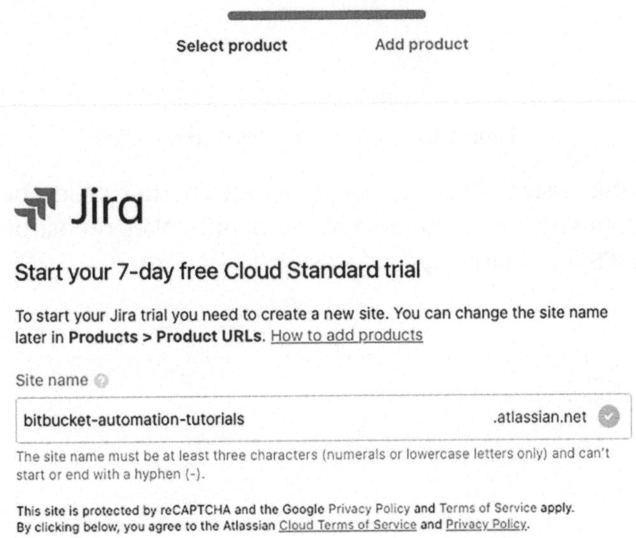


***Figure 4.11**: Jira Software Site Registration*

We have the site set up at https://bitbucket-automation-tutorials.atlassian.net with a default project called "My Scrum Project."

To integrate Bitbucket Cloud with Jira Cloud:

1. Navigate to your Bitbucket workspace (you must have admin permissions for both the workspace and the Jira instance).
2. Since we created the site, we have been granted default admin access.
3. In Bitbucket, go to **`Settings`** (gear icon) > **`Workspace Settings`**, and select **`Jira`** under Atlassian Integrations.
4. Choose the Jira Cloud instance (which should be listed as we created Jira using the same account) and click **`Connect`**.

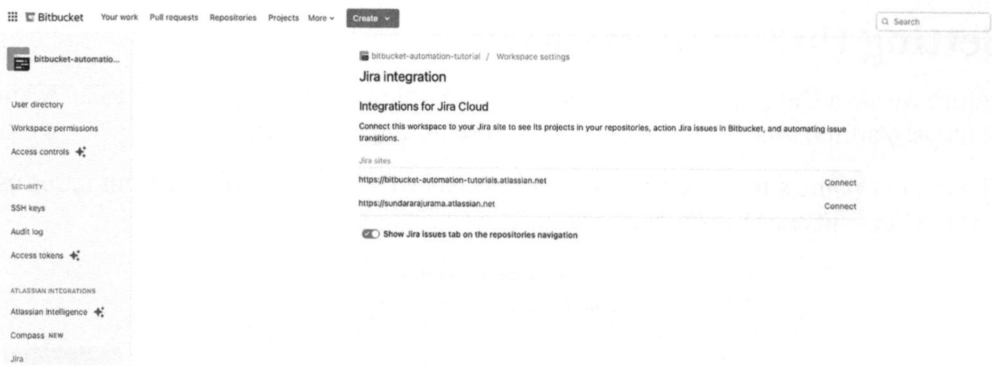


***Figure 4.12***: *Atlassian integrations - Jira*

We can also enable **`Smart Commits`**, allowing automatic syncing between Jira issues and Bitbucket commits. Once connected, your Bitbucket repositories will appear in Jira under the **`DVCS accounts`** page, accessible to Jira Admins.

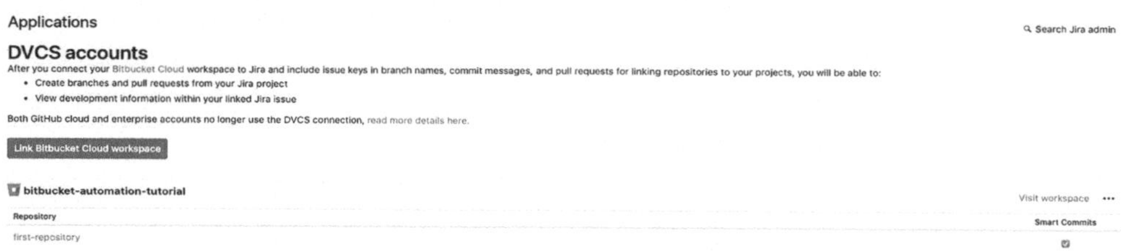


***Figure 4.13***: *Jira DVCS Settings*

To disconnect the integration, you can manage the connection from either Bitbucket or Jira by navigating to **`Workspace Settings`** and selecting **`Disconnect`**.

**Testing the Integration**

After the integration, let us test it by creating a Jira issue (task) under "**`My Scrum Project`**."

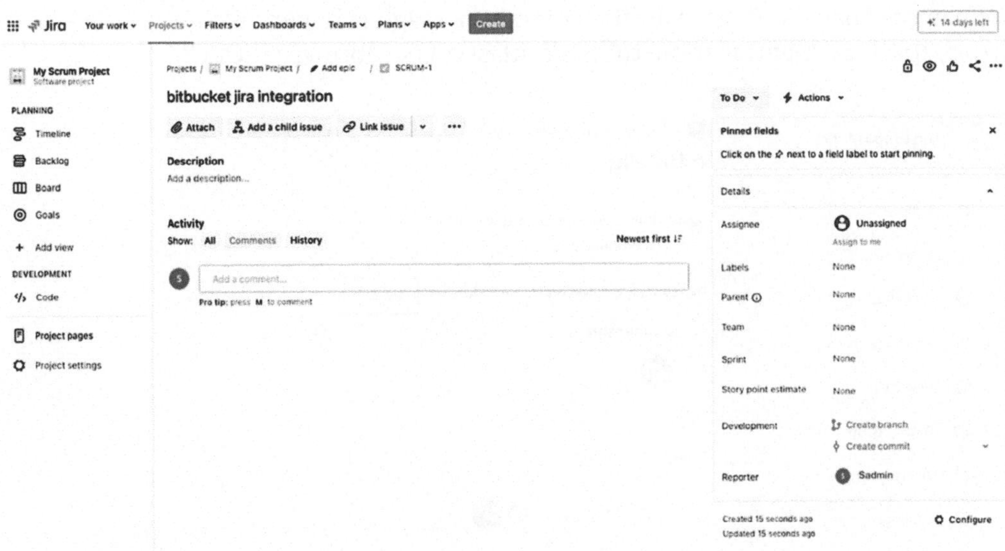


***Figure 4.14**: Jira Task*

We can see that the task is in "**`To Do`**" status and has a side panel labeled **`Development`**, which shows Bitbucket integration details of repositories where commit messages are issued with Jira keys or pull requests tagged with the Jira key **`SCRUM-1`**.

Let us issue the Jira key **`SCRUM-1`** in a commit message and check the integration. We created a file called "**`jira-commit`**," and while committing, we made sure to include **`SCRUM-1`** (the Jira key).

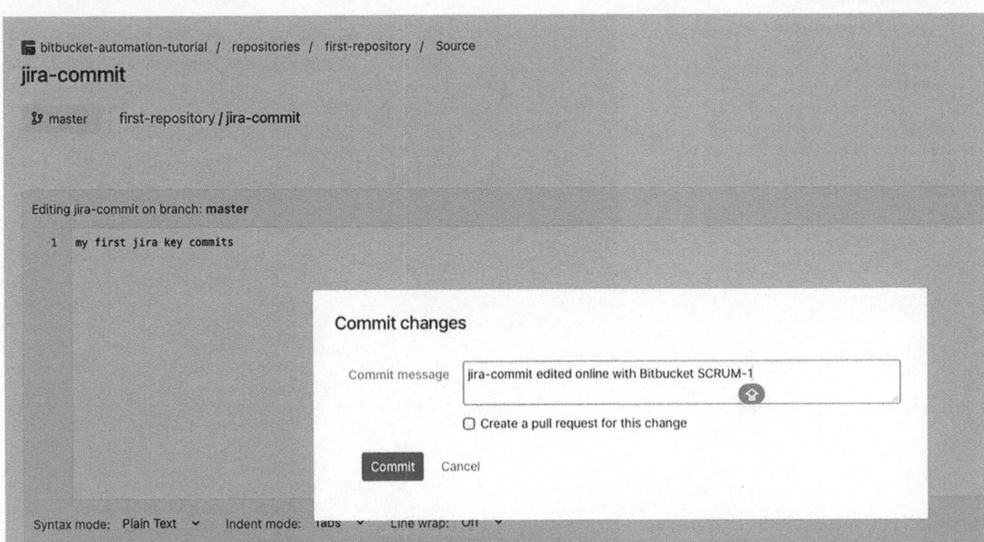


***Figure 4.15**: commit message with Jira Key*

We can see that the Jira key in the commit message is hyperlinked to the Jira issue: https://bitbucket-automation-tutorials.atlassian.net/browse/SCRUM-1.

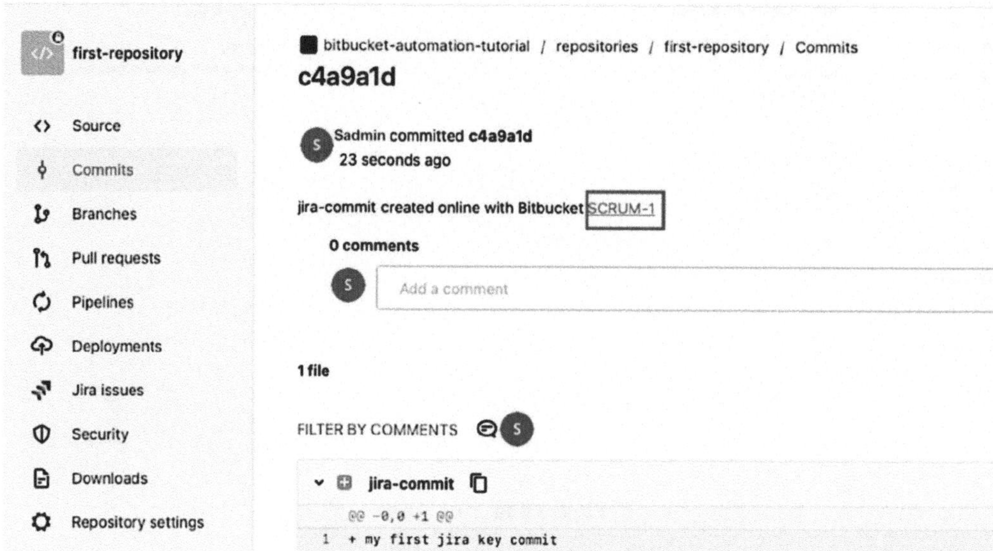


***Figure 4.16**: Jira key hyperlink (smart commit)*

In the Jira issue, the **`Development`** panel shows the newly added file with the commit on Bitbucket Cloud.

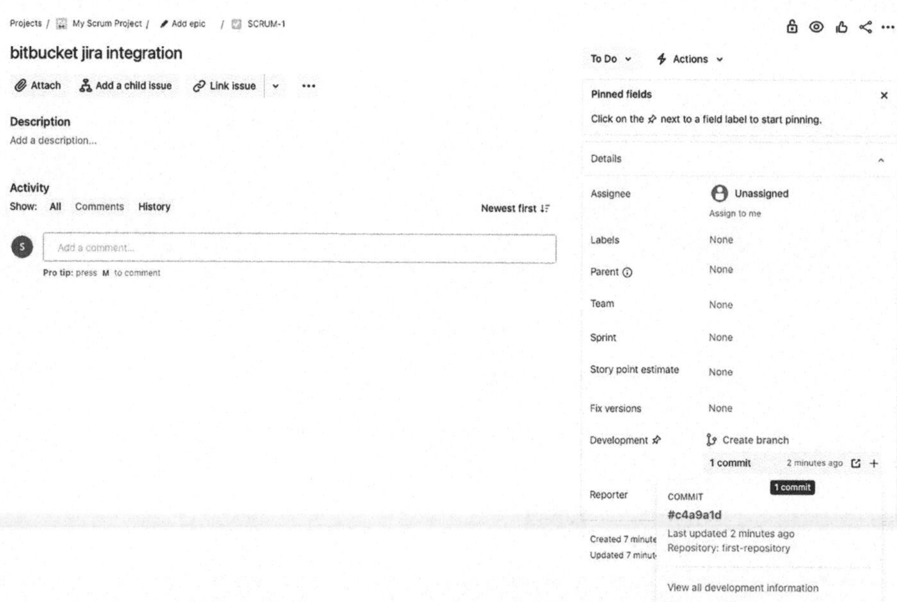


***Figure 4.17**: Jira Task with updated commit*

This integration is crucial for tracking features, bugs, and hotfixes in Jira, with actual code changes mapped to them and tracked under Bitbucket Cloud. Bitbucket Cloud and Jira Cloud have native integration, with more features such as automations that will be covered in subsequent chapters.

We will now explore how to integrate third-party apps from the Atlassian Marketplace to extend Bitbucket Cloud's functionality. In addition to Atlassian's built-in product integrations, third-party vendors host apps on the AtlassianMarketplace (https://marketplace.atlassian.com/) that enable powerful integrations for communication, code quality, reporting, and more. Examples include **`Slack`** for team communication, **SonarQube** for code quality and coverage, and **`Awesome Graphs for Bitbucket`** for tracking team activities.

We will walk through an example of integrating **`Awesome Graphs for Bitbucket`**, as well as covering how to create **`OAuth consumers`** to integrate with apps such as Jenkins, AWS CodeStar, and Azure DevOps.

**Integrating Awesome Graphs for Bitbucket**

1. **Search and Install the App:**
    a. Go to the **`Atlassian Marketplace`** and search for "**`Awesome Graphs`**."

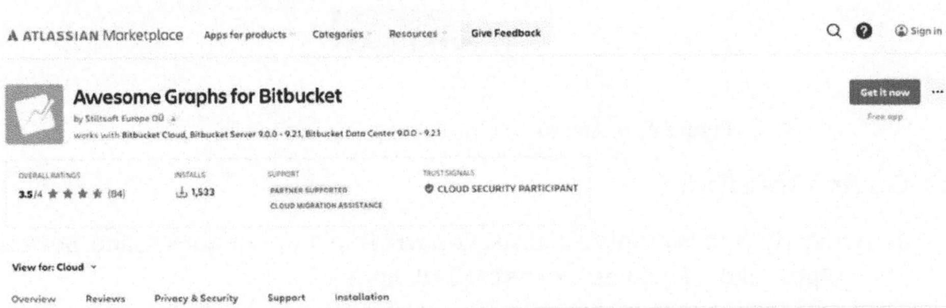


**Figure 4.18**: *Atlassian Marketplace*

    b. Click on "**`Get it now`**" and grant access to your Bitbucket workspace. For this example, we will be granting access to the "**`bitbucket-automation-tutorial`**" workspace.

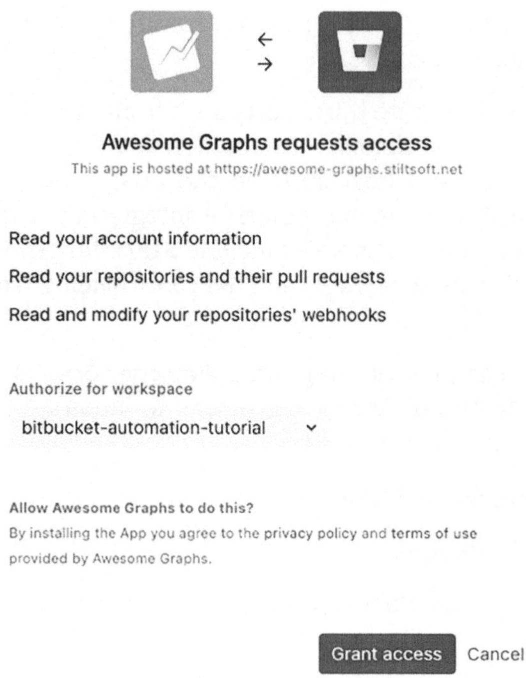


**Figure 4.19**: *Awesome Graphs App Permissions*

2. **Confirm Installation**:

    a. Once the app is granted access, you will find it under **`Workspace Settings`** → **`Apps and Features`** → **`Installed Apps`**.

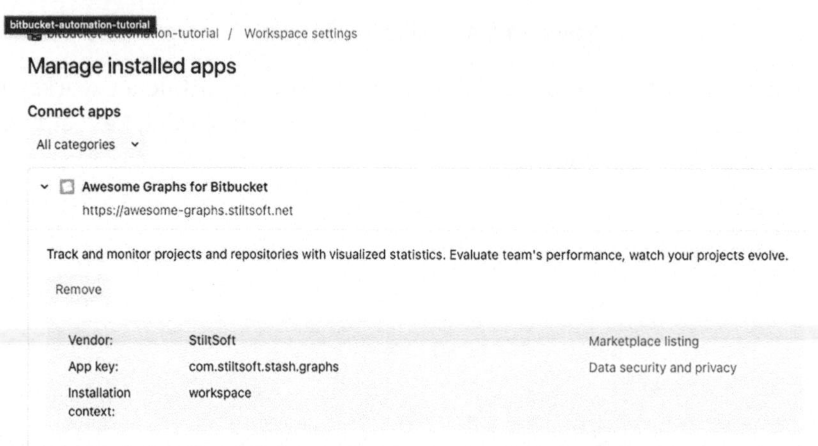


**Figure 4.20**: *Awesome Graphs App*

3. **Access Awesome Graphs**:

   a. Go to your repository (for example, "**`first-repository`**") and select **`Graphs`** from the navigation bar.

   b. Approve any access permissions requested by the app.

   c. View contributor activity graphs, commits, and other insights for the selected date range, helping you track and analyze team productivity.

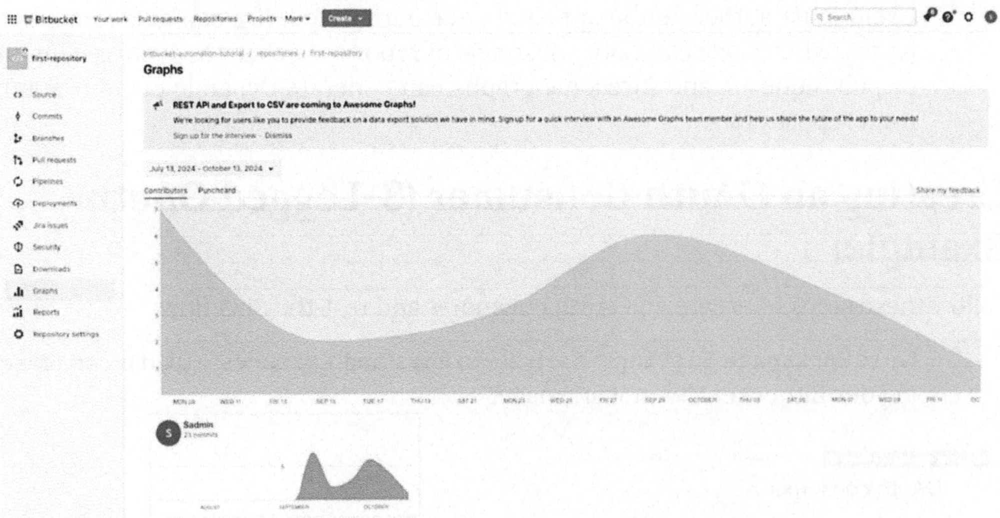


***Figure 4.21**: Awesome Graphs Commits Graph*

This is just one example of how to install and use a third-party app from the Atlassian Marketplace. We will cover more integrations for pull request automation and CI/CD in subsequent chapters.

# OAuth Consumers and Integration

Some third-party integrations require you to create OAuth consumers to securely authenticate and allow external apps access to your Bitbucket repositories. **`OAuth (Open Authorization)`** is a standard protocol that grants websites or applications limited access to user information without exposing sensitive credentials, such as passwords.

**Two Types of OAuth Flows in Bitbucket Cloud:**

- **2-Legged OAuth (2LO)**: This flow is typically used for automated processes, where a service (such as Jenkins) directly interacts with Bitbucket Cloud without user interaction. This is ideal for CI/CD pipelines, nightly builds, or deployments.

**Example**: Jenkins can use 2LO to authenticate with Bitbucket and pull code from repositories, trigger builds, run tests, and deploy applications without needing manual user input.

- **3-Legged OAuth (3LO)**: This flow involves three parties: a user, a third-party app (such as Jira or Slack), and Bitbucket Cloud. Users must explicitly grant permission to the third-party app to access their Bitbucket data.

  **Example**: Jira, Awesome Graphs, and Slack use 3LO to access repositories. Users must authorize the app, and once authorized, Jira can link commits to issues, while Slack can notify channels of repository changes such as commits or pull requests, and Awesome graphs can generate dynamic commit graphs from repositories.

# Creating an OAuth Consumer (3-Legged OAuth Example)

Follow these steps to create an OAuth consumer and test the 3LO flow:

1. **Go to `Workspace Settings`**: Navigate to **`Apps and Features`** → **`OAuth consumers`** in your Bitbucket Cloud workspace.

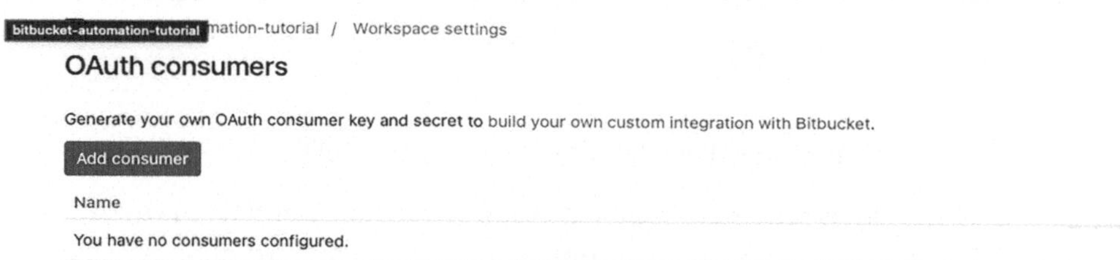


***Figure* 4.22**: *OAuth consumers*

2. **Add a New Consumer**: Click on "**`Add consumer`**" and fill in the necessary details:
   - **Name**: "**`Bitbucket Automation Tutorial`**"
   - **Description**: "**`Bitbucket automation tutorial test integration`**"
   - **Callback URL**: Use a placeholder (for example, https://www.google.com/) for now.
   - **Permissions**: Select **`Repository Read`**.

Here is a brief explanation of each field:

- **`Name`**: A human-readable identifier for the OAuth consumer (for example, "**`Bitbucket Automation Tutorial`**"). It helps you recognize the app or service you are integrating with Bitbucket.
- **`Description`**: A short explanation of what the OAuth consumer does (for

example, "**`Bitbucket automation tutorial test integration`**"). It helps others understand the purpose of the integration.

- **`Callback URL`**: The URL where users are redirected after authorizing your app (used in 3-legged OAuth). For now, a placeholder such as https://www.google.com/ can be used if not applicable.
- **`Permissions`**: Defines the scope of access the consumer has. For example, selecting **`Repository Read`** allows the app to read data from your repositories.

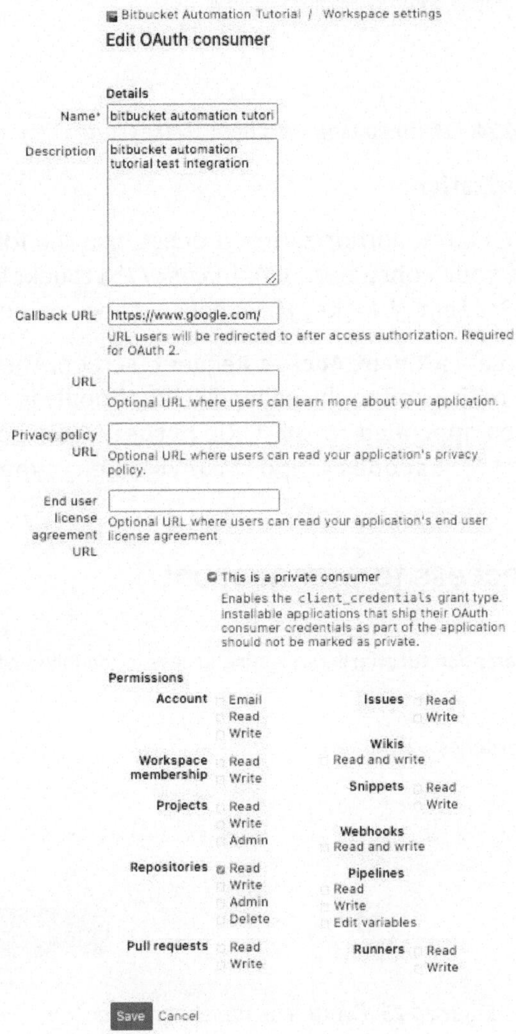


***Figure 4.23**: OAuth consumers Form*

3. **Save and Generate Client ID and Secret**: After saving, note down the **`Consumer Key (Client ID)`** and **`Consumer Secret`** for use in the authorization process.

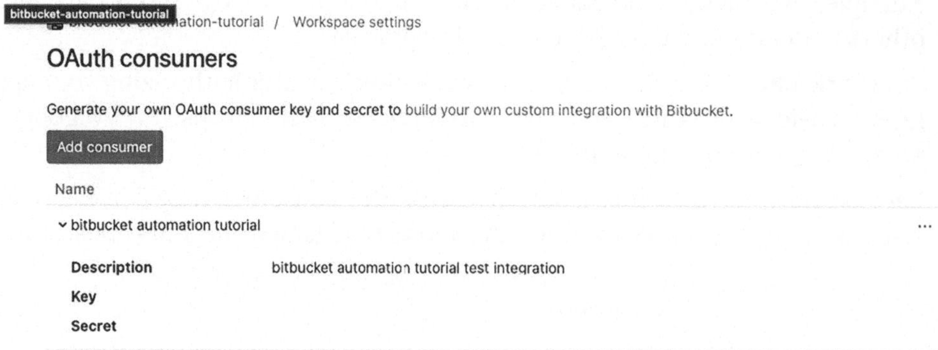


***Figure 4.24**: OAuth consumers client ID (key) and client secret*

4. **Request Authorization**:
   a. To start the OAuth authorization process, use the following URL (replace **`{key}`** with your consumer key): `https://bitbucket.org/site/oauth2/authorize?client_id={key}&response_type=token`
   b. This will prompt a "**`Grant Access Request`**" screen. Approve the request, and you will be redirected to the callback URL (Google in this example) with an access token appended to the URL: `https://www.google.com/#access_token=*******&scopes=repository&token_type=bearer&expires_in=7200`

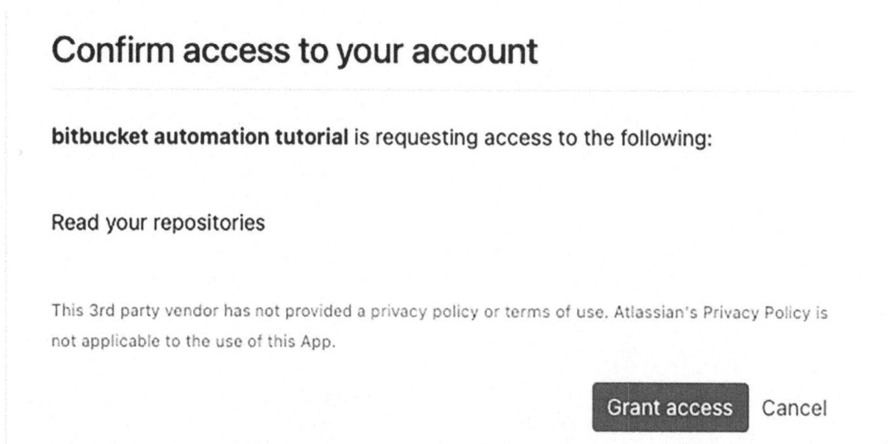


***Figure 4.25**: OAuth consumers grant access*

5. **Use the Access Token**: Extract the **`access_token`** from the URL and use it to clone:

```
git clone https://x-token-auth:{access_token}@bitbucket.org/bit-
bucket-automation-tutorial/first-repository.git
```

```
admin@Admins-MacBook-Pro Desktop % git clone https://<token>@bitbucket.org/bitbucket-automation-tutorial/first-repository.git
Cloning into 'first-repository'...
remote: Enumerating objects: 81, done.
remote: Counting objects: 100% (81/81), done.
remote: Compressing objects: 100% (65/65), done.
remote: Total 81 (delta 23), reused 0 (delta 0), pack-reused 0 (from 0)
Receiving objects: 100% (81/81), 9.26 KiB | 2.25 MiB/s, done.
Resolving deltas: 100% (23/23), done.
```

***Figure 4.26**: Git clone using OAuth tokens*

This process demonstrates how to authenticate and integrate third-party apps using OAuth in Bitbucket Cloud.

# Advanced Access Controls: IP Allowlisting and Two-Factor Authentication

To protect your workspace and repositories, Bitbucket Cloud offers advanced security features, such as IP Allowlisting and Two-Factor Authentication (2FA). These features ensure that only trusted users and devices can access sensitive data, adding an extra layer of security to prevent unauthorized access and protect your development processes.

## Two-Step Verification (2SV)

Two-Step Verification (2SV) adds another layer of security by requiring us to provide a one-time verification code in addition to their password.

1. Go to **`Personal Bitbucket Settings` (gear icon)** and click on **`Two-Step Verification`** under the **`Security`** section.

***Figure 4.27**: Two-Step Verification (2SV)*

2. Follow the prompts to set up 2SV by scanning a QR code with an authenticator app (for example, Duo, Google Authenticator, and Authy).
3. Store the recovery codes (important) provided for emergency access if the authenticator device is lost.
4. Once 2SV is enabled, users will be required to enter a verification code every time they log into their Bitbucket account.

***Figure 4.28***: *Two-Step Verification (2SV) Prompt*

**Enforcing Two-Step Verification (2SV)** is an admin-controlled setting that requires all users in your organization to enable two-factor authentication (2SV) on their accounts. To access repositories or workspaces, one must provide a second form of authentication (such as a code from an authenticator app) in addition to their password, significantly enhancing security. As an organization admin, navigate to admin.atlassian.com and select your organization.

1. Navigate to **`Bitbucket Cloud`** workspace settings (gear icon), and under **`Access Management`**, select **`Access Controls`**.
2. Select the checkbox **`Require two-step verification (2SV)`**. This ensures that users accessing the workspace **`bitbucket-automation-tutorial`** will be asked to enable 2SV. If already enabled, they will be prompted to enter their 2SV codes.

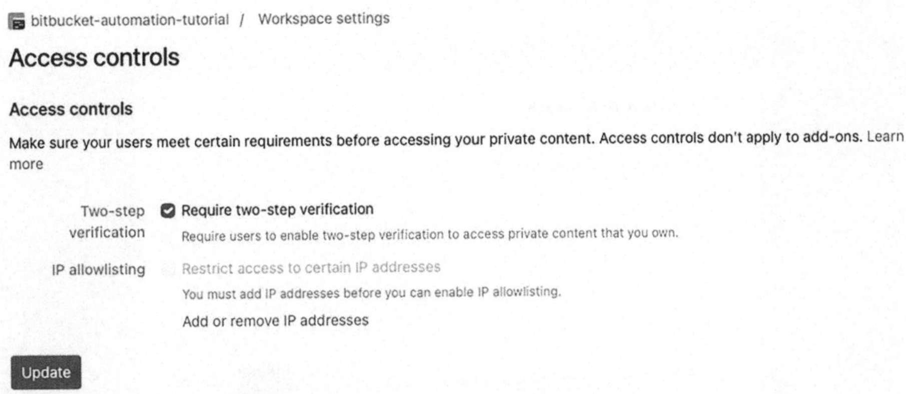


***Figure 4.29**: Enforce Two-Step Verification (2SV)*

**Note**: *The 2SV prompts are for web access. When users try to perform Git operations, such as git clone, or API operations, it will check if 2SV is enabled, but it does not prompt for codes. If 2SV is not enabled, the operation is blocked.*

## IP Allowlisting

**`IP allowlisting`** ensures that only requests from authorized IP addresses can access your workspace, limiting exposure to external threats.

1. Navigate to **`Bitbucket Cloud`** workspace settings (gear icon), and under **`Access Management`**, select **`Access Controls`**.
2. Under the **`IP Allowlisting`** section, add the specific IP addresses or CIDR ranges you want to allow access from.

   **Example**: If your team operates from a fixed office location, you can whitelist the office's IP range, blocking access from other networks.
3. Save the changes. Once configured, only requests from the allowed IP addresses will be permitted to access repositories and workspaces.

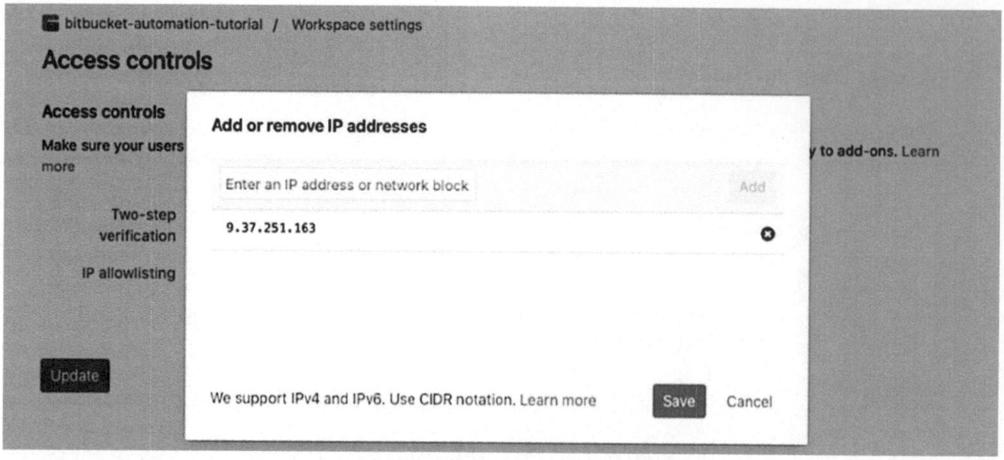


***Figure 4.30***: *IP Allowlisting*

By enabling **`IP Allowlisting`** and **`Two-Factor Authentication (premium features)`**, Bitbucket Cloud provides your team with robust, layered security. IP Allowlisting restricts access to trusted networks, while 2FA ensures that even if a password is compromised, the account remains secure with an additional verification step. These advanced controls help mitigate security risks and protect your repositories from unauthorized access.

# Audit Logs

Audit logs in Bitbucket Cloud provide a detailed record of activities and changes within your workspace. This helps ensure transparency and accountability, especially in environments with multiple users contributing to repositories.

**Accessing Audit Logs:**

> **Navigate to the Logs**: To view audit logs, go to the workspace settings (gear icon) click on "**`Audit logs`**" under security. This will display a list of activities, including user actions, permission changes, and repository updates.
>
> **Example**: If a user installs an app and enables the IP allowlisting feature, these actions will be logged with details, such as the **`username`**, **`time`**, and the specific action taken.

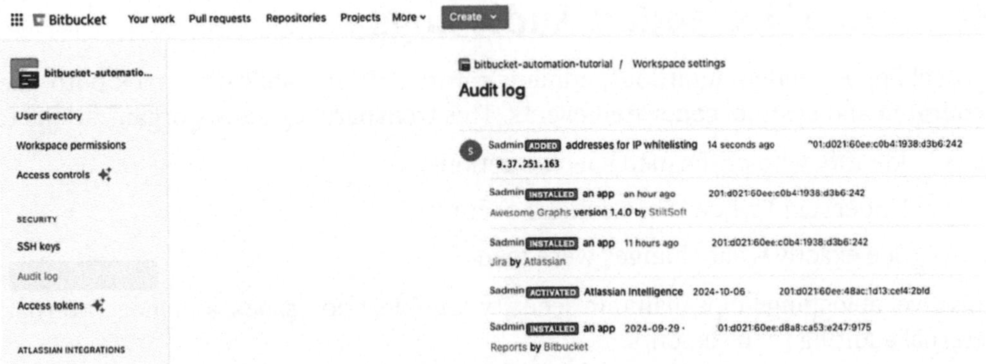


***Figure 4.31***: Audit Log

Bitbucket Cloud provides **`Extended Audit Logs`** for detailed tracking of critical events and actions performed within your repositories and workspaces. While the default audit logs under **`Workspace Settings`** offer limited tracking and lack filtering or export capabilities, the **`Extended Audit Logs`** provide more comprehensive insights.

**Key Features of Extended Audit Logs**

The extended audit logs track events, such as:

- **Branch restrictions added or removed**
- **Permission changes for users or groups**
- **Repository access updates**
- **Pull request modifications**
- **Other key security-related actions**

A complete list of audit log events can be found on Atlassian's documentation `https://confluence.atlassian.com/bbkb/bitbucket-cloud-audit-log-events-1178872155.html`

These logs are essential for:

- **Monitoring changes**: Track who made modifications to repositories or permissions.
- **Enhancing security**: Get visibility into unauthorized access or unexpected actions.
- **Ensuring compliance**: Maintain records for auditing and regulatory purposes.

## Benefits of Extended Audit Logs

By enabling extended audit logs, administrators gain the ability to track both **user-generated** and **system-generated** events. This transparency allows organizations to:

- Identify who performed specific actions.
- Understand when these actions occurred.
- See exactly what changes were made.

This level of logging helps maintain security, troubleshoot issues, and meet internal or external auditing requirements.

## Steps to Activate Extended Audit Logs

1. **Enable Atlassian Guard**:
    a. Go to the **`Atlassian Admin`** portal.
    b. Under **`Products`**, activate **`Atlassian Guard`**.
    c. Atlassian Guard is a suite of advanced security features and controls designed to help organizations protect their cloud environments. It ensures that only authorized users can access sensitive data in products, such as Bitbucket Cloud, Jira, and Confluence. Extended bitbucket cloud audit logs require Atlassian Guard subscription.
2. **Access Audit Logs:**
    a. Once Atlassian Guard is enabled, navigate to **`Security`** > **`Audit Logs`** in the **`Bitbucket Cloud workspace`**.
    b. You can now view detailed logs of activities, including permission changes, repository access, and pull request updates.
3. **Filter and Analyze Logs**:
    a. Use filters to narrow down the logs based on date, event type, user, or other criteria, making it easier to find specific actions.
    b. This filtering capability is particularly useful for auditing or investigating security incidents.

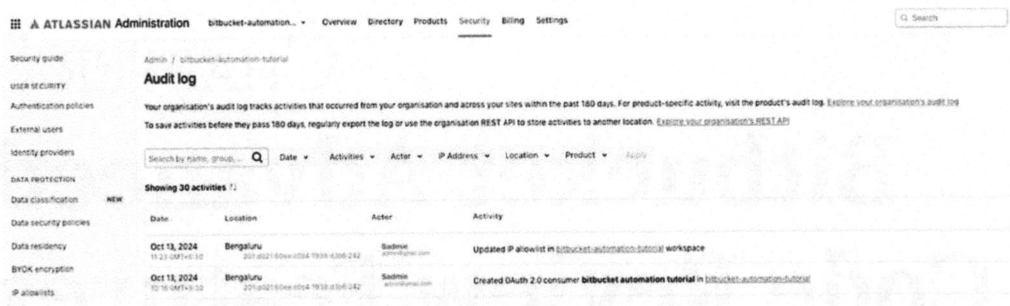

**Figure 4.32**: *Extended Audit Log*

# Conclusion

This chapter provided a comprehensive overview of managing Bitbucket Cloud workspaces, covering key topics such as user and group management, advanced security features such as IP allowlisting and two-factor authentication, and seamless integrations with Atlassian products and third-party apps from the Atlassian Marketplace. We explored how to enhance security and productivity through tools such as audit logs, extended audit logs, and webhooks for workflow automation. With these capabilities, you are now well-equipped to administer your Bitbucket environment effectively.

In the next chapter, we will focus on best practices for code reviews, including enforcing code quality standards through automated code reviews, configuring branch permissions, and setting up advanced merge checks. We will also explore how to automate workflows with Codeowners and improve collaboration.

# CHAPTER 5
# Bitbucket Advanced Code Review Features

## Introduction

In modern software development, code reviews are a crucial step to ensure that code changes meet quality, security, and functionality standards before being merged into the main branch. In *Chapter 3, Comprehensive Guide to Pull Requests*, we already covered the basic functionality of pull request-based code reviews. Now, we will dive into **advanced code review features** that help enhance collaboration and automate parts of the review process.

This chapter explores essential tools such as **branch permissions**, **advanced merge checks**, and the use of **`CODEOWNERS`** to ensure that only the right individuals can approve changes. By leveraging these tools, teams can streamline their code review workflows, elevate code quality, and maintain consistent coding standards across all projects. These features not only help automate key aspects of code reviews but also improve the efficiency and effectiveness of collaboration between team members.

## Structure

In this chapter, we will cover the following topics:

- Configuring Branch Permissions
- Advanced Merge Checks
- Configuring `CODEOWNERS` for Automated Code Reviews
- Collaborating on Code and Providing Feedback

**Best Practices for Code Reviews**

Effective code reviews help prevent bugs, enforce coding standards, and promote collaboration. Bitbucket Cloud provides tools to ensure that reviews are thorough and collaborative, focusing on assigning the right reviewers, managing pull request sizes, and tracking issues efficiently. Let us review the branch permissions and merge checks features for pull requests in the repository settings.

# Configuring Branch Permissions

In Bitbucket Cloud, branch restrictions allow you to control who can make changes to specific branches. To apply restrictions, navigate to your repository settings under Workflow and select Branch Restrictions. Add a new restriction, and you will land on a form for branch permissions.

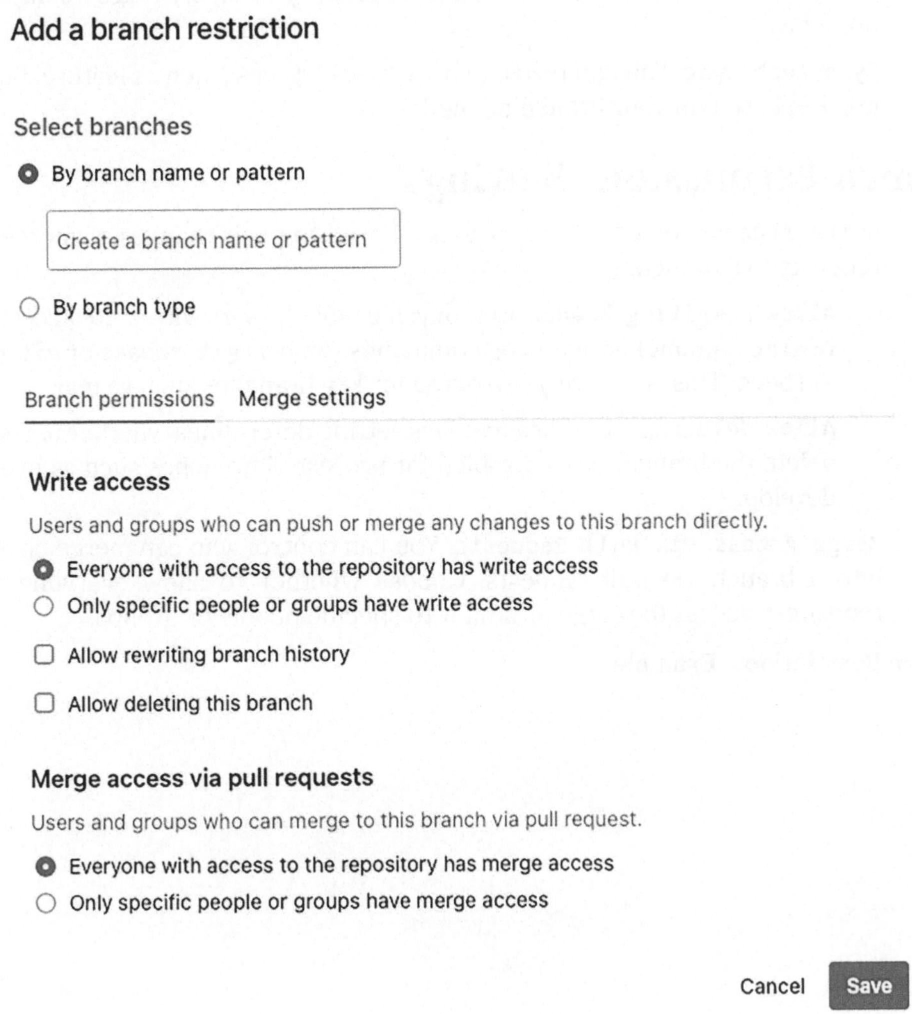


***Figure 5.1**: Branch Restrictions*

The options shown in this form are part of the branch restrictions and permissions feature, which helps enforce rules around who can push, merge, or delete branches. Here is a breakdown of each option:

## Select Branches

When setting branch restrictions, you will need to specify the branches to which the restrictions will apply. You can do this in two ways:

- **`By branch name or pattern`**: Use specific branch names (for example, **`main`**, **`develop`**) or patterns (for example, **`feature/*`**) to apply rules to multiple branches.
- **`By branch type`**: You can restrict entire branch types (such as feature, bugfix, release) based on your branching model.

## Branch Permissions Settings

- **`Write Access`**: You can define who is allowed to push changes or merge pull requests to a branch.
  - **`Allow rewriting branch history`**: If enabled, users with write access can rewrite commit history using commands, such as **`git rebase`** or **`git push --force`**. This is typically restricted for key branches such as main.
  - **`Allow deleting this branch`**: This setting determines whether users can delete the branch, often disabled for protected branches such as main or develop.
- **`Merge Access via Pull Requests`**: You can control who can merge changes into a branch via pull requests. Choose whether to allow everyone with repository access to merge or limit it to specific people or groups.

**Branch Restrictions Example**:

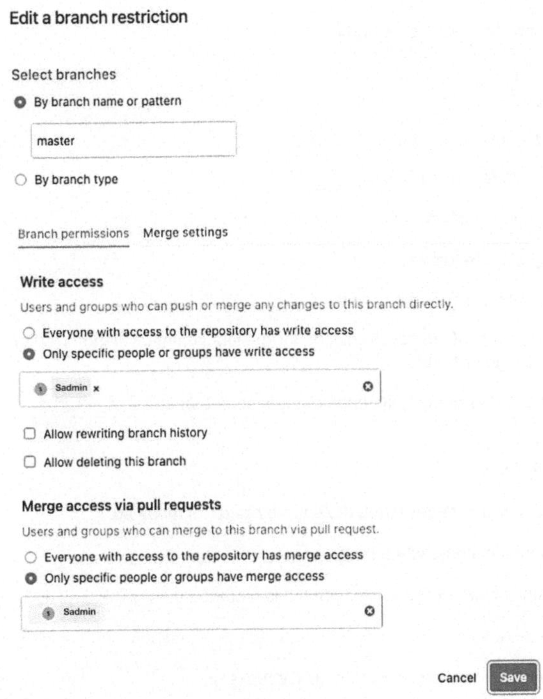


***Figure* 5.2**: *Example Branch Restrictions*

**`Select branches`**: The restriction is applied to the branch named **`master`**.

**`Branch permissions`**:

- **`Write access`**: Only specific people or groups can push or merge changes directly to this branch. In this case, only approver "**`Suhas`**" has write access.
- **`Allow rewriting branch history`** and **`Allow deleting this branch`** options are not checked, meaning that users cannot rewrite the branch history or delete the branch.
- **`Merge access via pull requests`**:
    - Only specific people or groups can merge pull requests into this branch. Again, only approver "**`Suhas`**" is specified as having merge access.

These settings effectively limit both direct write access and pull request merge access to the master branch, allowing only approver "**`Suhas`**" to perform these actions.

## Merge Settings and Merge Checks

Branch permissions are not the only layer of protection; merge settings and checks provide additional rules to ensure code quality and prevent incomplete or unreviewed code from being merged into a protected branch.

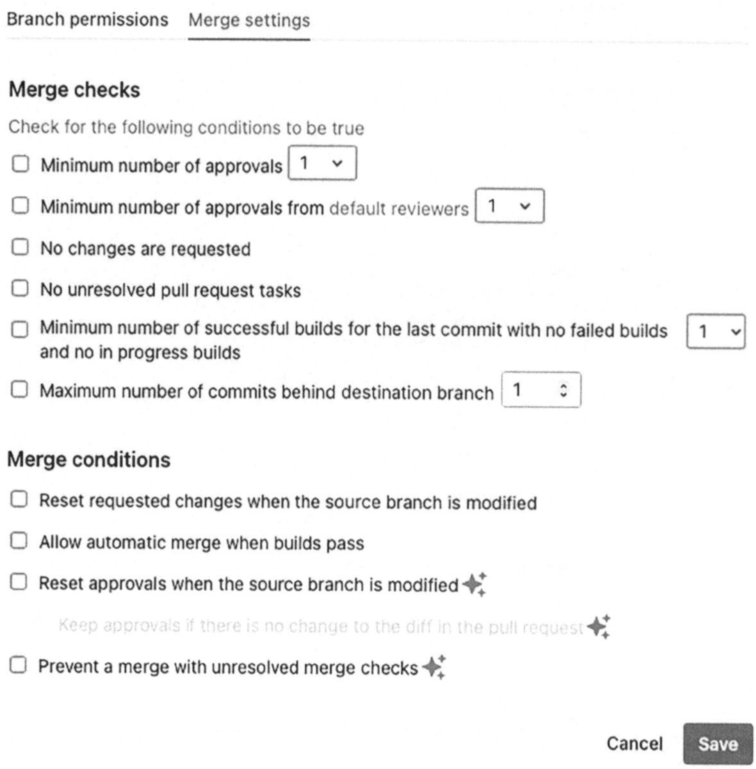


***Figure 5.3***: *Merge Checks*

Similar to write permissions, merge permissions ensure only authorized users or groups can merge changes into important branches, such as main or develop.

- Merge Settings (Conditions)

  These are the rules for handling pull requests before they are merged into the target branch:

  - **`Reset requested changes when the source branch is modified`**: If a reviewer requests changes and the source branch is updated, the "**`requested changes`**" status is reset; it ensures that the reviewer re-evaluates the updated code.
  - **`Allow automatic merge when builds pass`**: Bitbucket can automatically merge a pull request once all builds and merge checks are successful; it is useful for teams that want to merge changes as soon as their CI/CD pipelines succeed.
  - **`Reset approvals when the source branch is modified`**: When enabled, if the source branch is modified after a PR is approved, the previous approvals are reset, requiring the new changes to be reviewed.

    - `Keep approvals if there is no change to the diff`: This preserves approvals if the changes do not affect the actual content of the pull request (for example, rebasing or merging without altering the code itself).

- **Merge Checks**

  Merge checks are a crucial part of Bitbucket's workflow, enforcing specific conditions that need to be met before a pull request is merged:

    - `Minimum number of approvals`: Enforce that a certain number of reviewers must approve the PR before it can be merged.
    - `No unresolved pull request tasks`: All tasks assigned to the PR (for example, fixing a bug) must be resolved before the pull request can be merged.
    - `No changes requested`: If any reviewer has requested changes, the PR cannot be merged until those requests are addressed.
    - `Successful builds required`: The PR can only be merged if the CI pipeline passes successfully.
    - `Maximum number of commits behind the destination branch`: Prevents merging if the source branch is too far behind the target branch, encouraging the developer to rebase or merge the latest changes before proceeding.

**Common Scenarios for Merge Checks**

- **Scenario 1**: A pull request has one approval but requested changes from another reviewer. The PR cannot be merged until the requested changes are addressed.
- **Scenario 2**: A team may require that a pull request must have one successful build and no unresolved tasks and be no more than three commits behind the destination branch before merging.
- **Scenario 3**: The team can enable automatic merging, so once all checks pass, the pull request merges automatically without further intervention.

**Reasons to Use These Features**

The branch permissions, merge settings, and checks in Bitbucket Cloud offer a robust framework to maintain:

- **Code Quality**: Ensuring code passes through proper reviews, testing, and validation before being merged into a protected branch.
- **Consistency**: Pull requests cannot be merged unless they meet the same rigorous criteria, leading to a more stable and clean codebase.

- **Automation**: Automating merges once all checks are satisfied streamlines development workflows, reducing manual steps while maintaining control over quality.

By using these features, teams can ensure that code reviews are thorough, automated where possible, and aligned with organizational policies and coding standards.

**Testing the branch restrictions and merge checks workflow:**

1. **Create a Pull Request**: Another user (the pull request author) creates a pull request and requests a review from the designated reviewer. The pull request is now pending approval.

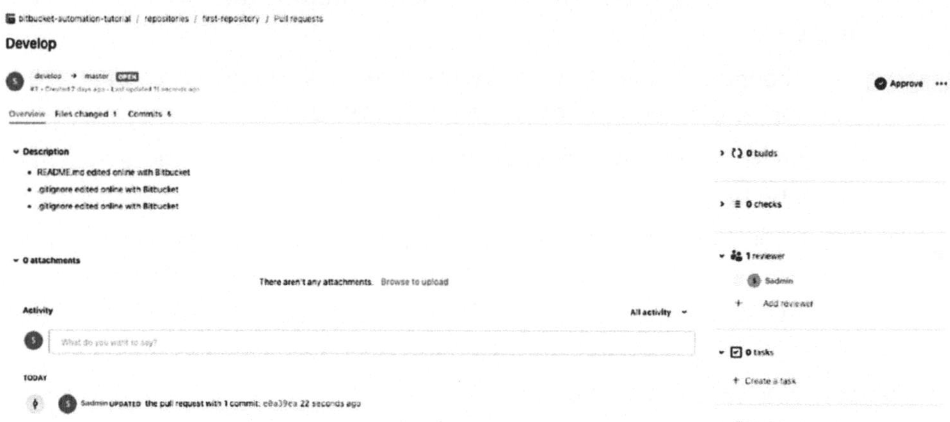


**Figure 5.4**: *Create PR for Approval*

2. **Approve the Pull Request**: The pull request reviewer reviews the changes and approves the pull request.

**Figure 5.5**: *Approve PR*

3. **Switch to the Pull Request Author**: When the author logs back in to the session, they will notice that there is no Merge button visible. This is because the author does not have write or merge access to the master branch.

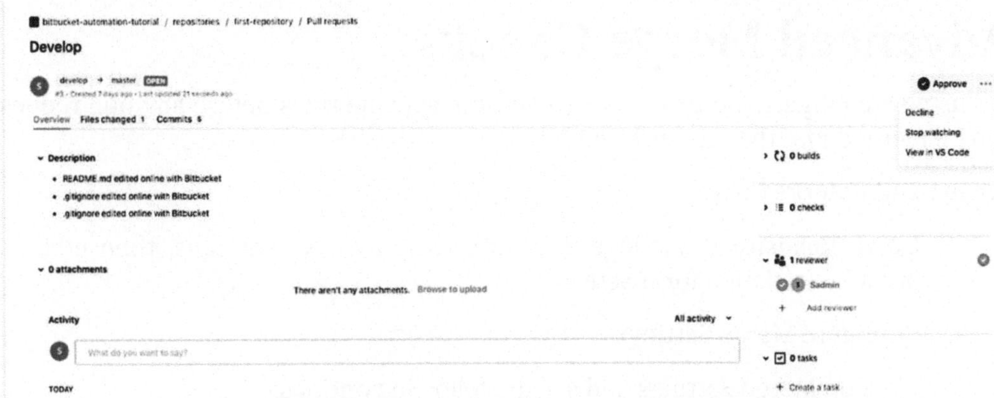


***Figure 5.6**: PR Merge is disabled due to branch permissions*

4. **Merge the Pull Request (Reviewer)**: To merge the pull request, switch back to the reviewer's session. Since the reviewer has write and merge access, they can go ahead and merge the pull request.

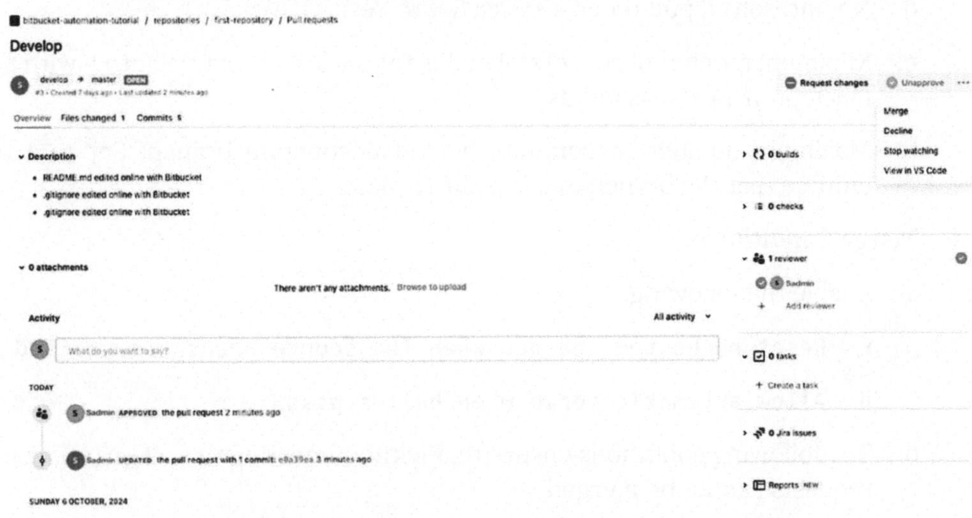


***Figure 5.7**: PR Merge allowed based on branch permissions*

In this example, we configured a basic branch permission to demonstrate how you can control who is allowed to merge changes into important branches such as master. This workflow ensures a controlled and secure process where only designated reviewers can approve and merge changes, preventing unauthorized users from directly modifying critical branches.

Next, let us explore and configure **merge checks**, which are advanced security features that further enhance the code review workflow by enforcing specific conditions, such as build success and required approvals, before a pull request can be merged.

# Advanced Merge Checks

Let us now configure merge checks to enforce specific rules before any pull request can be merged into the master branch.

**Steps to Add Merge Checks:**

1. **Go to Repository Settings**: Navigate to Branch Restrictions, then edit the branch restriction for master.
2. Configure Merge Settings
3. Click on Merge Settings and set the following options:
    a. Minimum number of approvals: Set to 1.
    b. Minimum number of approvals from default reviewers: Set to 1.
    c. No changes requested: Set to Yes.
    d. No unresolved pull request tasks: Set to Yes.
    e. Minimum number of successful builds for the last commit: Set to 1, with no failed or in-progress builds.
    f. Maximum number of commits behind destination branch: Set to 1 to enforce that the branch must be up-to-date.
4. **Merge Conditions**:
    a. Enable the following:
        i. **`Reset requested changes when the source branch is modified`**.
        ii. **`Allow automatic merge when builds pass`**.
    b. The following conditions ensure that without meeting the set criteria, pull requests cannot be merged.
        i. **`Reset approvals when the source branch is modified > Keep approvals if there is no change to the diff in the pull request`**
        ii. **`Prevent a merge with unresolved merge checks`**
    c. Note that these advanced checks are part of premium features, and for other subscriptions, the options might appear disabled. Even though

merge check failures are shown, the system might still allow you to merge the pull request.

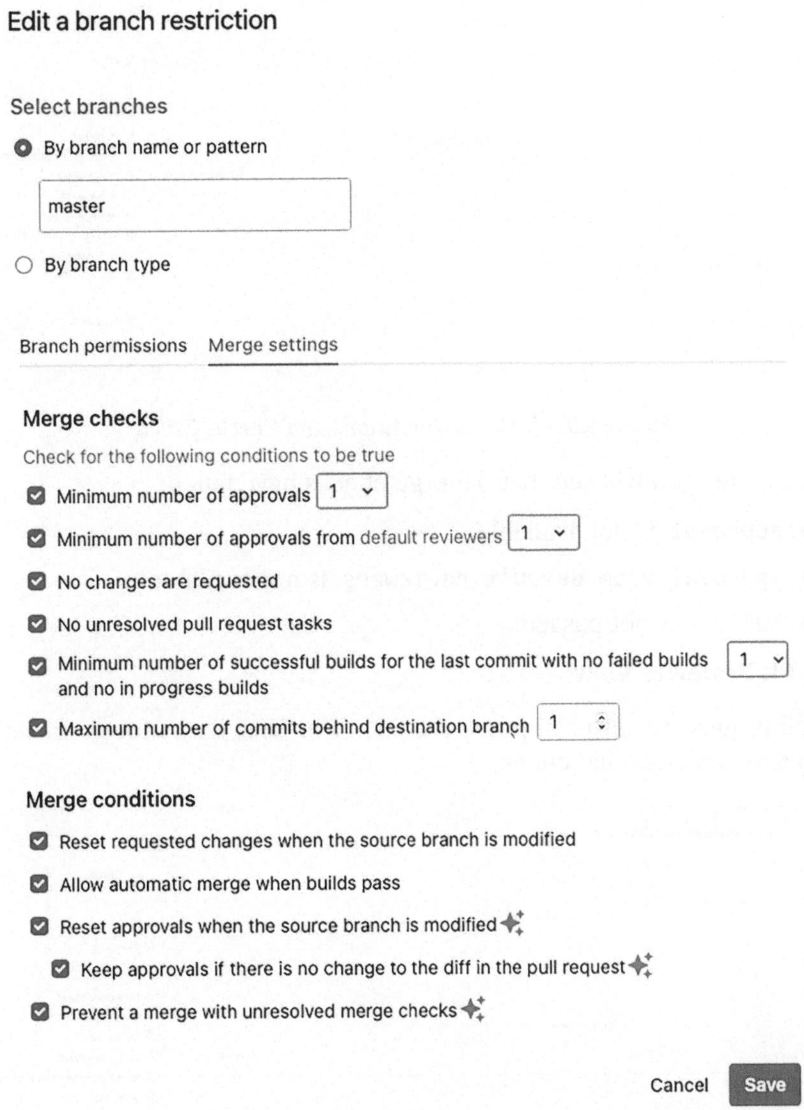


***Figure 5.8**: PR Merge Conditions and Checks Enforced*

Apply these settings to branches where they are required, typically for the master or develop branches.

- **Testing the Merge Checks:** Once the settings are in place, let us test them. Create a Pull Request and request a review.

**Figure 5.9**: *PR Merge Conditions and Checks Failed*

On the side panel, you will see that 3 merge checks have failed:

- `1+ approval` is not available.
- `1+ approval from default reviewers` is not available.
- `1+ build` has not passed.

**Switch to PR Reviewer View:**

Let the pull request reviewer approve the PR. After this, let us focus on setting up a sample pipeline for the build check.

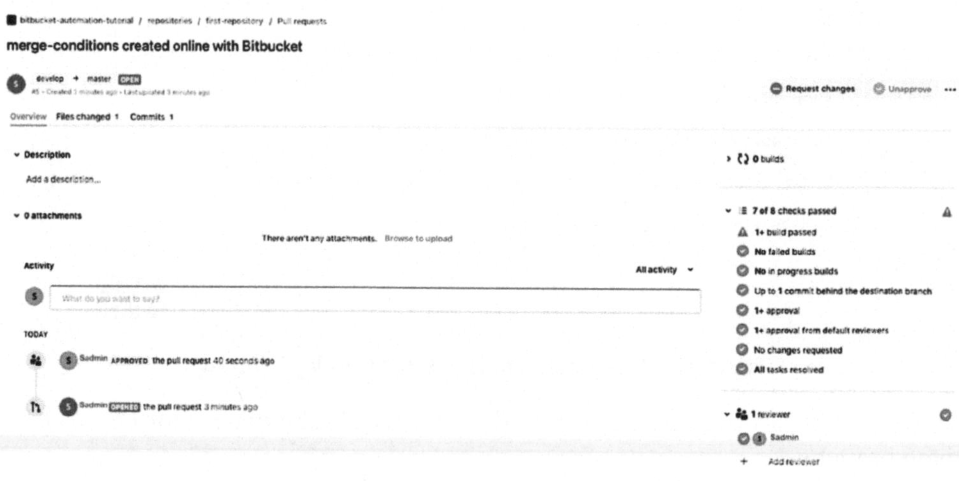


**Figure 5.10**: *PR Build Merge Checks failed*

**Enable Pipelines and Create a Sample Pipeline**: Bitbucket Pipelines is a CI/CD service integrated into Bitbucket Cloud that automates build and deployment tasks.

Let us enable pipelines:

- Go to **`Repository Settings`** > **`Pipelines Settings`** and enable Pipelines.
- Configure the pipeline using the starter template and create the bitbucket-**`pipelines.yml`** file

***Figure 5.11**: Pipelines Starter Templates*

Since branch restrictions are in place for the master branch, we will commit this file to the develop branch. Now, commit the pipeline file and check whether the pull request passes all checks.

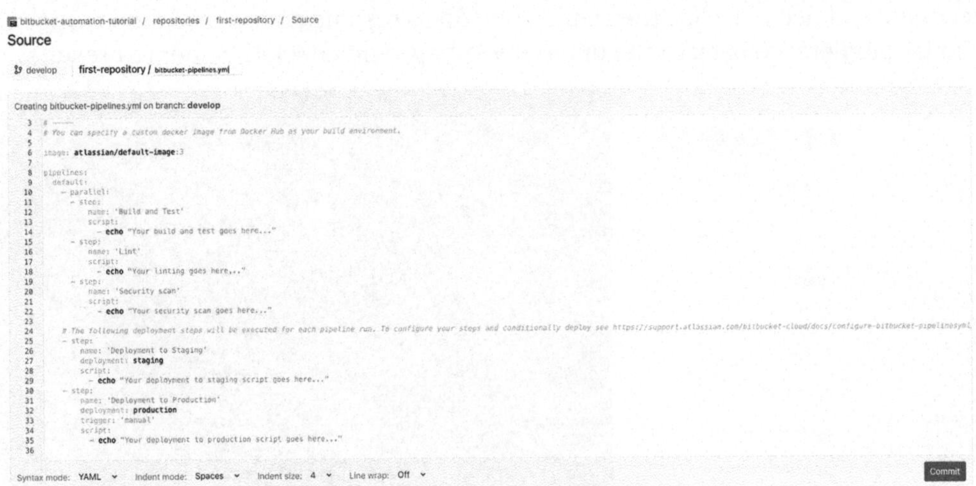


***Figure 5.12**: Pipelines Starter Template YAML*

**Handling Merge Check Failures:**

Once the pipeline is set up, you will notice:

- The approvals have been reset since the develop branch was updated with changes from the pipeline configuration.

*Figure 5.13: PR merge checks reset*

Also, go to the Pipelines page to ensure the pipeline steps are running and deployed successfully. If needed, click the Deploy button to resume any paused steps. Once the build is complete, go back to the pull request page and check the updated results.

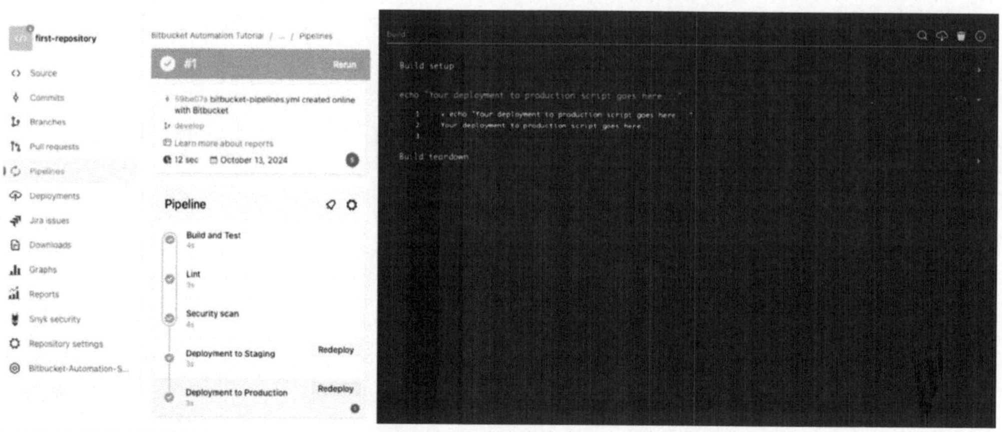


*Figure 5.14: Pipelines build*

**Check Build Status:**

Once the build status is updated, switch to the PR reviewer's session and approve the pull request again since the approvals were reset.

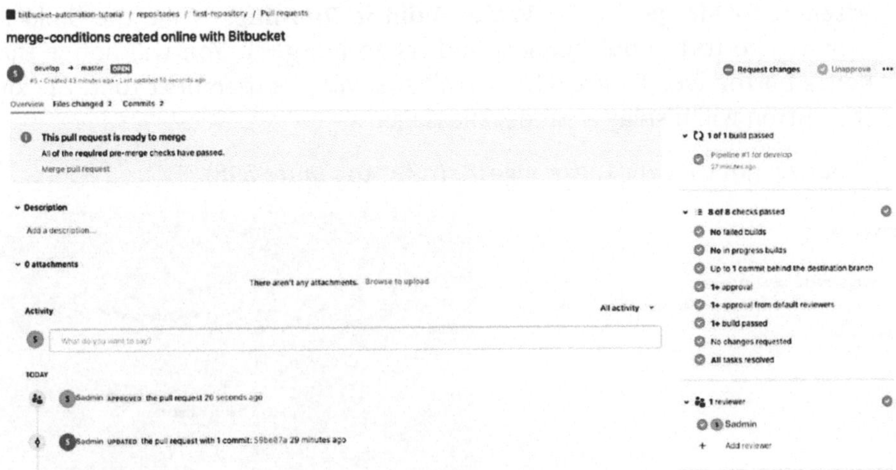


**Figure 5.15**: *Pull Request Ready for Merge*

Let us test another useful merge check: **automatic PR merge when builds pass**. This feature ensures that even while a build is running, you can queue the merge, and once the build passes, the PR will be automatically merged.

**Steps to Test:**

1. **Rerun the Pipeline Build**: After configuring the pipeline, rerun the build for the pull request. During this time, the pipeline will be actively processing the build.

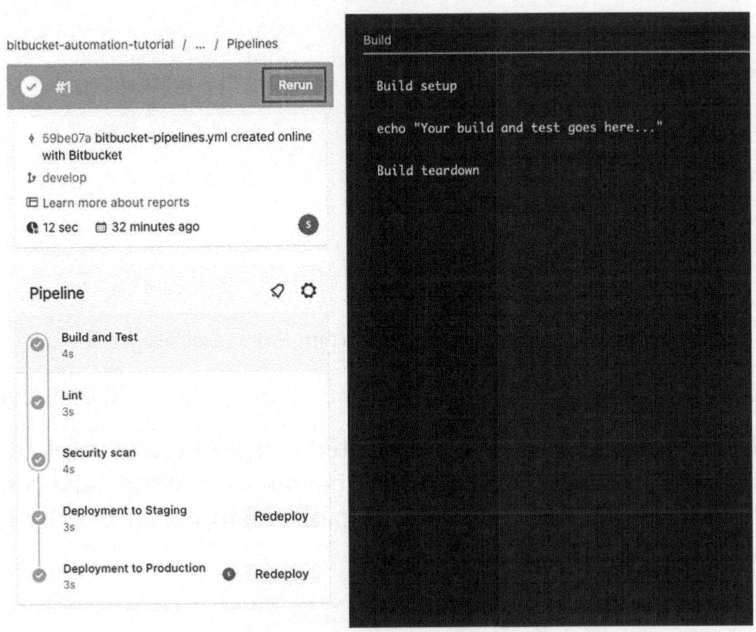


**Figure 5.16**: *Rerun pipeline build*

2. **Attempt to Merge the PR While Build is Running**: While the build is still running, go to the pull request and try to merge it. You will notice that the **`Merge`** button (see *Figure 5.17*) is available with a **`timer`** next to it. Clicking on the button will display a banner message:

   `"You've got a pending merge."` (refer to *Figure 5.18*)

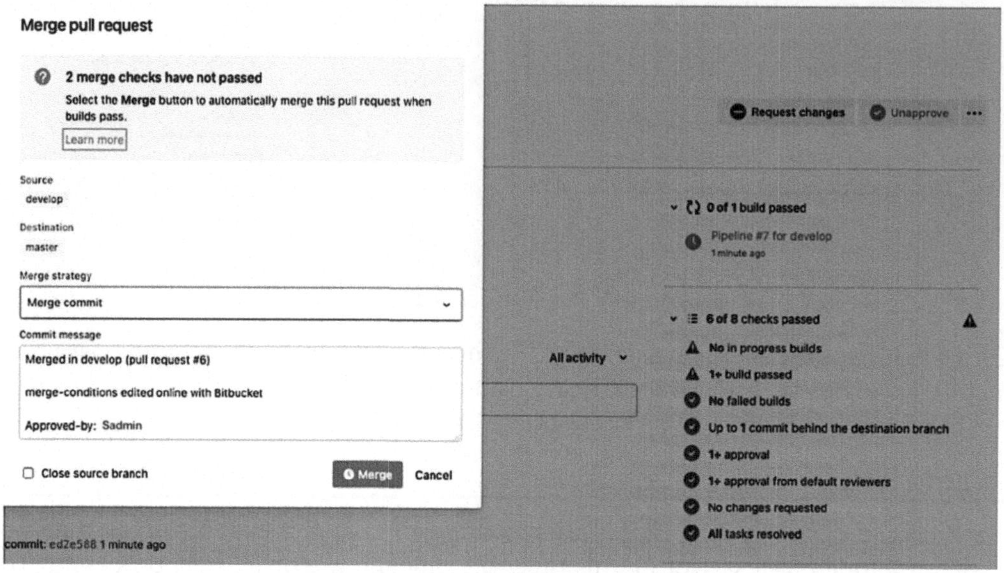


**Figure 5.17**: *Pull Request Ready for Merge*

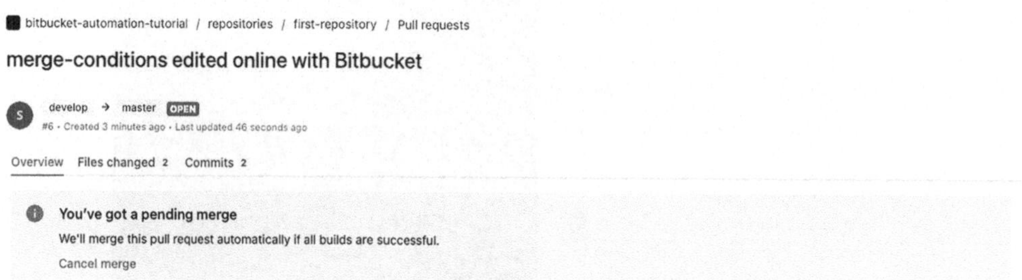


**Figure 5.18**: *Pull Request background merge in progress*

This indicates that the PR will automatically merge once the build completes.

3. **Pending Merge Process**: The automated merge check ensures that while the build is still running, the PR merge is pending. Once the build completes, the system will evaluate the build results (pass or fail) and automatically merge the PR if the build passes.

4. **Simulating a Build with Delay**: For this test, we are using a simple pipeline script that includes a sleep 300 command, which pauses the build for 5 minutes:

```
image: atlassian/default-image:3
pipelines:
  default:
    - step:
        script:
          - sleep 300
```

This allows us to observe the pending state for 5 minutes before the pipeline completes.

**Automatic Merge**: Once the build is finished and passes all required checks, the **`pending merge banner`** will be removed and the PR will be merged automatically.

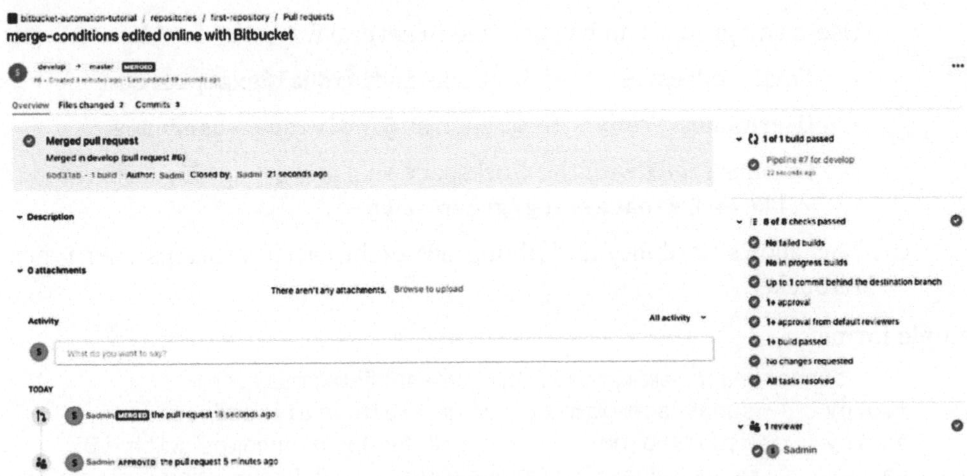


**Figure 5.19**: *Pull Request automatic merge in background after builds are passed*

We now configured merge checks and tested them with a pull request. The checks ensure that conditions such as approvals, passing builds, and resolved tasks must be met before any pull request is merged. This approach helps maintain code quality and security by enforcing the code review process. In the next chapters, we will cover Bitbucket Pipelines configuration and automated workflows in more detail.

# Configuring Code Owners for Automated Code Reviews

**Definition**: Code owners are designated individuals or teams responsible for reviewing specific parts of a codebase. By configuring a **`CODEOWNERS`** file, Bitbucket Cloud can automatically assign these reviewers based on defined ownership rules whenever a pull request involves their areas.

**Steps to Configure Code Owners**:

1. **Create the `CODEOWNERS` File**: Place the **`CODEOWNERS`** file in a directory named **`.bitbucket`** at the root of your repository.
2. **Define Ownership Rules**:
   - Each line in the **`CODEOWNERS`** file follows a specific format:
     - A file pattern is followed by one or more owners.
     - The pattern matching follows rules similar to **`.gitignore`** syntax, allowing for flexibility in specifying files or directories.
3. **Reference Users**:
   - Users and groups can be specified in several ways:
     - **Email addresses**: Directly add as **`individual@example.com`**.
     - **Usernames**: Prefix with @, such as **`@individual-username`**.
     - **Groups**: Prefix with the workspace slug and group slug, separated by a /, like **`@workspace-slug/group-slug`**.
   - This allows flexibility in defining ownership across various user types in Bitbucket.

**Example format:**

```
*           sundararajurama@gmail.com suhasrajmm@gmail.com
      foo.py      suhasrajmm@gmail.com # Plain email addresses
      bar.py     @suhasrajmm            # Prefix usernames with `@`
      baz.py     @workspace-slug/group-slug     # Prefix group slug with
      the workspace slug eg: bitbucket-automation-tutorial/code-reviewers
```

**Note**: *An asterisk (*) is a wildcard that matches* ***`all files`*** *in the repository. By using * as the file pattern, you can designate specific individuals or teams as responsible for reviewing any changes made to any file in the repository.*

4. **Commit the `CODEOWNERS` File**: Once the file is configured, commit it to the repository. Bitbucket will begin automatically assigning the specified owners to pull requests that affect the matching files or directories.

***Figure* 5.20**: *Bitbucket cloud* CODEOWNERS

In the preceding example,

- **The asterisk (*) acts as a wildcard**, applying this rule to all files in the repository.
- **`suhasrajmm@gmail.com` is specified as the code owner**, meaning this user will automatically be assigned as a reviewer for any pull requests that affect any file in this repository.

**Additional Steps and Process**

1. **Committing the `CODEOWNERS` file to the Master Branch**:
   a. The **`CODEOWNERS`** file is being committed to the master branch.
   b. Since **default reviewers** have been previously enabled for "**`Suhas`**," and **branch restrictions** are set to allow merges only via pull requests, this configuration will prompt the creation of a **`pull request from a temporary branch to the master branch`**.
2. **Merging the `CODEOWNERS` File**: To merge the **`CODEOWNERS`** file into the master branch, follow the previously discussed merge conditions, which include required approvals and any additional merge checks.
3. **Post-Merge Steps**:
   a. Once the **`CODEOWNERS`** file is merged to master, remove user "**`Suhas`**" from the **default reviewers** list.
   b. Next, create a new pull request between the develop and master branches.

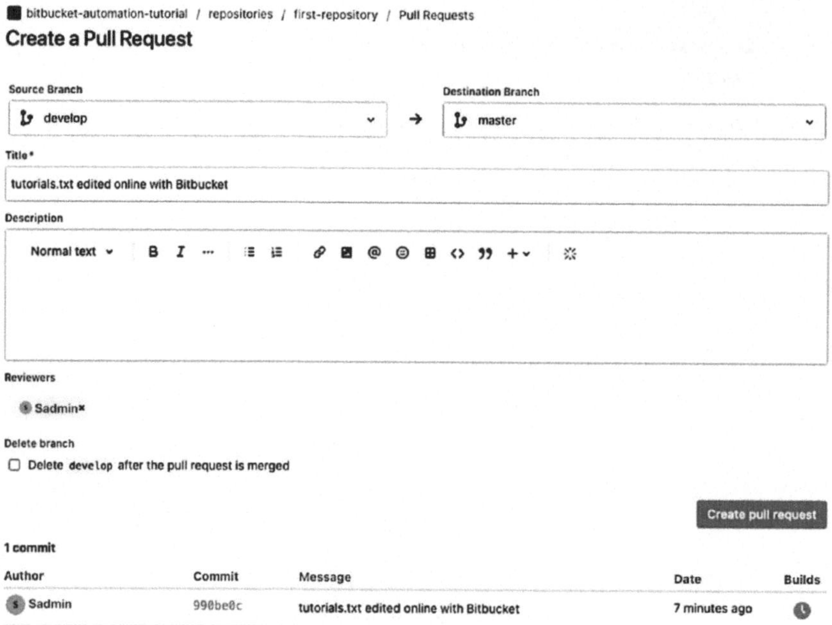


***Figure 5.21**: Bitbucket cloud CODEOWNERS assignment in a PR*

For this new pull request (from develop to master), you should now see user "**Suhas**" automatically added as an approver, the CODEOWNERS configuration applied to the master branch. This automation ensures that Suhas is designated to review changes to any file in the codebase.

The idea behind the **CODEOWNERS** feature is to manage code reviews through a configuration file (similar to **.gitignore**) and provide flexible options for assigning reviewers. This approach allows you to define specific reviewers–whether individuals, groups, or teams–to review changes to particular files, folders, or the entire codebase associated with a branch.

# Collaborating on Code and Providing Feedback

Collaboration during code reviews is essential to improving code quality. Bitbucket Cloud provides features such as inline comments, tasks, and file viewing status to facilitate efficient code review discussions.

## Steps to Collaborate on Code and Provide Feedback

Bitbucket simplifies code collaboration and review processes by integrating features such as inline comments, tasks, and file viewing statuses. These features enhance team collaboration by ensuring reviewers can provide actionable feedback, assign tasks, and track review progress efficiently.

The following steps illustrate functionalities, such as commenting, requesting changes, resolving comments, and marking files as reviewed, offering a practical view of how these features work during a pull request.

# Steps for Effective Code Reviews in Bitbucket

1. **Adding and Viewing Comments**
    a. Inline comments allow reviewers to provide feedback on specific lines of code within a pull request.
    b. Reviewers can directly select a line in the pull request and add comments for clarification or suggestions.
    c. Authors can engage in discussions by replying to comments, facilitating a productive feedback loop.
2. **To add a comment at each level**
    a. **Pull request**: Under `Comments` on the pull request, click in the `Add a comment` text field. Add your comment and select `Add comment now`.

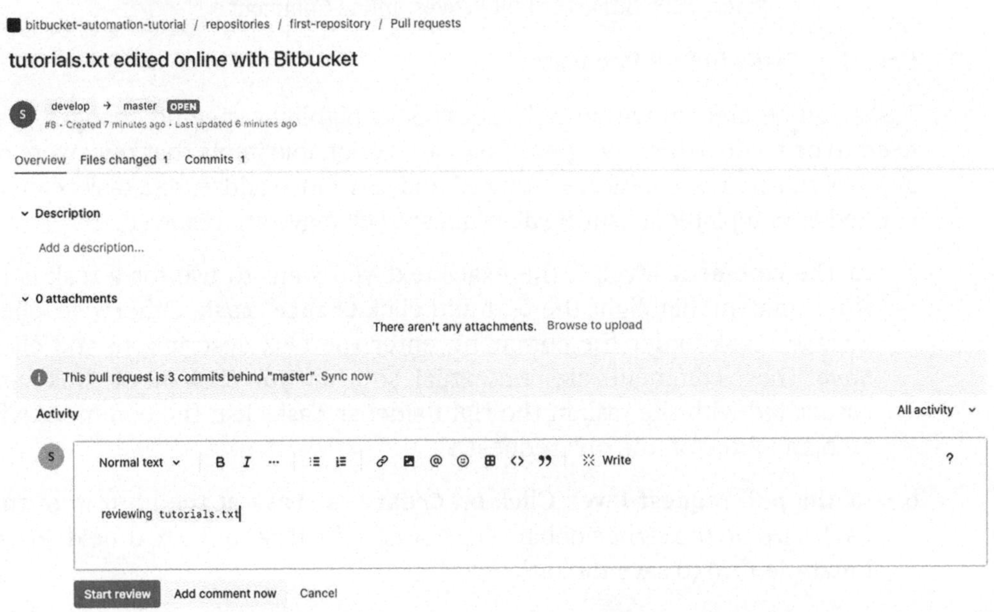


**Figure 5.22**: *Bitbucket Pull Request Comment*

Continue to review the PR and add any other comments and tasks you would like to be part of your review by selecting **`Add comment`**.

a. **Inline**: Click the '**`+`**' associated with the line in the diff you want to comment on and/or add a task to **>** select **`Add comment`** now. Add your comment to the text field and click **`Save`**. You can also add a comment to the entire **`diff`** by selecting the Add comment button on the right side of the **`diff's`** header.

   In the following example, an inline comment is being added to the tutorials.txt file with feedback such as "**`Please add a code comment here`**."

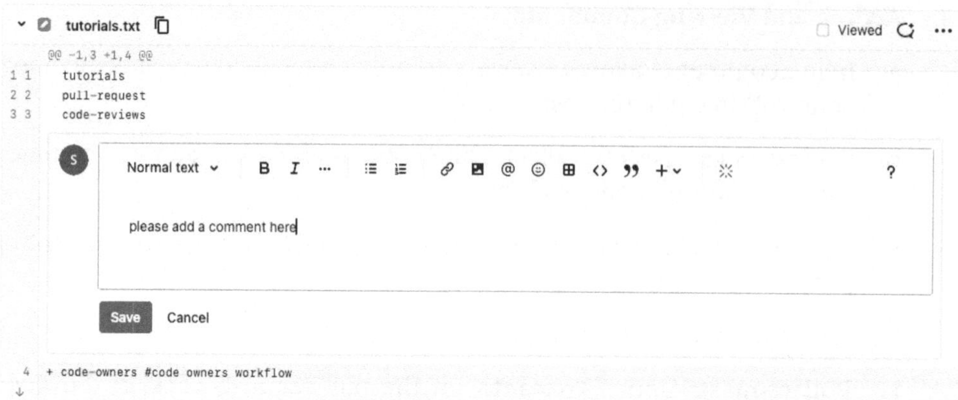


***Figure* 5.23**: *Bitbucket Pull Request Inline Comment*

3. **Creating Tasks in Pull Requests**

   Tasks can be created within pull requests to highlight specific changes that need to be made before merging. Tasks are actionable items that reviewers or authors can create to indicate required updates. Once addressed, tasks can be marked as completed, ensuring all requested changes are resolved.

   a. **At the comment level:** If the exact text you want to use for a task is in the comment, highlight the text and click **`Create task`**. Otherwise, click **`Create task`** under the comment, enter the task description, and click **`Save`**. These comments are contextual, so when you click on the link icon associated with the task in the right sidebar Tasks list, the comment will be highlighted on the pull request.

   b. **At the pull request level:** Click on **`Create a task`** at the bottom of the **`Task`** card on the right sidebar. Type or add the task to the text field. Press *Enter (Return)* to save the task.

The following example describes how comments or feedback can be converted into tasks, ensuring accountability and clarity in the review process.

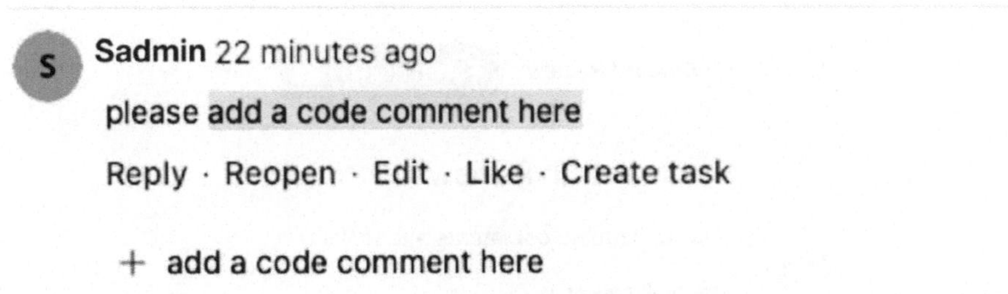


***Figure 5.24***: *Bitbucket Pull Request Tasks*

4. **Marking Files as Viewed**

   Marking files as viewed helps reviewers keep track of their progress during the review.

   Reviewers can mark files as "**`Viewed`**" after thoroughly reviewing them. This feature reduces the chance of revisiting already-reviewed files and ensures efficient code reviews. The following example describes the use of the "**`Viewed`**" option for a file in the pull request, showing how reviewers track their progress.

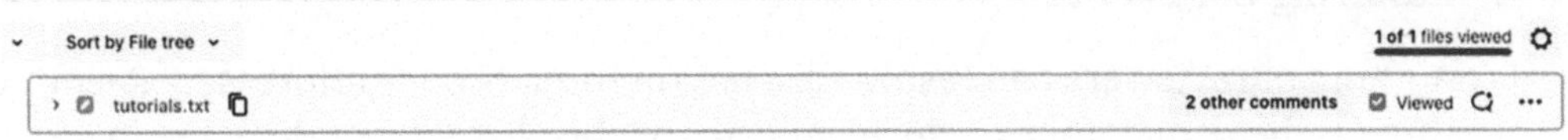


***Figure 5.25***: *Bitbucket Pull Request mark files as "Viewed"*

5. **Requesting Changes or Approving**

   Reviewers can either approve a pull request or request changes based on the review. After reviewing, a reviewer can either approve the changes or submit feedback indicating what must be resolved.

   The request for changes option ensures quality control before merging.

   The following example describes the "**`Request Changes`**" and "**`Approve`**" options being selected during the review.

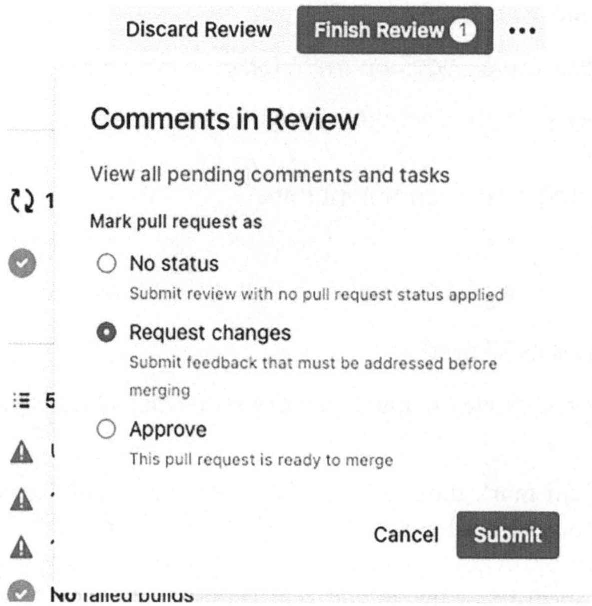


**Figure 5.26**: *Bitbucket Pull Request Finish Review Button*

6. **Resolving Comments**

   Authors or reviewers can resolve discussion threads once addressed. Resolved threads help maintain a clean and actionable list of pending feedback; it ensures completed feedback is closed, keeping the review streamlined.

   The following image describes a resolved thread for a comment added earlier, demonstrating how feedback is managed effectively.

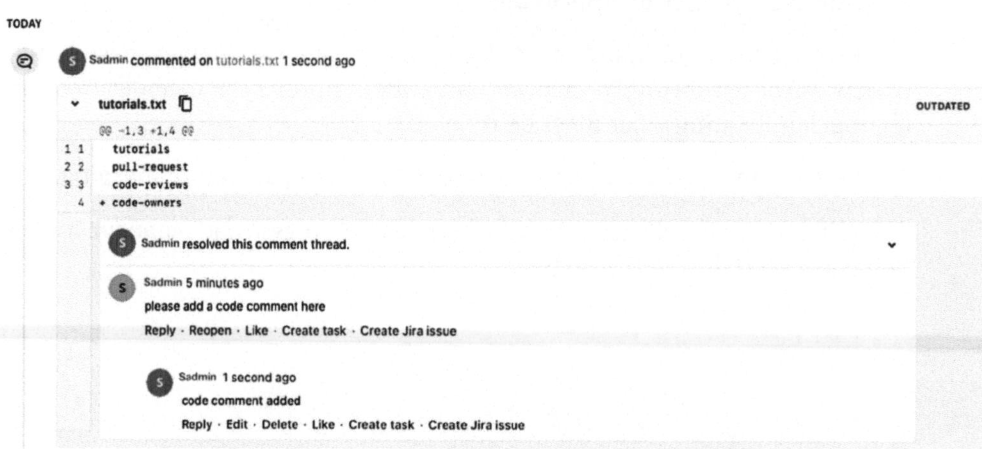


**Figure 5.27**: *Bitbucket Pull Request Resolve Comments*

# Conclusion

Advanced code review features in Bitbucket Cloud allow teams to automate critical parts of the review process, enforce quality standards, and enhance collaboration. By configuring branch permissions, setting up advanced merge checks, and automating reviewer assignments with Codeowners, teams can ensure that the right people are reviewing the right code, that code meets quality standards, and that security and workflow integrity are maintained. These tools, combined with best practices for providing feedback and reviewing code efficiently, enable teams to improve their codebase quality while fostering a collaborative development environment. The next chapter explores Bitbucket Pipelines and the essential concepts of continuous integration and continuous deployment (CI/CD).

# CHAPTER 6

# Mastering Bitbucket Pipelines and CI/CD Integration

## Introduction

Bitbucket Pipelines is a built-in continuous integration and delivery service for Bitbucket repositories. It empowers teams to automate code builds, tests, and deployments using a simple configuration file in their codebase. By integrating these actions directly into Bitbucket, development teams can reduce integration headaches, spot problems sooner, and streamline their release cycles.

In this chapter, we will explore the fundamental concepts behind Bitbucket Pipelines and walk through how to configure these workflows in YAML. We will also discuss key features such as test reporting, connections to Jira, and extending pipelines with specialized "*pipes*" for external tools. By the end, you will be equipped to create reliable, automated pipelines that support the unique needs of your project.

## Structure

In this chapter, we will cover the following topics:

- The Importance of CI/CD
- Understanding Bitbucket Pipeline Concepts
- Overview of Pipelines UI and Key Features
- Running a Sample Pipeline
- Using Predefined Templates
- YAML Configuration for Pipelines
- Setting up Pipeline Configurations

- Test Reporting in Pipelines and Analyzing Build Test Results
- Integrating Pipelines with Jira
- Using Pipes for Third-party Integration

# The Importance of CI/CD

Continuous Integration (CI) and Continuous Deployment (CD) form the backbone of modern software development. **Continuous Integration (CI)** ensures that each new code change is integrated frequently, preventing the dreaded "*merge hell*" by catching conflicts and bugs early. **Continuous Deployment (CD)** streamlines the process of pushing new features or fixes into production, minimizing manual intervention and risk.

**Why CI/CD Matters:**

- **Higher Code Quality:** Automated tests and checks run on every code commit, spotting issues quickly instead of later in the process.
- **Faster Delivery:** By removing human-driven deployment steps, organizations can release updates more frequently and confidently.
- **Improved Team Collaboration:** Developers can merge small, incremental changes more often, reducing the complexity of large integrations and lengthy review cycles.

**Example Use Case:**

Imagine updating a web application every week. Without CI/CD, you must manually run tests, build the application, and deploy it. A CI/CD build job automates these tasks by running tests automatically whenever changes are pushed, then deploying the new build to the environment once everything passes.

# Understanding Bitbucket Pipeline Concepts

In Bitbucket Pipelines, you declare your build, test, or deployment process as steps in a YAML file '**`bitbucket-pipelines.yml`**' committed to your repository. This approach makes it easy to version the pipeline definition alongside your code.

**Key Elements:**

- **Pipeline**: An overall sequence of operations (for example, build, test, deploy) that runs when triggered by an event such as a new commit or pull request.

- **Step**: A set of commands that run in a Docker container. When a step fails, the pipeline halts unless configured otherwise.
- **Services**: Supplementary containers running alongside your main step, useful for databases, caches, or other resources needed during tests.
- **Conditions**: Rules defining when and how specific pipelines or steps will execute (for example, a step condition to execute the build only on the master branch or only for pull requests).

  **Example**: A pipeline with two steps: (i) building a Node.js app in the first step and then (ii) deploying to a staging server might look as follows:

```
pipelines:
  default:
    - step:
        name: Build
        script:
          - npm install
          - npm run build
    - step:
        name: Deploy to Staging
        script:
          - ./deploy.sh
```

# Overview of the Pipelines UI and Key Features

Once you push code to a Bitbucket repository, the Pipelines tab becomes your control center for all automated runs. Here are some features that help you manage and understand your pipelines more effectively:

- **Live Log Streaming:** Observe log output from each step in real time, making it easier to spot errors as they happen.

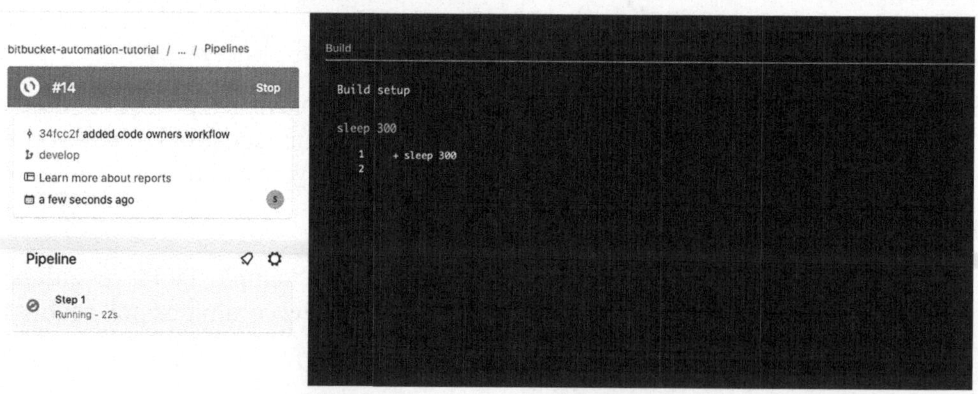


**Figure 6.1**: *Pipelines log streaming*

- **Build Status Indicators:** Each pipeline's status—pass or fail—is plainly displayed, and you can drill down to see precisely which step malfunctioned.

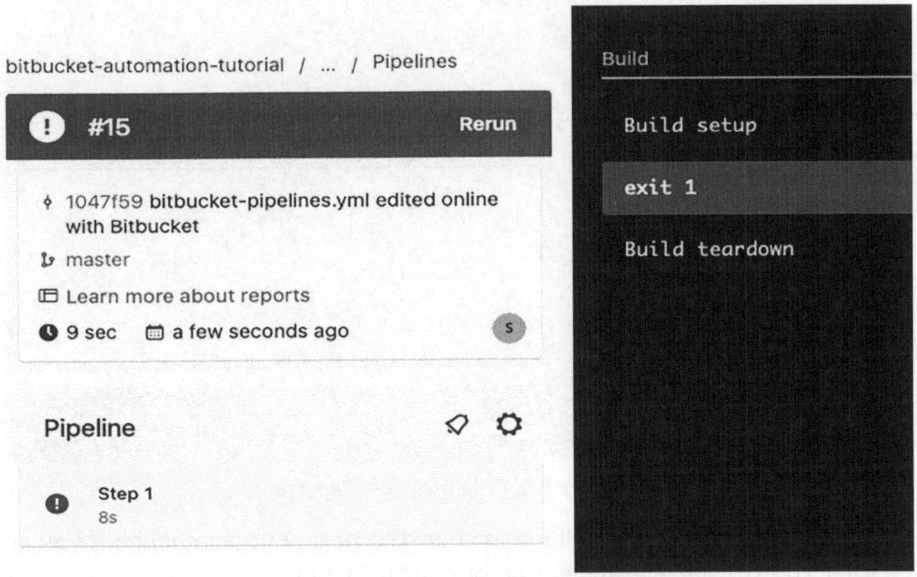


**Figure 6.2**: *Pipelines Status – failed build*

- **Artifacts and Test Summaries**: Configure pipeline steps to save build outputs or to display failed test reports, which can be reused by subsequent steps or inspected for debugging.

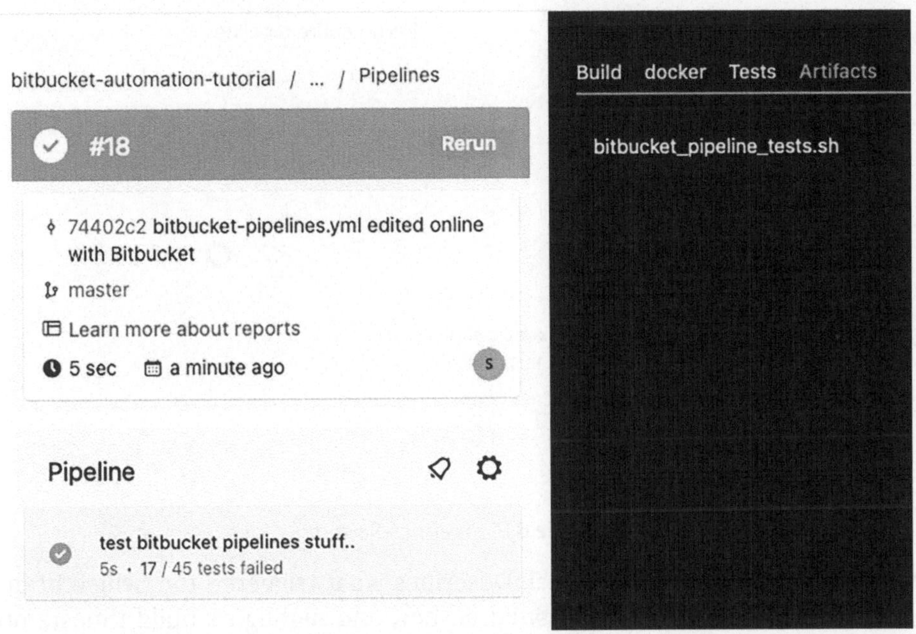


**Figure 6.3**: *Pipelines Artifacts*

*Figure* 6.4 shows the pipeline test report:

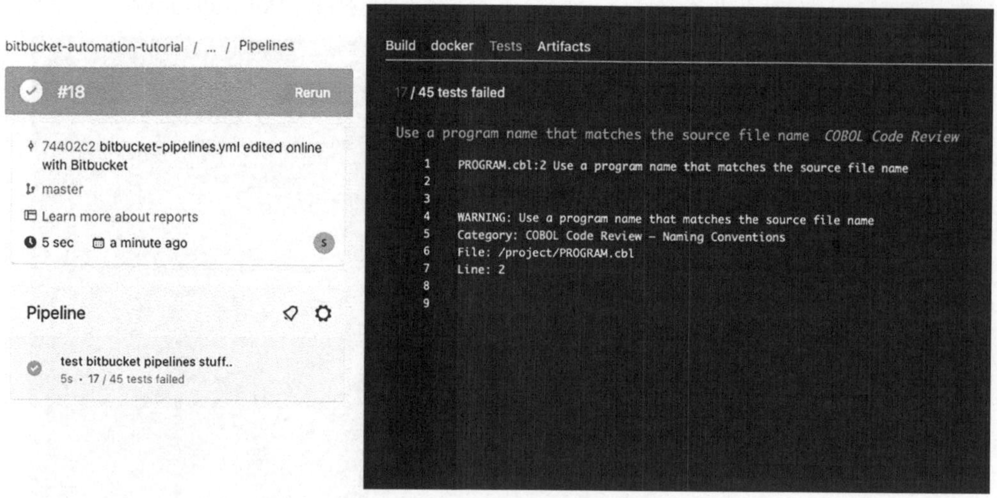


**Figure 6.4**: *Pipelines Test Reports*

- **Restart and Rerun**: Quickly re-run a step or an entire pipeline if you suspect that an external or transient error caused the failure.

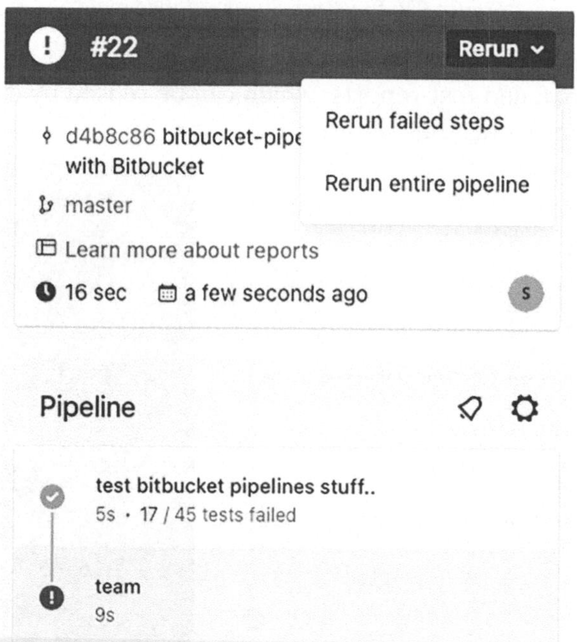


**Figure 6.5**: *Pipelines Re-run*

- **Pipelines Information Panel**: Describes what triggered the (which branch or pull request), the pipeline build author, and highlights build timestamp and build minutes usage information..

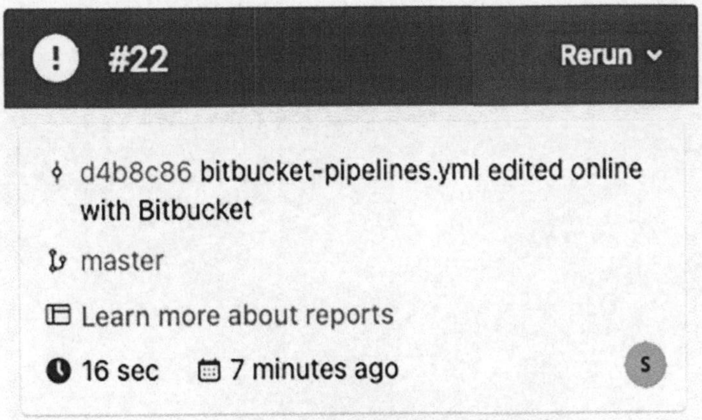


***Figure 6.6***: *Pipelines Information Panel*

- **Pipeline Steps**: Lists each sequential action (build, test, deploy), along with durations and statuses.

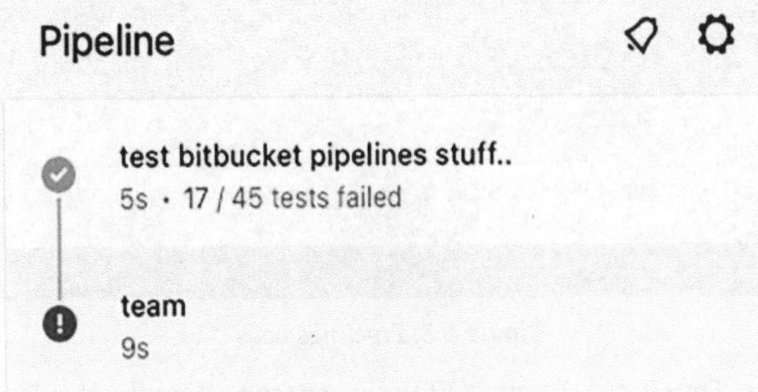


***Figure 6.7***: *Pipelines Steps*

- **Log Segments**: Split into setup, user commands, and teardown, showing every line that was executed.

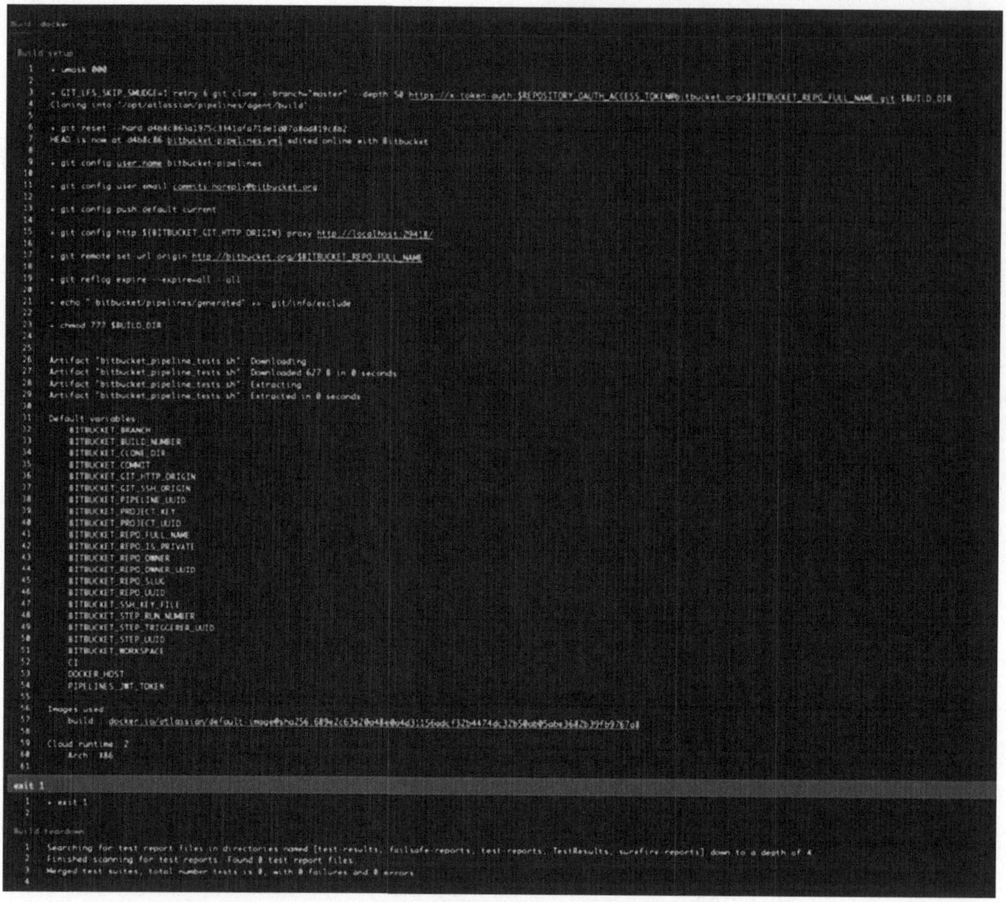

**Figure 6.8**: *Pipelines Logs*

- **Pipelines Top-Right Icons**: Offer log search, download, clearing, and help documentation.

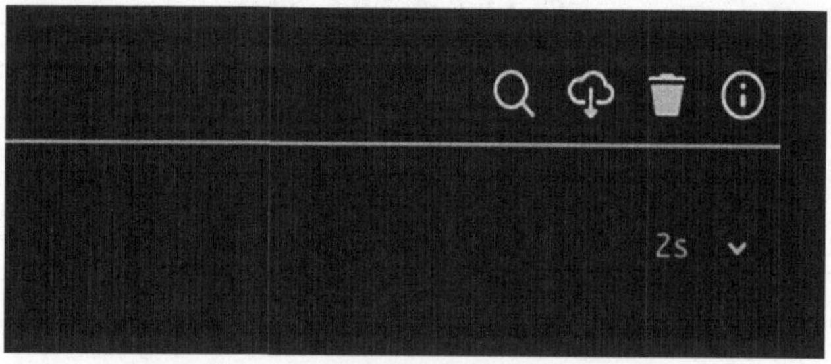


**Figure 6.9**: *Pipelines Top Right Icons*

# Running a Sample Pipeline

Let us run a simple **`'Hello, World!'`** pipeline to understand the structure of pipelines.

1. **Enable Pipelines:** In repository's settings, turn on the Pipelines feature.

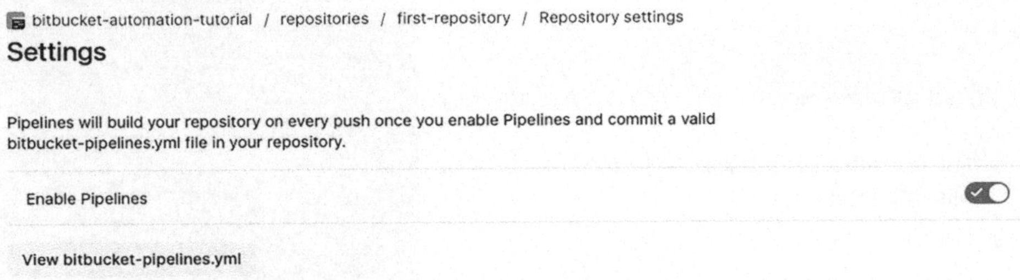


***Figure 6.10**: Pipelines Settings*

2. **Create the Configuration:** At the root of your repository, add a file named **`bitbucket-pipelines.yml`**:

```
pipelines:
  default:
    - step:
        script:
          - echo "Hello, World!"
```

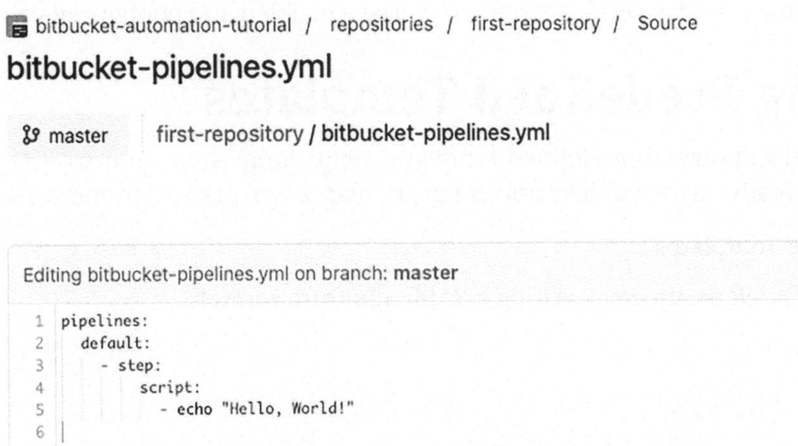


***Figure 6.11**: Pipelines YAML syntax*

3. **Commit the File:** Once you push your changes, Bitbucket automatically starts a pipeline run.

4. **View in the UI:** Go to the Pipelines tab to see the log output and confirm **`"Hello, World!"`** was printed.

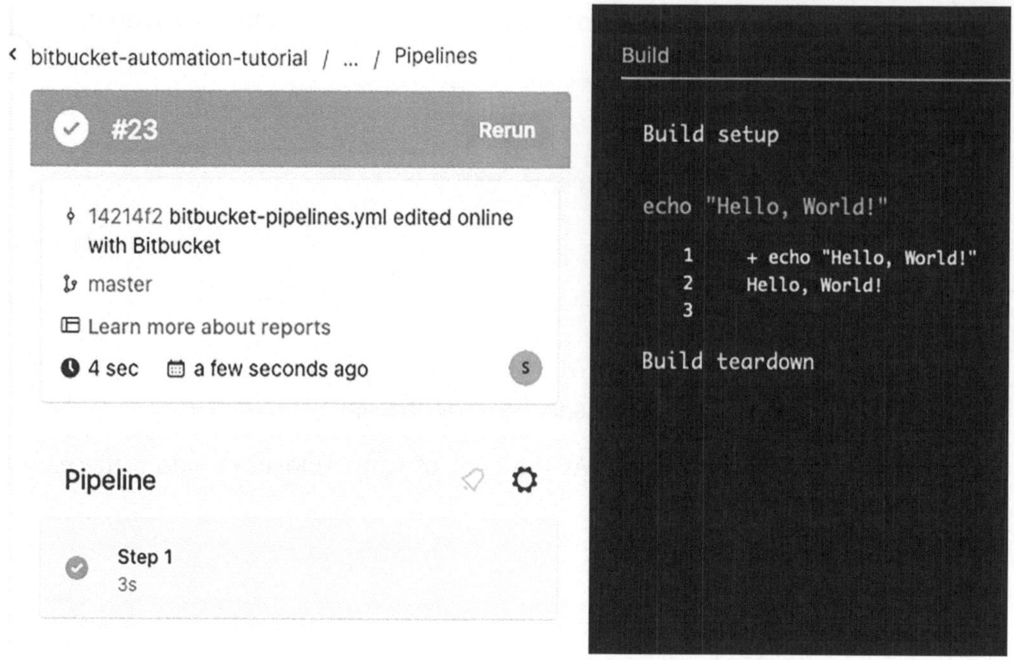


***Figure 6.12**: Pipelines step results*

This simple exercise verifies that pipelines are enabled and configured properly.

# Using Predefined Templates

Bitbucket's library of predefined templates helps jump-start your CI/CD process by offering ready-made configurations for popular languages and frameworks.

**Why Use Templates?**

- **Quick Setup**: Skip writing a YAML file from scratch.

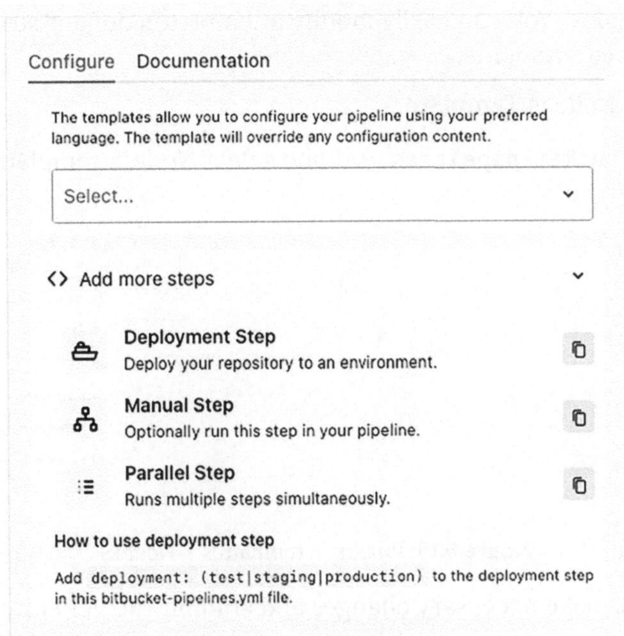


***Figure 6.13**: Pipelines templates - steps*

- **Recommended Practices**: Templates often include standard commands such as installing dependencies and running tests.

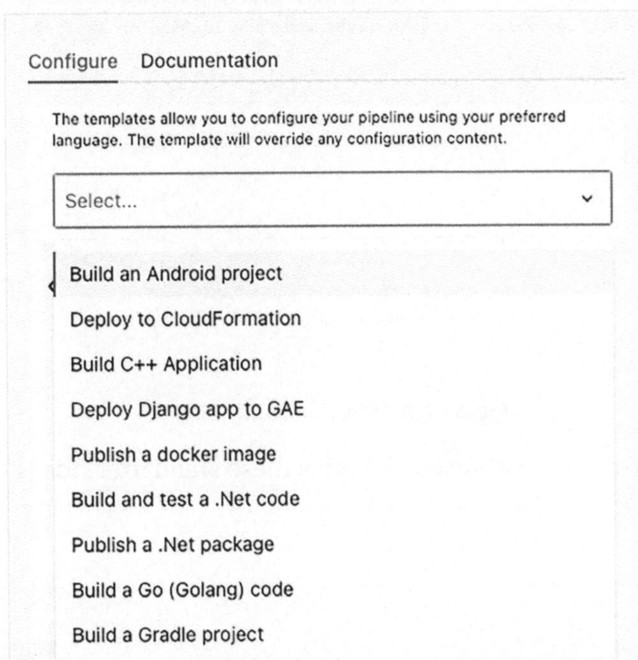


***Figure 6.14**: Pipelines templates – preferred language*

- **Customizable**: You can easily modify a template's default steps to match your project's requirements.

  **Example: Node.js Template**

  Go to **`bitbucket-pipelines.yml`** and select NodeJS template

***Figure 6.15***: *Pipelines templates – NodeJS*

Review the YAML, make necessary changes and commit the generated YAML.

first-repository / **bitbucket-pipelines.yml**

```yaml
#  Template NodeJS build

#  This template allows you to validate your NodeJS code.
#  The workflow allows running tests and code linting on the default branch.

image: node:16

pipelines:
  default:
    - parallel:
        - step:
            name: Build and Test
            script:
              - npm install esbuild
              - node node-build/build.js

```

***Figure 6.16***: *Pipeline build– NodeJS*

Next time you push code, Bitbucket executes these standard Node.js build commands automatically.

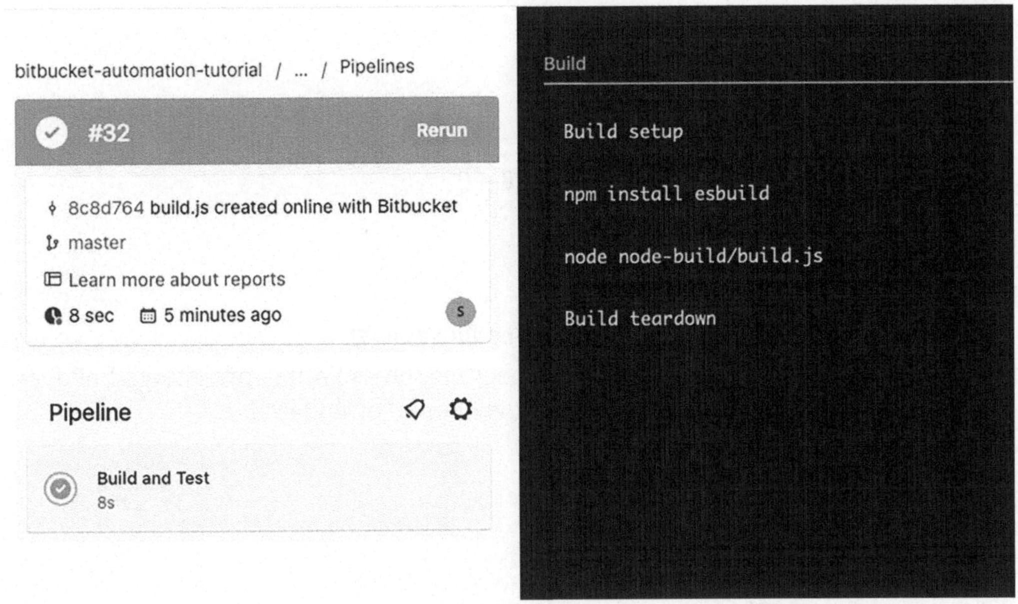


***Figure 6.17**: Pipeline build results – NodeJS*

# YAML Configuration for Pipelines

The **`bitbucket-pipelines.yml`** file is your blueprint for how and when the pipeline runs. Here are several key sections you might use:

- **Default**: Runs whenever you push code and no other branch- or tag-specific pipeline applies.

  *Pipelines Syntax*

  ```
  pipelines:
    default:
        - step:
            name: "Run Tests and Build"
            script:
              - echo "build successful"
  ```

- **Branches or Tag**: Allows specifying behaviors for different branches or tags. For instance, you might only deploy to your staging environment if changes are pushed to a "**`staging`**" branch or run a build for "**`test`**" tag push.

  **Branch-Specific build**

  *Pipelines Syntax*

```
pipelines:
  branches:
    staging:
      - step:
          script:
            - ./deploy-staging.sh
    tags:
      'test':
         - step:
             script:
                - ./deploy-production.sh
```

- **Pull-requests build:** Automates checks (such as linting, pre-merge build, and unit tests) whenever a pull request is opened or updated.

  *Pipelines Syntax*

```
pipelines:
  pull-requests:
    develop:
      - step:
          name: Build for develop branch pull request
          script:
            - echo "Hello, develop branch PR!"
```

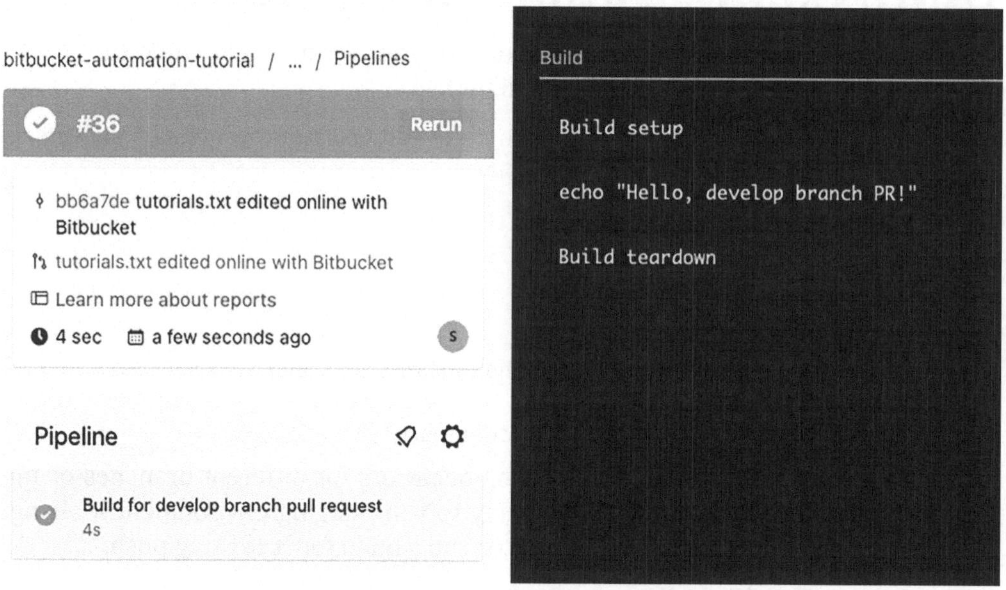


**Figure 6.18**: *Pipeline pull request step condition*

- **Custom build:** Let us create pipelines that only run when manually triggered, perfect for one-off tasks such as large data migrations.

Custom pipelines are manually triggered and are useful for tasks, such as running deployments, migrations, or performing maintenance.

*Pipelines Syntax*

```
pipelines:
  custom:
    deployment:
      - step:
          name: deployment
          script:
            - echo "Hello, deployed to staging!"
```

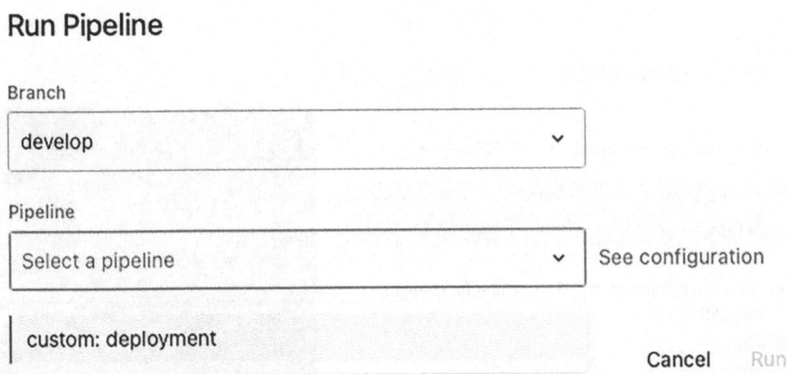


**Figure 6.19**: *Pipeline custom step condition*

**Figure 6.20** displays Pipeline custom step build:

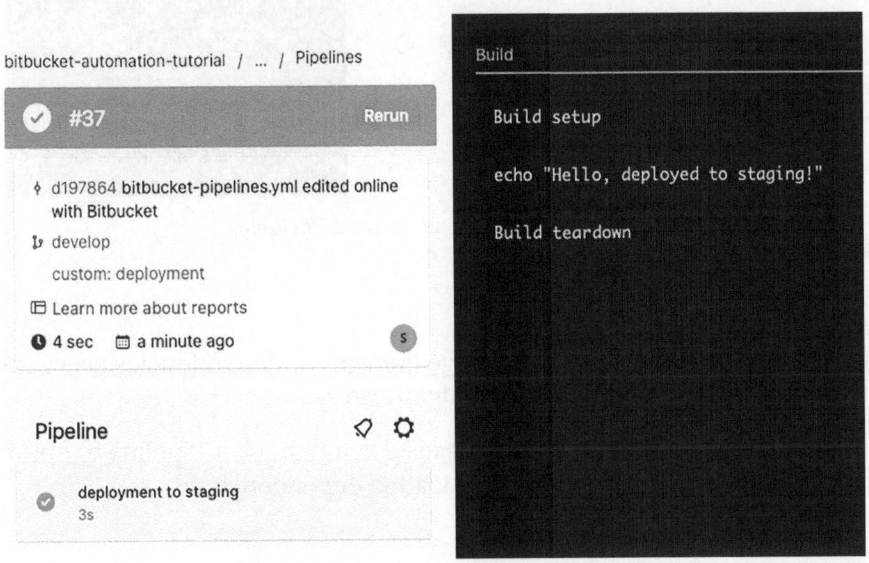


**Figure 6.20**: *Pipeline custom step build*

# Setting Up Pipeline Configurations

As you refine your pipelines, you will often need to incorporate additional settings that improve security, speed, and flexibility.

## Secure Variables

Store sensitive details (for example, API keys, credentials) in the pipelines repository's settings rather than hardcoding them in plain text. Use environment variables such as **$API_KEY** in your YAML, which remain encrypted at rest in Bitbucket pipelines log output.

```
script:
  - echo $API_KEY
```

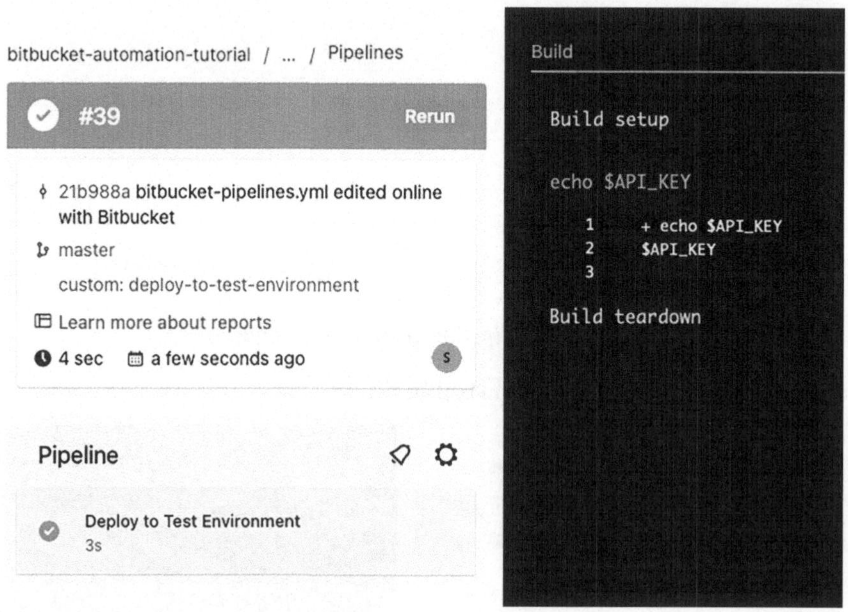


***Figure 6.21**: Pipeline Secured Variables*

## Dependency Caching

Leverage caching to avoid reinstalling large libraries or dependencies every time your pipeline runs, thus reducing build times significantly.

In the following example, **Node caching** is used in a Bitbucket Pipeline to optimize the build process by reusing previously downloaded dependencies:

*Pipelines Syntax*

```
pipelines:
  default:
    - step:
        caches:
          - node
        script:
          - npm install esbuild
          - node node-build/build.js
```

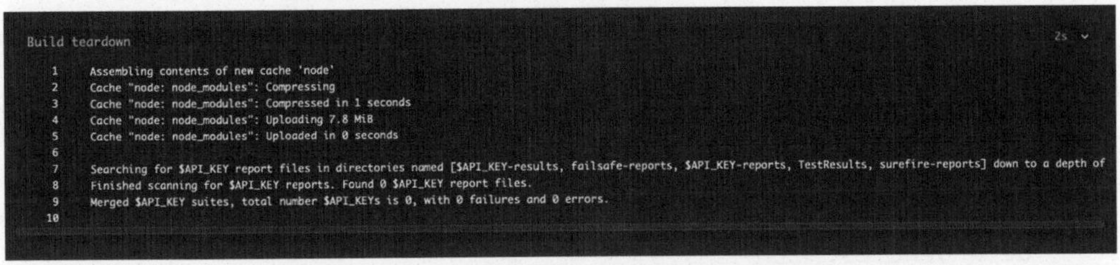


***Figure 6.22**: Pipeline Caching feature upload logs*

The following image shows Pipeline Caching versions under pipelines tab.

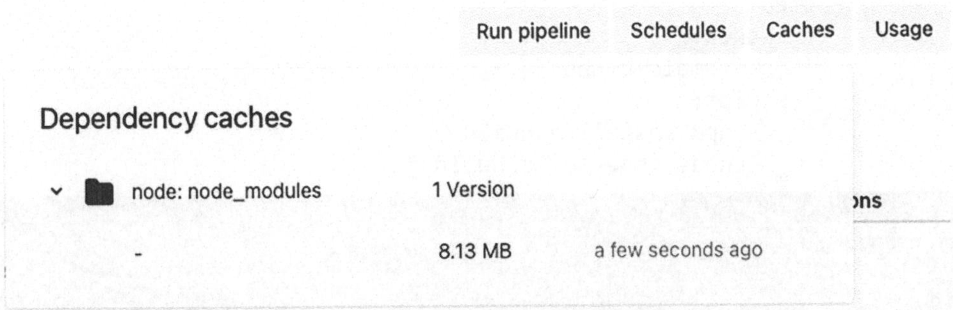


***Figure 6.23**: Pipeline Caching versions under pipelines tab*

Bitbucket supports the following pre-defined caches to speed up builds by reusing dependencies:

- **docker**: Caches Docker build layers.
- **node**: Caches node_modules.
- **maven**: Caches dependencies in ~/.m2/repository.
- **pip**: Caches Python packages in ~/.cache/pip.
- **gradle**: Caches dependencies in ~/.gradle/caches.
- **composer**: Caches PHP dependencies in ~/.composer/cache.
- **dotnetcore**: Caches .NET dependencies in ~/.nuget/packages.

- **ivy2**: Caches dependencies in ~/.ivy2/cache.
- **sbt**: Caches Scala dependencies in ~/.sbt and ~/.ivy2/cache.

# Custom Caching

Custom caching in Bitbucket Pipelines lets you define your own cache. In the following example, **`sample-cache`** is a custom cache name tied to **`package.json`** for detecting changes. The **`build`** directory is cached and reused across pipeline runs, speeding up tasks such as dependency installs or build processes.

```
definitions:
  caches:
    sample-cache:
      key:
        files: # the files you want pipelines to check for changes when deciding whether to use the cache, or download fresh dependencies.
          - package.json
      path: build # the directory you want to be cached.

pipelines:
  default:
    - step:
        caches:
          - sample-cache
        script:
          - npm install esbuild
          - node node-build/build.js
```

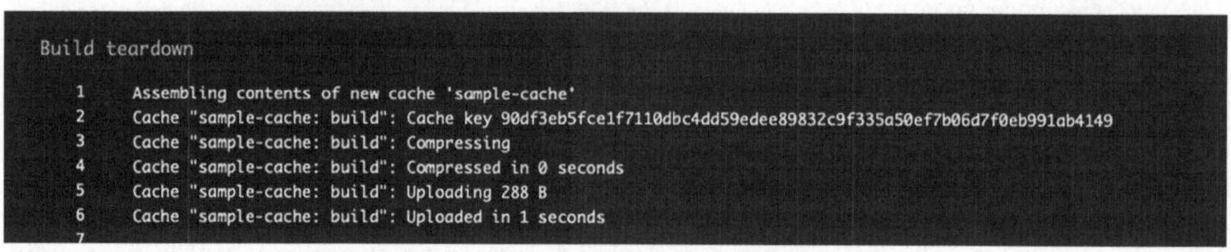


**Figure 6.24**: *Pipeline custom caching*

# Parallel Steps

Run tasks such as build, unit tests, and linting simultaneously to speed up overall pipeline time. If these tasks have no dependency on each other, parallel steps can cut waiting time.

*Pipelines Syntax*

```
pipelines:
  default:
    - parallel:
        - step:
            script:
              - echo "step 1"
        - step:
            script:
              - echo "step 2"
```

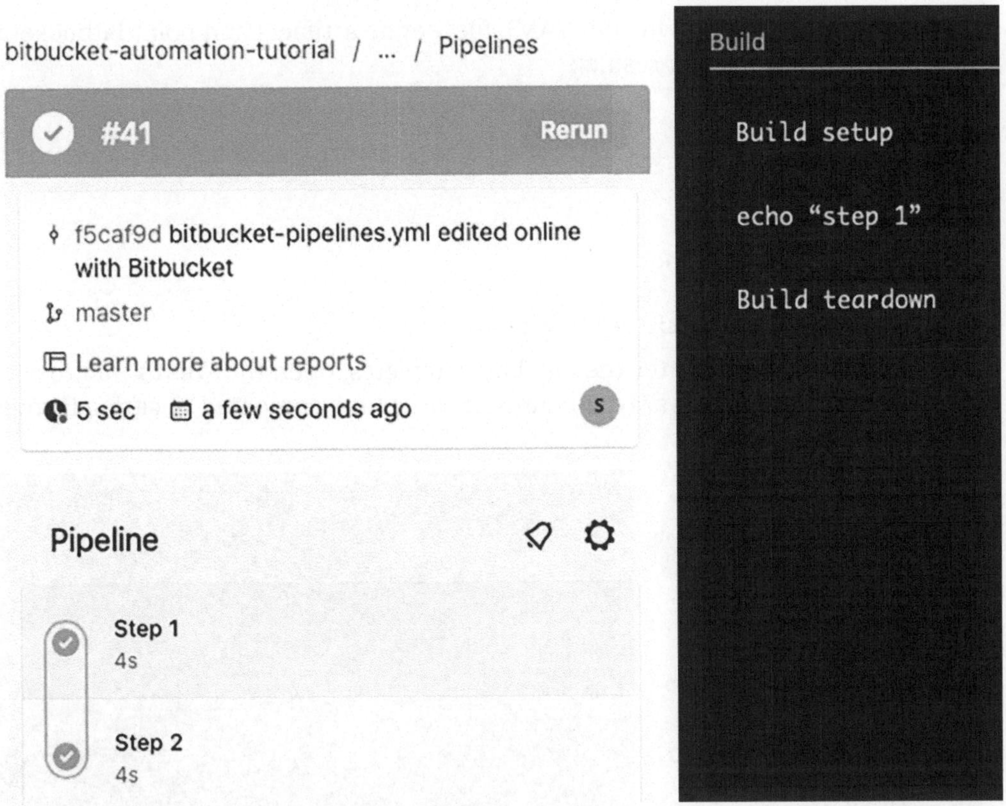


***Figure 6.25**: Pipeline parallel steps*

## Test Reporting in Pipelines and Analyzing Build Test Results

Bitbucket Pipelines can display test results in an easy-to-read format, making it simpler to spot failing tests.

- **Generate Test Reports**: Use your test runner's built-in functionality to produce an XML or JSON output (for example, junit.xml). Ensure that build test reports are generated in one of the supported default locations (with a directory depth of 3 levels):

```
./**/surefire-reports/**/*.xml
./**/failsafe-reports/**/*.xml
./**/test-results/**/*.xml
./**/test-reports/**/*.xml
./**/TestResults/**/*.xml
```

The test report file scanner will begin searching from the base directory of your build: **`/opt/atlassian/pipelines/agent/build`**

- **Publish the Report**: In your YAML file, define artifacts and point Bitbucket to the path of your test results:

  *Pipelines Syntax*

```
pipelines:
  default:
    - step:
       name:Testing
       script:
        - /bin/bash tests.sh
```

- **Review in the UI**: After the pipeline completes, open the "**`Tests`**" tab to see a summary of test **`pass/fail`** counts; it saves time compared to sifting through raw logs.

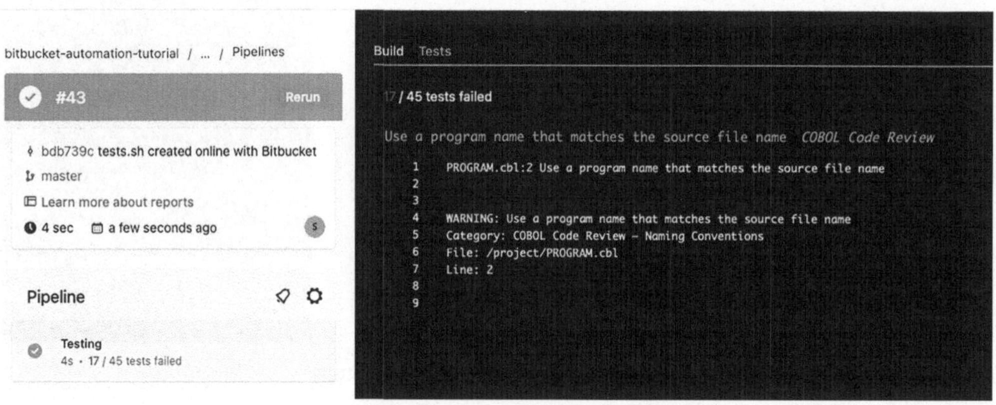


***Figure 6.26***: *Pipeline Tests Reporting*

# Integrating Pipelines with Jira Cloud

Connecting pipelines to Jira allows you to track development progress directly inside Jira tickets:

1. **Link Bitbucket cloud to Jira**: Go to your workspace settings to connect Bitbucket with Jira Cloud.

2. **`Workspace settings`** -> **`Security`** -> **`Jira`** -> **`connect`**

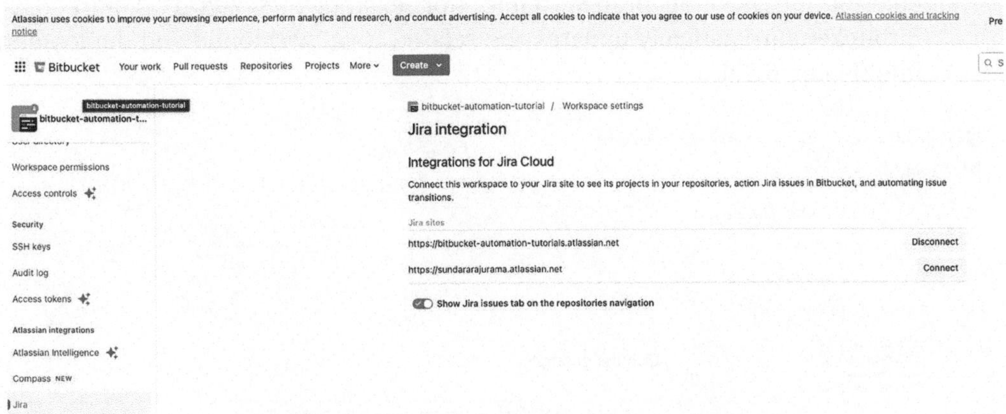


**Figure 6.27**: *Bitbucket cloud – Jira integration*

Jira integration requires access to administer repositories. Click on "**`Grant access`**" to approve it.

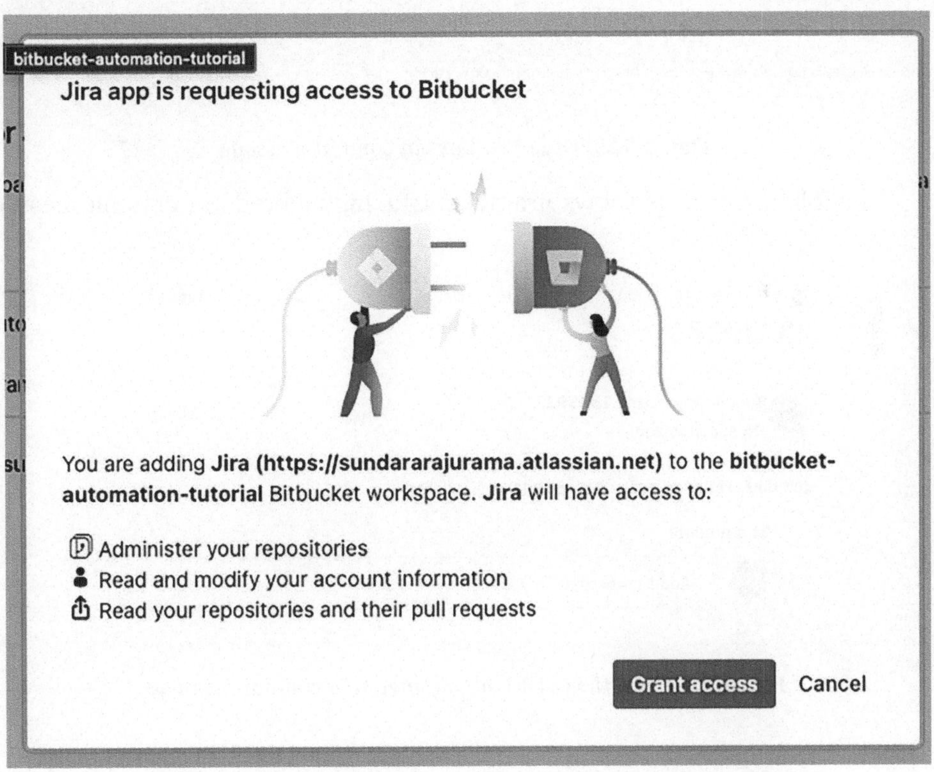


**Figure 6.28**: *Bitbucket cloud – Jira integration Authorization*

3. **Include Jira Keys in Commits**: By referencing a Jira ticket number in your commit message or branch name (for example, "`SCRUM-1`", *Figure* 6.29), Bitbucket automatically updates the related issue with build and deployment info (*Figure* 6.30).

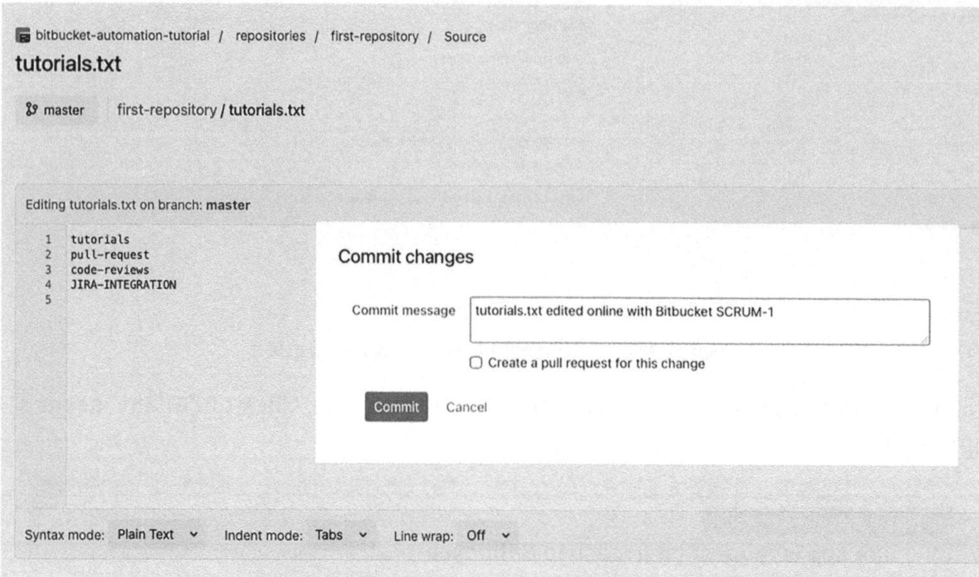


***Figure 6.29**: Issue Jira Keys in commit message*

The following image shows Jira ticket URL highlighted in a commit message.

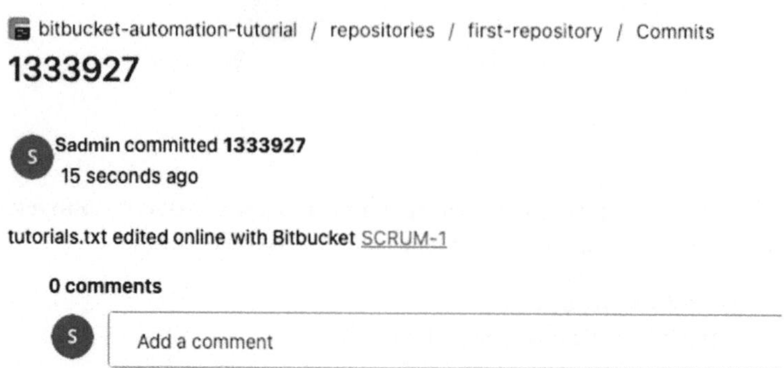


***Figure 6.30**: Jira ticket URL highlighted in a commit message*

Create a branch with a Jira issue key in its name to start tracking builds.

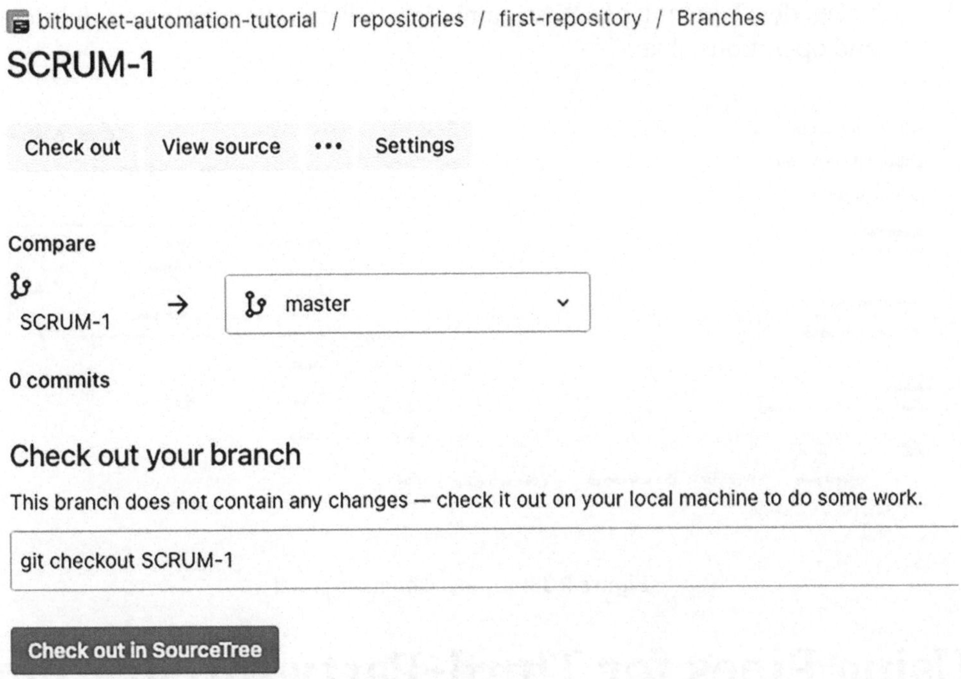


***Figure 6.31**: Issue Jira Keys as a branch name*

Issue a Jira key as a commit message of a source branch in an open pull request or as a pull request description or with the source branch name with the Jira key:

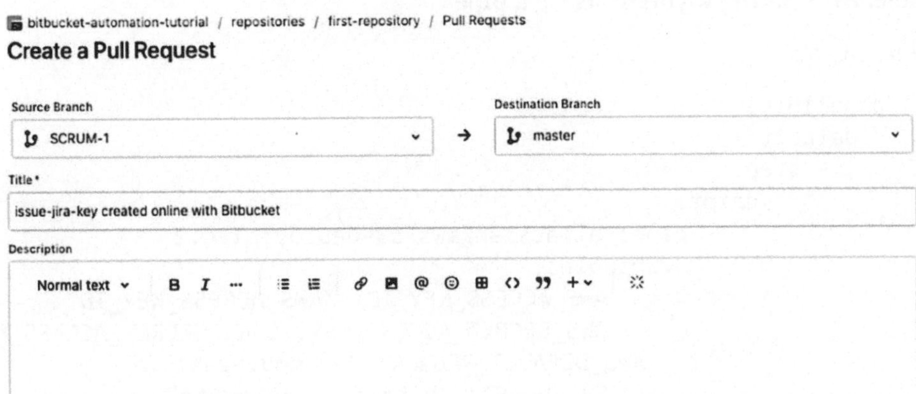


***Figure 6.32**: pull request with source branch name containing the Jira key*

4. **Visibility in Jira**: Your teammates can now see whether a fix is passing tests and code can be merged or has been deployed without leaving Jira, under the ticket development panel, streamlining collaboration between development and operations alike.

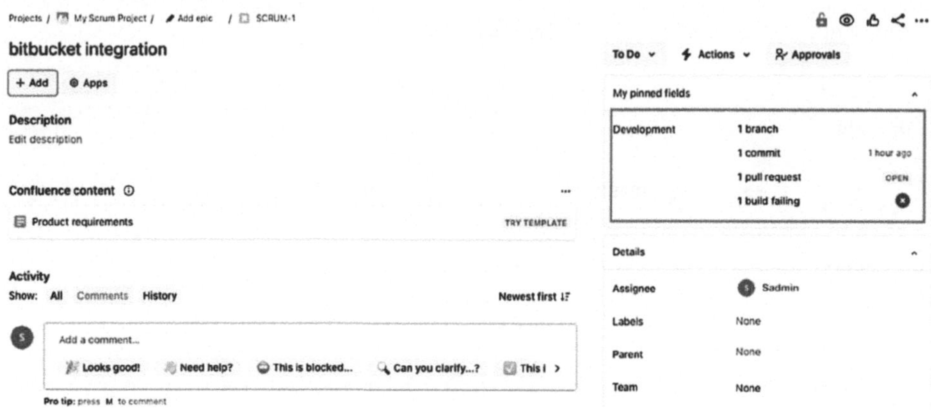


***Figure 6.33***: *Jira development panel*

# Using Pipes for Third-Party Integration

Pipes are pre-built configurations that let you use external tools or services more easily in your pipeline. Rather than writing custom scripts, you can plug in a pipe for tasks such as deploying to cloud services, sending notifications, or scanning for security vulnerabilities.

**Example: AWS S3 Deployment using a pipe**

*Pipelines Syntax*

```
pipelines:
  default:
    - step:
        script:
          - pipe: atlassian/aws-s3-deploy: 1.6.2
             variables:
                 AWS_ACCESS_KEY_ID: $AWS_ACCESS_KEY_ID
                 AWS_SECRET_ACCESS_KEY: $AWS_SECRET_ACCESS_KEY
               AWS_DEFAULT_REGION: "ap-southeast-2"
                 S3_BUCKET: "bitbucket-automate"
                 LOCAL_PATH: "build/"
```

**Store credentials** in your repo's secure variables.

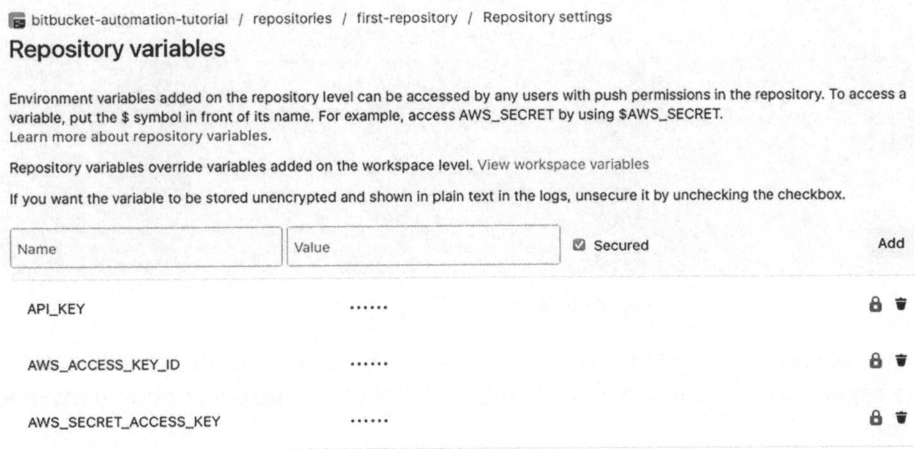


***Figure 6.34***: *AWS credentials as repository secured variables*

**Deploy**: The pipe takes care of uploading your compiled files from the **`build/`** directory to S3.

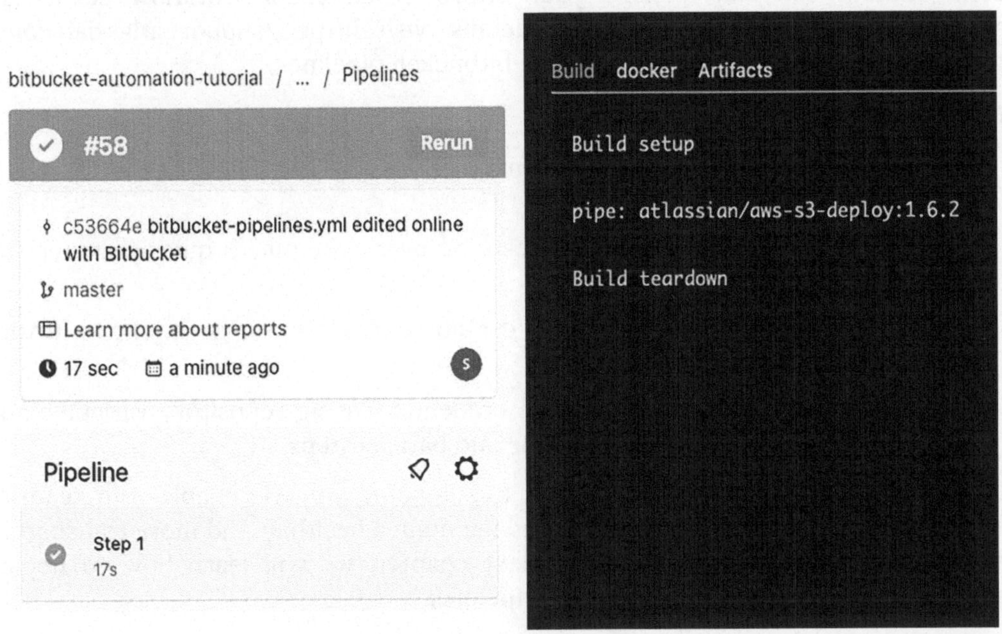


***Figure 6.35***: *AWS S3 Deploy pipe*

**Monitor logs** to confirm a successful deployment or troubleshoot any problems.

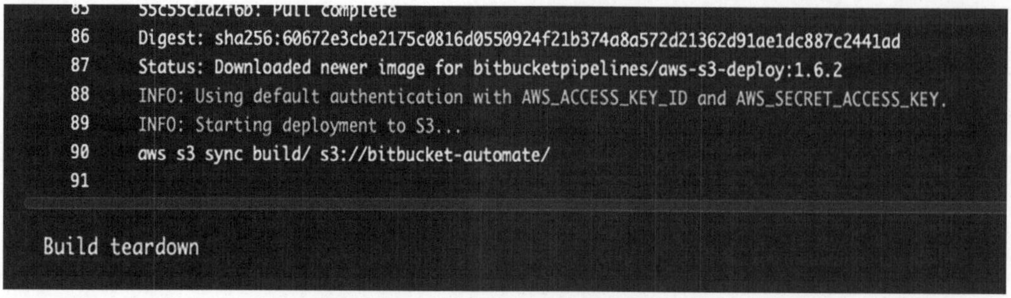


***Figure 6.36***: *AWS S3 Deploy pipe logs*

You can also create custom pipes if you need something more specialized. This approach can be especially valuable if you have unique deployment targets or company-specific workflows.

# Conclusion

Bitbucket Pipelines integrates CI/CD directly into your repository, streamlining the building, testing, and deployment of software. By leveraging a simple YAML configuration, you can manage your entire development workflow seamlessly alongside your codebase. For more details, visit https://support.atlassian.com/bitbucket-cloud/docs/write-a-pipe-for-bitbucket-pipelines/

**Highlights:**

- **Automate Everything**: Minimize manual tasks by integrating builds, tests, and deployments.
- **Keep Code Quality High**: Run tests on every commit to quickly detect and address issues.
- **Expand with Add-ons**: Use pipes, caching, and integrations with Jira to further enhance your workflow.
- **Secure and Efficient**: Safeguard credentials using repository variables and optimize build speed with caching and parallel steps.

By adopting the strategies discussed in this chapter, you will enable your team to release features faster, reduce errors, and maintain a healthier and more transparent development process overall. In the next chapter, we will learn how to deploy applications efficiently using Bitbucket Pipelines.

# CHAPTER 7
# Pipelines Deployments and Self-Hosted Runners

## Introduction

This chapter explores how to deploy applications efficiently using Bitbucket Pipelines. From managing deployment environments to monitoring progress via the Deployment Dashboard, we will examine best practices for streamlining your CI/CD workflows. Additionally, this chapter delves into setting up self-hosted runners, allowing the readers to execute pipelines on their custom infrastructure, offering flexibility, control, and scalability.

## Structure

In this chapter, we will discuss the following topics:

- Deployment Processes in Bitbucket Pipelines
- Setting Up Deployment Environments
- Configuring Deployments for AWS S3 and EKS
- Introduction to Self-Hosted Runners
- Hybrid Build Model Using Self-hosted Runners
- Kubernetes-Based Runners with Autoscalers

## Deployment Processes in Bitbucket Pipelines

Bitbucket Pipelines offers a streamlined method to deploy code efficiently across various environments. From development to production, deployment workflows are managed through YAML configuration files, ensuring a smooth and reliable transition of code.

By setting up deployment environments, you can:

- Define a promotion sequence (for example, **`testing`** → **`staging`** → **`production`**).
- Configure environment-specific variables to inject dynamically during deployments.
- Control access to deployment permissions, specifying who can deploy to each environment.

# Setting Up Deployment Environments

By default, Bitbucket provides three basic environments:

- **`Test`**: For running initial validations and exploratory testing.
- **`Staging`**: Used as a pre-production environment to simulate real-world conditions.
- **`Production`**: The final environment where your application goes live.

***Figure 7.1***: *Deployment Environments*

You can either modify these existing environments or add more environments to suit your workflow.

**Steps to Configure Environments**

1. Navigate to **`Repository Settings`** > **`Pipelines`** > **`Deployments`**.
2. Select **`Test`**, **`Staging`**, or **`Production`**, click "**`add environment`**" to create a new environment
3. Configure the environment details

   **Example**: New "**`dev-env`**" environment created

***Figure 7.2:*** *add deployment environment*

Define your deployment in the bitbucket-pipelines.yml file to activate the environment.

```
pipelines:
  default:
    - step:
        name: Deploy to dev
        deployment: dev-env
        script:
          - echo "deploying in dev"
```

Once the deployment pipeline is executed, the deployment details can be tracked in the deployment dashboard.

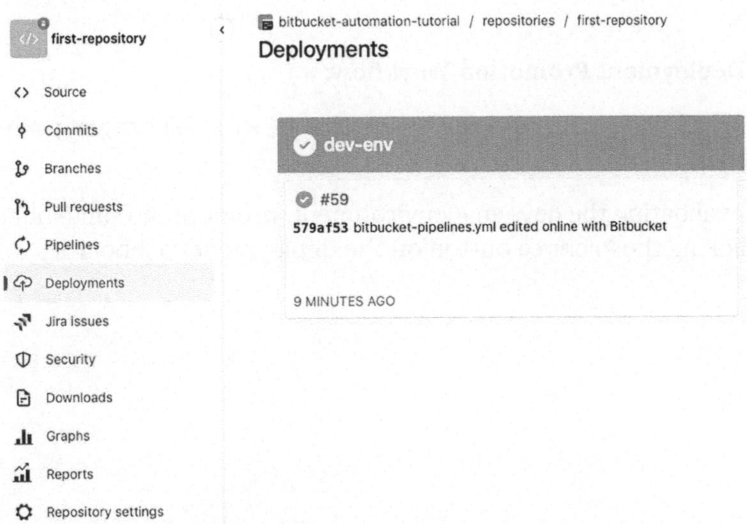


***Figure 7.3:*** *deployment dashboard*

When a deployment banner is selected in the deployment dashboard (for example, **`dev-env`**), it displays the environment history, including details such as the pipeline build number and the commit associated with the deployment. This provides a clear overview of the changes applied in each deployment.

***Figure 7.4:*** *Environment history*

# Deployment Triggers

Deployment triggers in Bitbucket pipelines operate similarly to standard pipeline job triggers such as branch or tag-based triggers, pull request based triggers, and manual triggers, providing flexibility to initiate deployments based on specific criteria or manual intervention. These triggers can be tailored to align with your team's workflow and deployment needs.

# Deployment Promotion

One unique feature of deployments is the ability to promote builds to higher environments, such as moving a deployment from staging to production. This eliminates the need to rebuild the application for each environment, ensuring consistency across deployments.

**Example of Deployment Promotion Workflow**:

1. Deploy a build to the **`dev-env`** environment, with the **`staging-env`** step set as manual.
2. After validating the **`dev-env`** environment, promote the same build to staging by clicking the **`Promote`** button on the deployment dashboard.

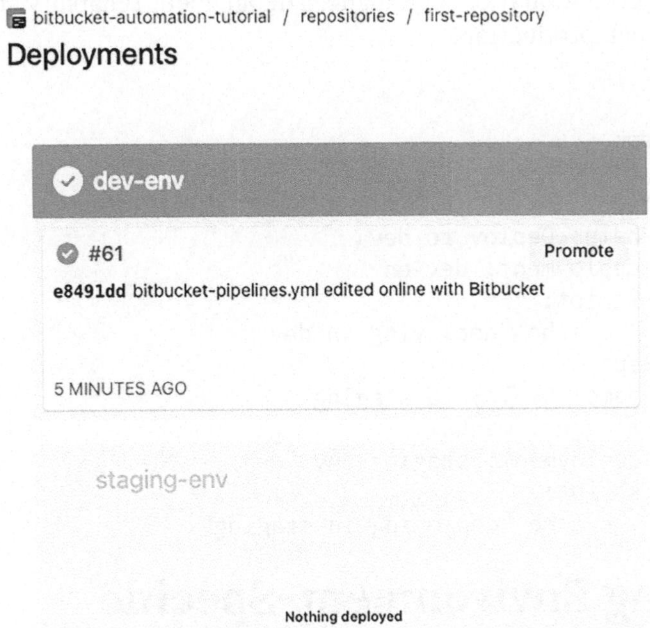


**Figure 7.5:** *Deployment promote button*

3. Review changes and click **`Deploy`** to finalize the promotion.

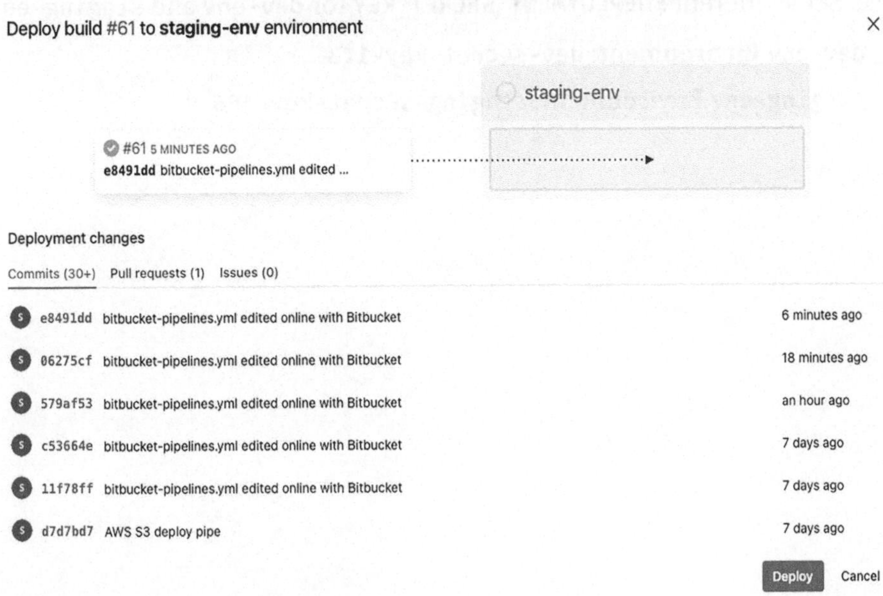


**Figure 7.6:** *Deploy to finalize the promotion*

This structured promotion process enhances deployment reliability and ensures only verified builds reach production.

*Pipelines* YAML:

```
pipelines:
  default:
    - step:
        name: Deploy to dev
        deployment: dev-env
        script:
          - echo "deploying in dev"
    - step:
        name: Deploy to staging
        trigger: manual
        deployment: staging-env
        script:
          - echo "deploying in staging"
```

# Leveraging Environment-Specific Deployment Variables

Environment variables allow you to securely store sensitive data, such as API keys or database credentials, without hardcoding them. These variables override team and repository-level variables, providing flexibility for each deployment.

Example: Set a different **`$DEPLOYMENT_SECRET_KEY`** for **`dev-env`** and **`staging-env`**:

- **`dev-env` Environment**: **`dev-secret-key-123`**
- **`staging-env` Environment**: **`staging-secret-key-456`**

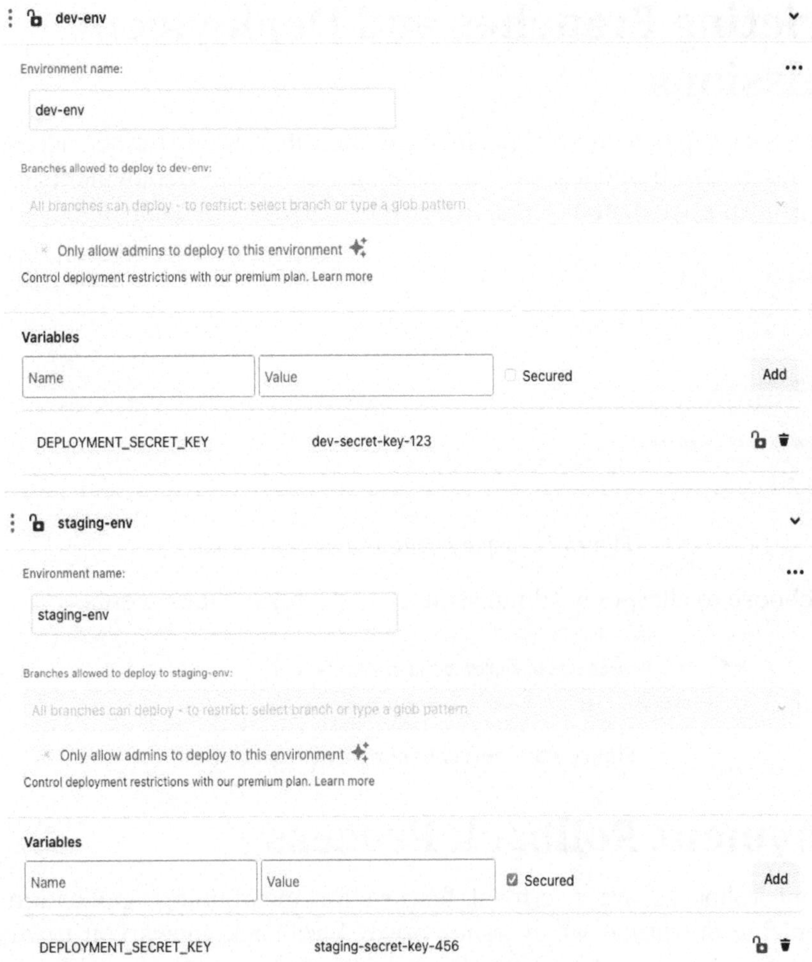


**Figure 7.7:** *Deployment variables*

```
pipelines:
  default:
    - step:
        name: Deploy with Secret Key
        deployment: dev-env
        script:
          - echo $DEPLOYMENT_SECRET_KEY
    - step:
        name: Deploy with Secret Key
        deployment: staging-env
        script:
          - echo $DEPLOYMENT_SECRET_KEY
```

During deployment, the appropriate value will be injected based on the target environment.

# Restricting Branches and Deployment Permissions

You can restrict deployments to specific branches. Restricting branch access ensures that only designated branches, such as develop, can trigger deployments to the **dev-env**. This prevents accidental or unauthorized changes from being deployed.

***Figure 7.8**: deployment branch restrictions*

You may choose to allow only administrators to perform deployments.

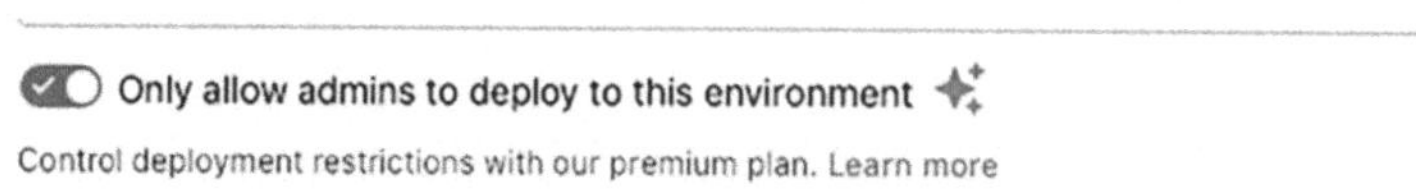


***Figure 7.9**: Control deployment restrictions*

# Deployment Rollback Process

Deployment rollbacks are a critical feature for maintaining application stability and minimizing downtime when issues arise. A rollback allows you to restore the last successful deployment, effectively undoing changes introduced by a failed or problematic deployment. This process ensures that your application continues running smoothly while giving you time to troubleshoot the issue.

**When to Use a Rollback:**

- **Critical Failures**: If a new deployment introduces bugs or crashes your application.
- **Unexpected Behavior**: When the deployment causes performance issues or breaks existing functionality.
- **Security Concerns**: To revert a deployment containing a vulnerability or misconfiguration.

**Steps to Perform a Rollback:**

1. **Navigate to the Deployment Dashboard**: Access the deployment history for the environment in question.

2. **Select the Environment and Redeploy**: Locate the last successful build and click the Redeploy button. This action initiates the rollback process.
3. **Review and Confirm**: Before redeploying, review the changes to ensure you are restoring the correct version. Once confirmed, proceed with the redeployment.

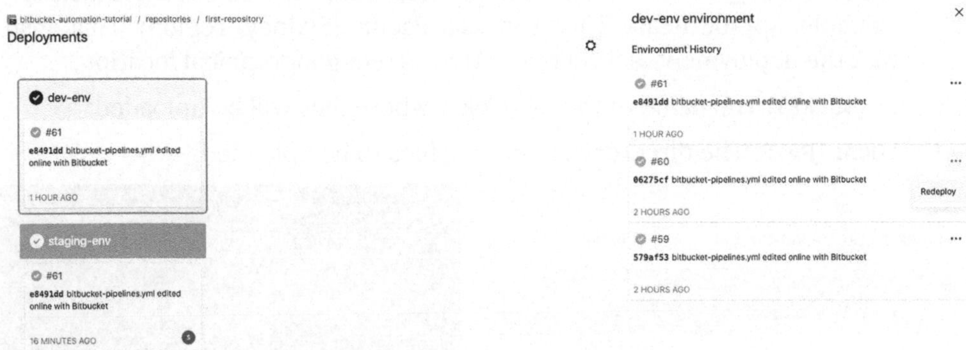


***Figure 7.10**: deployment rollback*

# Configuring Deployments for AWS S3 and EKS

In this section, we will explore sample pipelines for deploying applications to AWS S3 and Amazon Elastic Kubernetes Service (EKS). These examples leverage Bitbucket's built-in pipes, simplifying the deployment process while maintaining flexibility and security.

## AWS S3 Deployment

Using the Bitbucket pipe atlassian/aws-s3-deploy, you can easily automate the upload of your files to an S3 bucket.

```
pipelines:
  default:
    - step:
        name: Deploy to S3
        deployment: dev-env
        script:
          - pipe: atlassian/aws-s3-deploy:1.6.2
            variables:
              AWS_ACCESS_KEY_ID: $AWS_ACCESS_KEY_ID
              AWS_SECRET_ACCESS_KEY: $AWS_SECRET_ACCESS_KEY
```

```
              AWS_DEFAULT_REGION: "ap-southeast-2"
              S3_BUCKET: "bitbucket-automate"
              LOCAL_PATH: "build/"
```

- **AWS_ACCESS_KEY_ID** and **AWS_SECRET_ACCESS_KEY**: Secure credentials stored as environment variables.
- **AWS_DEFAULT_REGION**: Specifies the region where the S3 bucket is located (for example, ap-southeast-2 for the Asia Pacific (Sydney) region). This ensures that the deployment is directed to the correct geographical location.
- **S3_BUCKET**: The name of the S3 bucket where files will be uploaded.
- **LOCAL_PATH**: The directory containing files to be uploaded.

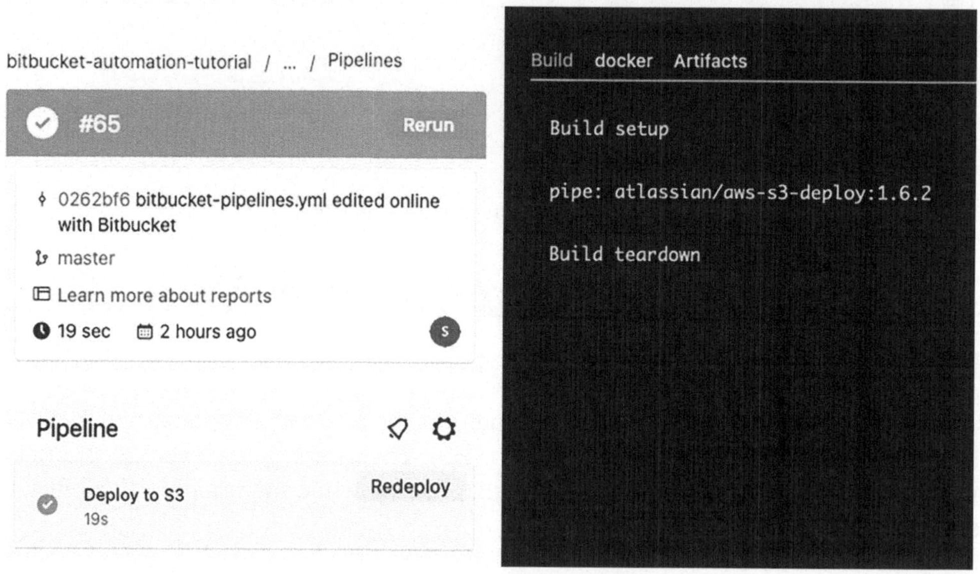


***Figure 7.11:*** *S3 pipe deployment*

# Amazon EKS Deployment

Deploying to EKS involves applying Kubernetes manifests to the cluster, which can also be automated using Bitbucket pipe deployments.

```
pipelines:
  default:
    - step:
        name: Deploy to EKS
        deployment: dev-env
        script:
          - pipe: atlassian/aws-eks-kubectl-run:3.0.0
            variables:
              AWS_ACCESS_KEY_ID: ${AWS_ACCESS_KEY_ID}
```

```
                AWS_SECRET_ACCESS_KEY: ${AWS_SECRET_ACCESS_KEY}
                AWS_DEFAULT_REGION: "us-east-1"
                CLUSTER_NAME: "floral-dance-duck"
                KUBECTL_COMMAND: "apply"
                RESOURCE_PATH: "hello-world-pod.yaml"
                DEBUG: "true"
```

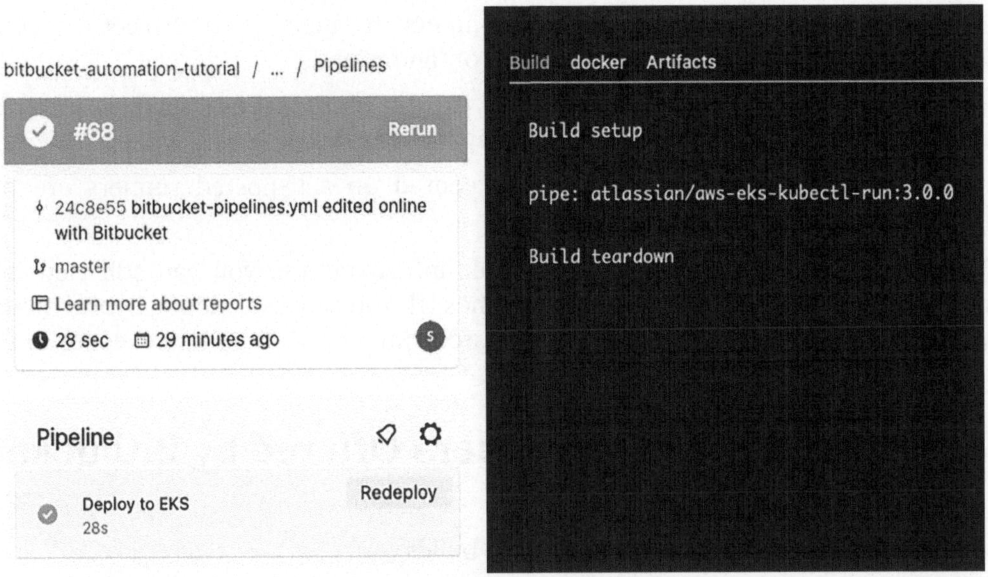


***Figure 7.12:*** *EKS pipe deployment*

- **CLUSTER_NAME:** Specifies the name of your EKS cluster to connect to. In this case, it is set to "**floral-dance-duck**".
- **KUBECTL_COMMAND:** Defines the **kubectl** command to execute on the cluster. Here, it is set to "**apply**", which applies the Kubernetes manifest file to the cluster.
- **AWS_ACCESS_KEY_ID and AWS_SECRET_ACCESS_KEY:** Securely authenticate and authorize access to your AWS account. These values are stored as environment variables for security.
- **AWS_DEFAULT_REGION:** Specifies the AWS region where your EKS cluster is located. In this example, it is set to "**us-east-1**".
- **RESOURCE_PATH:** Points to the Kubernetes manifest file to be applied. Here, it is set to "**hello-world-pod.yaml**".
- **DEBUG:** Enables detailed logging to assist with troubleshooting. This is set to "**true**" for this deployment.

# Introduction to Self-Hosted Runners

Self-hosted runners are agents that can be installed on your own servers or infrastructure, allowing you to execute pipeline builds locally. This setup offers several advantages:

- **Flexibility**: Customize the environment to meet your project's specific requirements, including hardware configurations.
- **Compliance:** Run builds on your organizations secure servers, ensuring adherence to data security and compliance policies.
- **Cost Efficiency:** Build minutes executed on self-hosted runners are not charged by Bitbucket.

Despite the builds being executed on your infrastructure, you can still view and monitor them in the Bitbucket Cloud Pipelines UI. You can also adopt a hybrid model, where some pipeline steps run on self-hosted runners while others execute in the cloud.

## Types of Self-Hosted Runners Offered by Bitbucket

- Docker-Based Linux Runners
    - Ideal for isolated, containerized builds.
    - Pipelines run within Docker containers.
- Linux Shell-Based Runners
    - A lightweight option for running pipelines directly on the Linux host without Docker.
- Windows and macOS Runners
    - Platform-specific builds, such as .NET applications on Windows or iOS applications on macOS.
- ARM-Based Runners (Beta)
    - Suitable for low-power devices such as Raspberry Pi.
    - Perfect for IoT projects and specialized hardware.
- Docker Linux Runners on Kubernetes and Autoscalers
    - Scalable solutions for dynamic pipeline demand.
    - Kubernetes runners can horizontally scale runner instances (nodes).

# Setting Up Self-Hosted Runners

**Prerequisites**

The prerequisites depend on the type of runner:

- **Docker Linux Runners**: Requires Docker v19.03 or newer.
- **Linux Shell, Windows, and macOS Runners**: Requires OpenJDK 11 (11.0.15 or newer) and Git 2.35.0 or newer.
    - **Linux Shell Runners**: Bash 3.2 or newer.
    - **Windows Runners**: PowerShell 5.4.0 or newer.

**Common Requirements**

- Minimum 8 GB RAM.
- For Docker runner containers: Allocate at least 512 MB of memory.

Refer to the Bitbucket Runner Documentation https://support.atlassian.com/bitbucket-cloud/docs/runners/ for the latest updates.

**Repository versus Workspace Level Runners Setup**

- **Repository-Level Runners:** Provide finer control, as they are dedicated to specific repositories.
- **Workspace-Level Runners:** Offer flexibility by allowing multiple repositories to share and manage runners centrally.

**Setting Up a Sample Repository-Level Docker Linux Runner**

1. Go to **`Repository Settings`** → **`Pipelines`** → **`Runners`**.
2. Click **`Add Runner`** and select **`Linux Docker`** Runner.
3. Name the runner and add labels (for example, "**`test`**") for targeted usage.
    - Labels help select specific runners for different pipeline steps.

      **Example**: Use a "**`test`**" label for lightweight test builds.

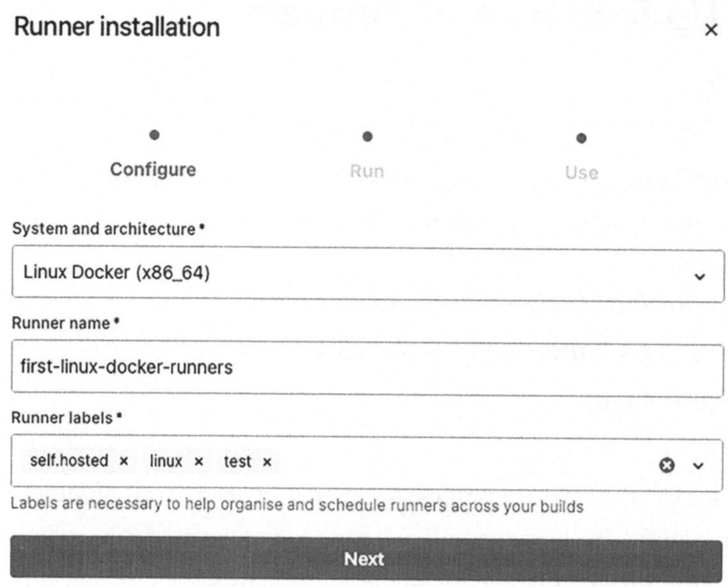


***Figure 7.13:*** *Runner installation*

4. Click **Next**, copy the provided Docker container run command, and execute it on your server where the runner will be installed.

```
docker container run -itd \
-v /tmp:/tmp \
-v /var/run/docker.sock:/var/run/docker.sock \
-v /var/lib/docker/containers:/var/lib/docker/containers:ro \
-e ACCOUNT_UUID={****} \
-e REPOSITORY_UUID={****} \
-e RUNNER_UUID={****} \
-e RUNTIME_PREREQUISITES_ENABLED=**** \
-e OAUTH_CLIENT_ID=**** \
-e OAUTH_CLIENT_SECRET=**** \
-e WORKING_DIRECTORY=/tmp \
--name runner-**** \
docker-public.packages.atlassian.com/sox/atlassian/bitbuck-
et-pipelines-runner
```

# Understanding the Docker `Run` Command

The command creates a containerized runner. Here is a breakdown:

1. **`docker container run`**: Creates and runs a Docker container.
2. **Options**:

- **`-it`**: Interactive terminal.
- **`-v`**: Mounts volumes for sharing data between host and container:
  - **`/tmp`** → **`/tmp`**
  - **`/var/run/docker.sock`** → Docker daemon socket.
  - **`/var/lib/docker/containers`** → Metadata for running containers.
- Environment Variables:
  - **`ACCOUNT_UUID`**, **`REPOSITORY_UUID`**, **`RUNNER_UUID`**: Unique identifiers for account, repository, and runner.
  - **`RUNTIME_PREREQUISITES_ENABLED=true`**: Enables runtime checks.
  - **`OAUTH_CLIENT_ID & OAUTH_CLIENT_SECRET`**: For authentication.
  - **`WORKING_DIRECTORY=/tmp`**: Specifies runner's working directory.

3. **Docker Image**: Uses **`docker-public.packages.atlassian.com/sox/atlassian/bitbucket-pipelines-runner`** for the runner setup.

# Verify Runner Online Status

Run the following command to check the runner status:

```
docker logs <runner container_id>
```

**Example output:**

```
[2025-01-12 09:09:48,973] Runner version: 3.15.0
[2025-01-12 09:09:48,980] Runner runtime: linux-docker
[2025-01-12 09:09:51,164] Updating runner state to "ONLINE".
```

Once the runner is online, proceed to the runner registration page in Bitbucket and finalize the setup.

Let us use the following sample pipeline YAML to run a build on the self-hosted runner:

```
pipelines:
  default:
    - step:
        runs-on:
          - self.hosted
          - linux
          - test
        script:
          - echo "Running sample build on self-hosted Docker
Linux runner"
```

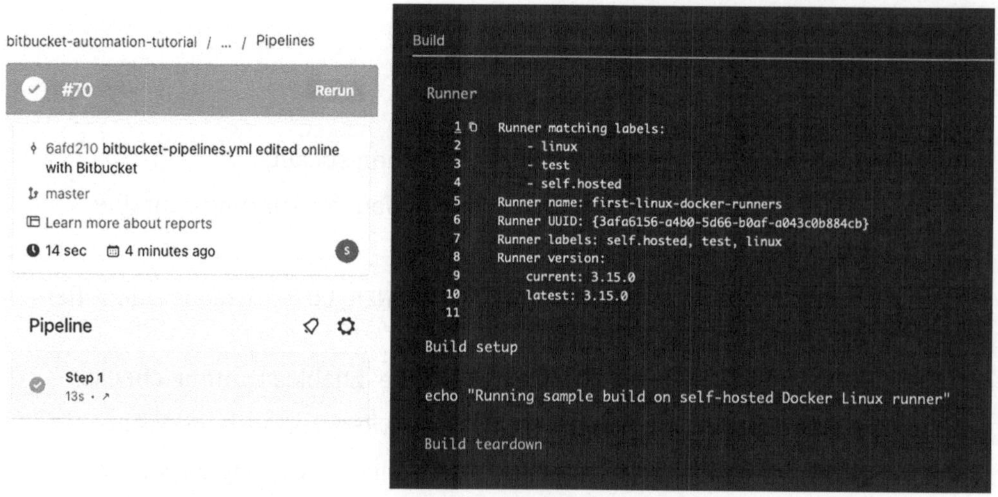


***Figure 7.14:** build on self-hosted runners*

The setup process of ARM based runners is similar to linux docker runners and Bitbucket's default Docker image, **`atlassian/default-image:4`**, supports both ARM and Intel architectures, ensuring compatibility across pipelines.

```
image: atlassian/default-image:4

pipelines:
  default:
    - step:
        name: Build and Test
        runs-on:
          - self.hosted
          - linux.arm64
        script:
          - npm run build
          - npm run test
```

Linux shell, macOS, or Windows runners require downloading the runner startup script atlassian-bitbucket-pipelines-runner.tar.gz, which must be executed using Bash or PowerShell (depending on the runner type) along with input parameters, such as the account ID, runner ID, and credentials to register the runners.

# Hybrid Build Model Using Self-hosted Runners

As explained earlier, a **hybrid model** can leverage self-hosted runners to run selected pipeline steps while executing the remaining steps on cloud-hosted pipelines. This allows for optimized resource usage and flexibility in your CI/CD process.

**Example:**

**Step 1** runs on an ARM-based self-hosted runner to build the application, while **Step 2** deploys the output to S3 using Bitbucket Cloud pipelines.

```
image: atlassian/default-image:4

pipelines:
  default:
    - parallel:
        - step:
            name: Build and Test
            runs-on:
              - self.hosted
              - linux.arm64
            script:
              - npm install
              - npm run build
              - npm run test
            artifacts:
              - build/** # Replace with your actual build output
path

        - step:
            name: Deployment to S3
            script:
              - pipe: atlassian/aws-s3-deploy:1.1.0
                variables:
                  AWS_ACCESS_KEY_ID: $AWS_ACCESS_KEY_ID
                  AWS_SECRET_ACCESS_KEY: $AWS_SECRET_ACCESS_KEY
                  AWS_DEFAULT_REGION: "us-east-1" # Replace with
your region
                  S3_BUCKET: "<your-s3-bucket-name>" # Replace
with your S3 bucket
                  LOCAL_PATH: "build/" # Path to your build output
                  S3_PATH: "my-app/" # Path in the S3 bucket
where files will be deployed
```

# Kubernetes-Based Runners with Autoscalers

Autoscaler is a service deployed into an existing Kubernetes cluster, allowing for dynamic management of self-hosted runners. With autoscalers, you can configure a scaling policy via configuration files, enabling the autoscaler to poll the Bitbucket Cloud Runner API and automatically increase or decrease the number of runners available to handle builds.

# Setting Up Autoscaler-Based Kubernetes Runners

**Prerequisites**

To deploy autoscaler-based Kubernetes runners, ensure the following prerequisites are met:

- Kubernetes cluster (v1.24+).
- Access to Bitbucket Cloud with an App Password or OAuth credentials.
- Base64-encoded credentials for secure storage.

# Steps to Deploy Autoscaler

**Step 1:** Clone the Autoscaler Repository

```
git clone git@bitbucket.org:bitbucketpipelines/runners-auto
scaler.git
cd runners-autoscaler/kustomize
```

**Step 2:** Encode Credentials

Encode your credentials in Base64 for secure storage:

- **For OAuth:**

```
echo -n "<BITBUCKET_OAUTH_CLIENT_ID>" | base64
echo -n "<BITBUCKET_OAUTH_CLIENT_SECRET>" | base64
```

- **For App Password:**

```
echo -n "<BITBUCKET_USERNAME>" | base64
echo -n "<BITBUCKET_APP_PASSWORD>" | base64
```

**Step 3:** Update Configuration Files

Edit the following files:

- **`runner_config.yaml`**:
  - Set **`workspace_uuid`** and **`repository_uuid`**.
  - Review and adjust scaling parameters as needed.
- **`kustomization.yaml`**: Uncomment and configure the Secret and Deployment sections based on your chosen authentication method.

**Step 4:** Verify and Apply Configuration

Run the following command to apply the configuration:

```
kubectl kustomize values | kubectl apply -k values
```

**Step 5:** Verify Deployment

- **Check the controller pod logs:**
  ```
  kubectl logs -f -l app=runner-controller -n bitbucket-runner-
  control-plane
  ```
- **Verify runner creation:**
  ```
  kubectl logs -l runner_uuid -c runner
  ```

# Escalator Setup (For Node Autoscaling)

Escalator provides node autoscaling capabilities to manage cluster resources efficiently.

**Step 1:** Deploy Escalator

Clone the Escalator repository:

```
git clone https://github.com/atlassian/escalator.git
cd escalator/docs/deployment/aws
```

Apply the Escalator configuration:

```
kubectl create -f escalator-rbac.yaml
kubectl create -f escalator-cm.yaml
kubectl create -f escalator-deployment-aws.yaml
```

**Step 2:** Label Nodes for Runner Jobs

Label nodes to specify where runner jobs should be executed:

```
kubectl label nodes <node-name> customer=shared
```

**Step 3:** Configure Node Groups

Edit the **`nodegroups_config.yaml`** file in the **`Escalator configMap`** to define node groups and scaling policies.

**Step 4:** Monitor Escalator

Check the Escalator logs to ensure it is functioning correctly:

```
kubectl logs -f deployment/escalator -n kube-system
```

# Verification

Once the setup is complete, verify that the runners are updated and running online. Workspace-based Kubernetes autoscaler runners should appear in the Bitbucket Cloud UI.

**Figure 7.15:** *Kubernetes autoscaler runners*

## Sample Pipeline on Autoscaler Runners

```
pipelines:
  default:
    - step:
        runs-on:
          - self.hosted
          - linux
        script:
          - echo "Running sample build on self-hosted kubernetes
autoscaler runner"
```

**Build output:**

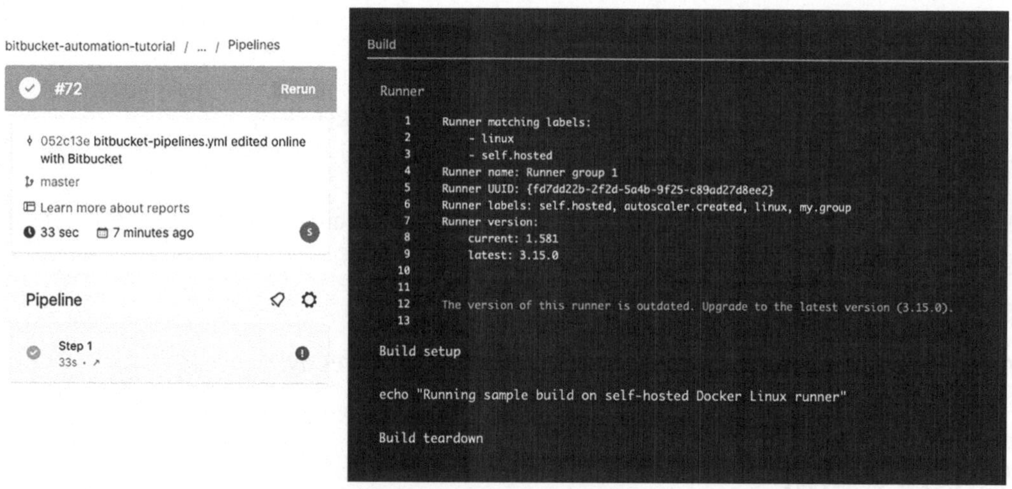


**Figure 7.16:** *Kubernetes autoscaler runners builds*

With Escalator in place, the number of nodes will automatically scale based on concurrent build demand, ensuring optimal resource usage.

# Conclusion

Bitbucket Pipelines and self-hosted runners provide a powerful framework for deploying applications with precision and control. By mastering these tools, you can streamline your CI/CD workflows, ensure deployment consistency, and optimize your infrastructure for scalability.

In the next chapter, we will explore pipeline integrations with third-party applications such as SonarCloud for automated code quality reviews and Snyk for identifying and fixing code vulnerabilities, along with other integrations to enhance your development workflow.

# CHAPTER 8
# Code Quality, Security, and Integrations in Bitbucket Cloud

## Introduction

Ensuring high-quality, secure code while maintaining efficient CI/CD workflows is essential for modern software development. Bitbucket Cloud allows seamless integration with various third-party tools for automated code quality reviews, security vulnerability detection, and CI/CD pipeline enhancements. This chapter explores integrating SonarCloud for automated code quality analysis, Snyk for security vulnerability checks, Jenkins for extended CI/CD capabilities, and Slack and Microsoft Teams for real-time build and deployment notifications.

## Structure

In this chapter, the following topics will be covered:

- Integrating SonarCloud with Bitbucket Pipelines
- Automated Code Quality Reviews
- Performing Code Vulnerability Checks with Snyk
- Integrating Jenkins with Bitbucket Cloud Using Webhooks
- Setting Up Notifications in Slack
- Integrating Microsoft Teams with Bitbucket
- Custom Notifications via Email in Bitbucket Pipelines

# Integrating Sonar Cloud with Bitbucket Pipelines

SonarCloud is a cloud-based service that helps developers ensure code quality and security by detecting code smells, bugs, and vulnerabilities. Bitbucket Pipelines can integrate with SonarCloud to perform static code analysis during the CI/CD process.

**Steps to Integrate SonarCloud:**

1. **Create a SonarCloud Account**: Sign up at SonarCloud.io and create an organization.
2. **Generate a SonarCloud Token**: Navigate to **`My Account`** > **`Security`** > **`Generate Token`**.
3. **Add SonarCloud to Your Repository**: Go to **`Repository Settings`** > **`Repository Variables`**, add **`SONAR_TOKEN`** with the generated token.
4. **Modify `bitbucket-pipelines.yml` to Include SonarCloud**:

   **Example:**

```
image: node:18
pipelines:
  default:
    - step:
        name: SonarCloud Analysis
        clone:
          depth: full    # SonarQube Cloud scanner needs the full
history to assign issues properly
        size: 2x
        script:
          - npm install
          - npm test
          - pipe: sonarsource/sonarcloud-scan:3.0.0
          - pipe: sonarsource/sonarcloud-quality-gate:0.1.6
definitions:
  services:
    docker:
      memory: 5124 #set memory based on resource requirement to
run the sonar scan pipe
```

**Pipeline SonarCloud build:**

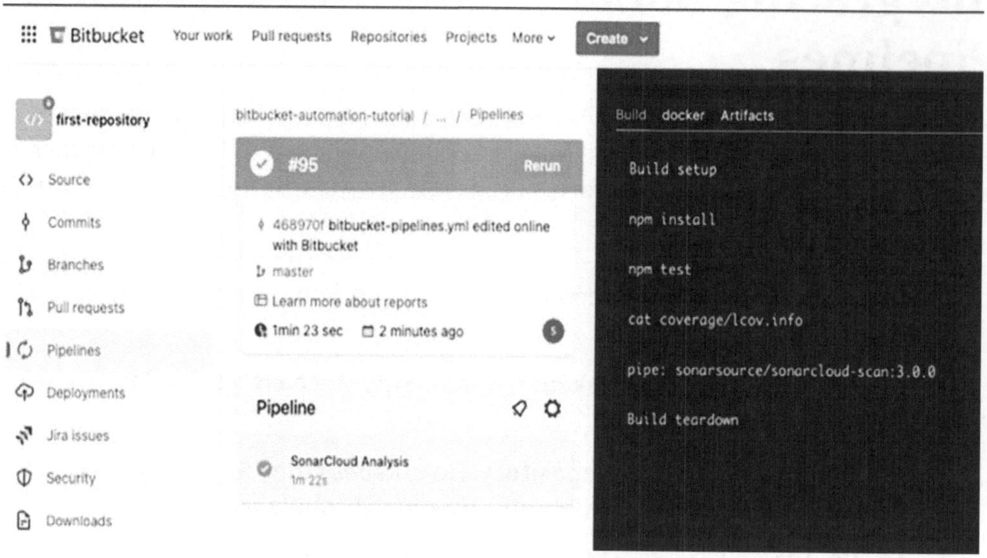


***Figure 8.1**: SonarCloud – pipeline build*

5. **Analyze Results in SonarCloud**: Once the pipeline runs, view code analysis reports in SonarCloud.

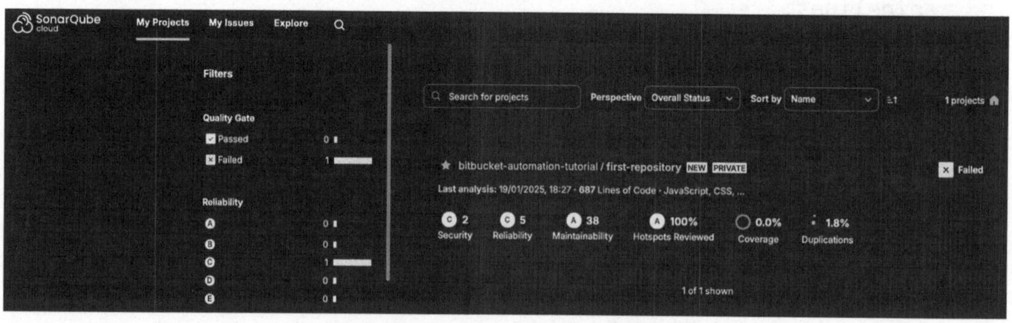


***Figure 8.2**: SonarCloud Analysis*

**Note**: *This is an example configuration demonstrating the integration of SonarCloud with Bitbucket Cloud for code scanning and quality gate enforcement.*

It includes a sample Node.js build and test setup. The values shown are indicative only, and the scan reports and quality gate results will be based on your actual test results.

# Automated Code Quality Reviews

Automated code quality checks play a crucial role in maintaining a clean, efficient, and maintainable codebase. These checks enforce coding standards, help detect issues early, and provide actionable feedback to developers before the code is merged.

By integrating SonarCloud with Bitbucket Pipelines, teams can automate static code analysis, ensuring that all code meets predefined quality standards.

**Key Benefits:**

- Detects code smells, duplications, and complexity issues.
- Helps maintain a clean codebase by identifying inefficiencies.
    - Reduces technical debt by ensuring best practices are followed.
- Improves code maintainability and readability.
    - Ensures that code is consistent, well-structured, and easy to understand.
    - Helps prevent future rework by proactively resolving issues.
- Enhances team collaboration with automated feedback.
    - Developers receive instant feedback on pull requests.
    - Encourages adherence to best practices across the team.

**Example Workflow for Code Quality Checks**

This is a typical workflow integrating **SonarCloud** with **Bitbucket Pipelines**:

- Developers push code to a feature branch in Bitbucket.
- Bitbucket triggers a pipeline that includes SonarCloud analysis.
- SonarCloud scans the code for issues such as Code smells and Duplications.
- SonarCloud show the report details directly on the pull request with issues and suggestions.

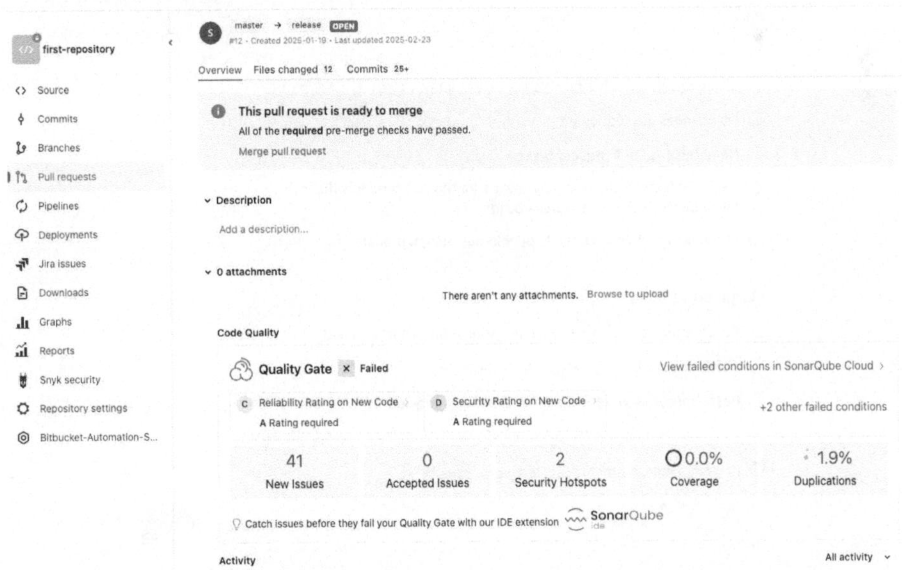


**Figure 8.3**: *SonarCloud reports in pull requests*

**Preventing Pull Request Merges When the Quality Gate Fails:**

To enforce code quality before merging, you need to configure branch restrictions:

**Steps to Restrict Merging for Failed Quality Gates**

1. Navigate to: **`Repository settings`** → **`Branch restrictions`**.
2. Choose Add a branch restriction or edit an existing restriction.

Under the **`Merge settings`** tab, enable the following:

- Minimum number of successful builds for the last commit.
    - Ensure there are no failed builds and no in-progress builds before merging.
- Prevent merging with unresolved merge checks
    - This blocks merging if the SonarCloud Quality Gate has failed.

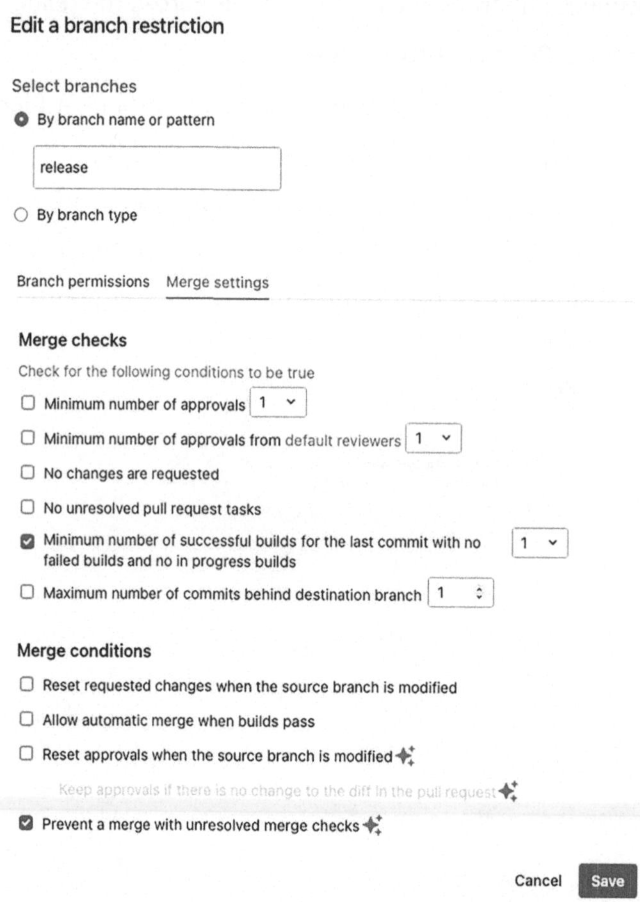


***Figure 8.4**: Branch restrictions for Quality Gate Fails*

This ensures that only high-quality, reviewed code is merged into the repository and prevents code merges for quality gate failures.

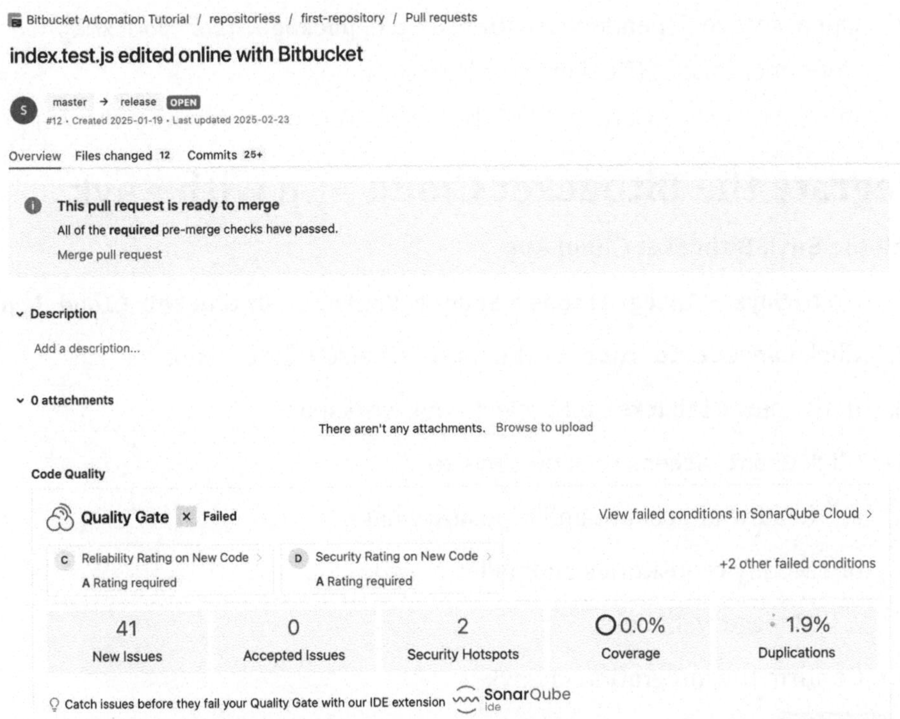


***Figure 8.5**: Pull request merge check - Quality gate Failures*

By integrating SonarCloud with Bitbucket Pipelines, teams can:

- Automate code quality checks to maintain high standards.
- Receive real-time feedback on code issues.
- Enforce strict merge rules to prevent low-quality code from being merged.
- Improve overall code health, making maintenance easier and reducing future technical debt.

With automated code quality reviews, teams can focus on building great software while ensuring compliance with best practices.

# Performing Code Vulnerability Checks with Snyk

Security vulnerabilities in dependencies can expose applications to attacks. Snyk integrates with Bitbucket to scan dependencies and suggest fixes.

**Why Use Snyk?**

Snyk integrates with Bitbucket to detect vulnerabilities in:

- Open-source dependencies (for example, **`package.json`**, **`pom.xml`**).
- Container images (Docker security scanning).
- Infrastructure as Code (IaC) (Kubernetes, Terraform security checks).

# Integrate the Bitbucket Cloud App with Snyk

### Install the Snyk Bitbucket Cloud App

1. Go to **`Snyk`** → **`Integrations`** > **`Source Control`** > **`Bitbucket Cloud App`**.
2. Click **`Connect to install`** the Snyk Bitbucket Cloud App.
3. In the new **`Bitbucket`** tab, select your workspace.
4. Click **`Grant Access`** to allow Snyk to:
    a. Read your account and repository data.
    b. Modify repositories and pull requests.
    c. Manage webhooks.
5. Confirm the integration in Snyk.

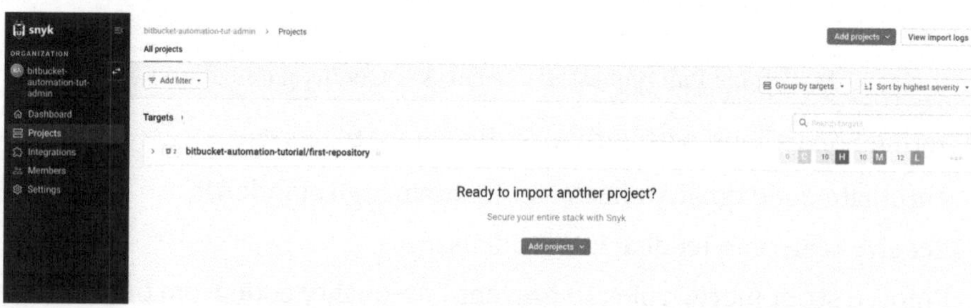


***Figure 8.6**: Snyk Bitbucket Cloud Integration*

- Snyk automatically scans all repositories in Bitbucket Cloud.
- Go to **`Snyk`** → **`Projects`** and check for security alerts.

**Example:**

The file **`hello-world-pod.yaml`** has been scanned in the repository with the following findings:

- 1 High vulnerability
- 4 Medium vulnerabilities
- 6 Low vulnerabilities

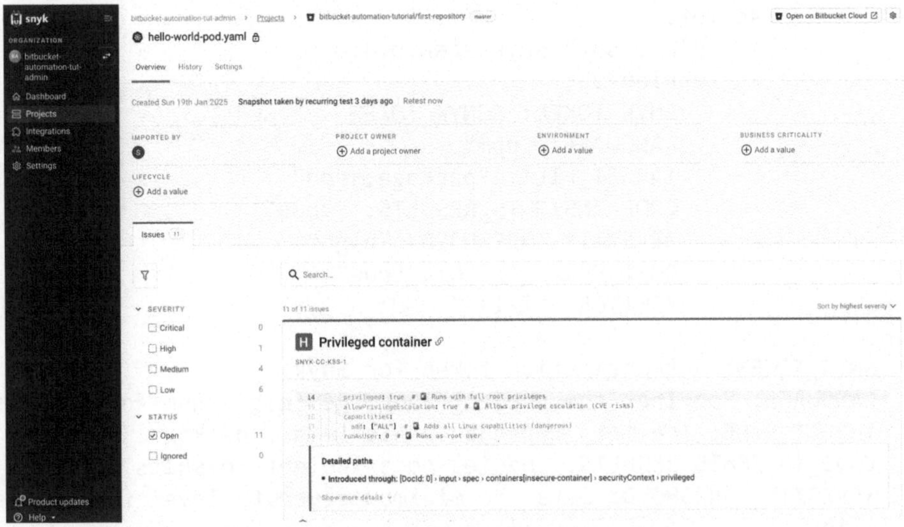


***Figure 8.7***: *Snyk Vulnerability Report*

# Configure Snyk in Bitbucket Pipelines

We can also integrate Snyk with Bitbucket Pipelines, scanning for both application dependencies and container images as part of your DevSecOps workflow.

Step 1: Add the Snyk API/Auth Token

a. Navigate to **`Bitbucket Repository Settings`** > **`Repository Variables`**.

b. Click **`Add`** a new variable:

i. Name: **`SNYK_TOKEN`**

ii. Value: *(Paste your Snyk* API *Token)*

**Step 2**: Modify Your **`bitbucket-pipelines.yml`** File

Update Bitbucket Pipelines configuration to include Snyk scans for both application dependencies and container images.

The following Bitbucket pipeline configuration scans Node.js project dependencies defined in **`package.json`** for security vulnerabilities using Snyk, ensuring that only open-source packages with a severity level of high or above are flagged, while reporting results in Bitbucket Code Insights.

```
pipelines:
  default:
    - step:
        name: "Scan Open Source Dependencies"
        caches:
          - node
```

```
script:
  - pipe: snyk/snyk-scan:0.4.3
    variables:
      SNYK_TOKEN: $SNYK_TOKEN
      LANGUAGE: "npm"
      TARGET_FILE: "package.json"
      CODE_INSIGHTS_RESULTS: "true"
      SEVERITY_THRESHOLD: "high"
      DONT_BREAK_BUILD: "true"
      MONITOR: "false"
```

**SNYK_TOKEN**: Authentication token for Snyk.
**LANGUAGE**: Specifies the project language (e.g., npm for Node.js).
**TARGET_FILE**: The main dependency file (e.g., package.json).
**CODE_INSIGHTS_RESULTS**: Enables code insights results (true).
**SEVERITY_THRESHOLD**: Sets the minimum severity level for issues (high).
**DONT_BREAK_BUILD**: Determines if the build should fail on vulnerabilities (false = fail on high severity issues).
**MONITOR**: Controls whether to monitor the project in Snyk (false = no monitoring).

We can notice that the Snyk security scan detected 21 vulnerabilities, including 9 Critical, 9 High, and 6 Medium severity issues.

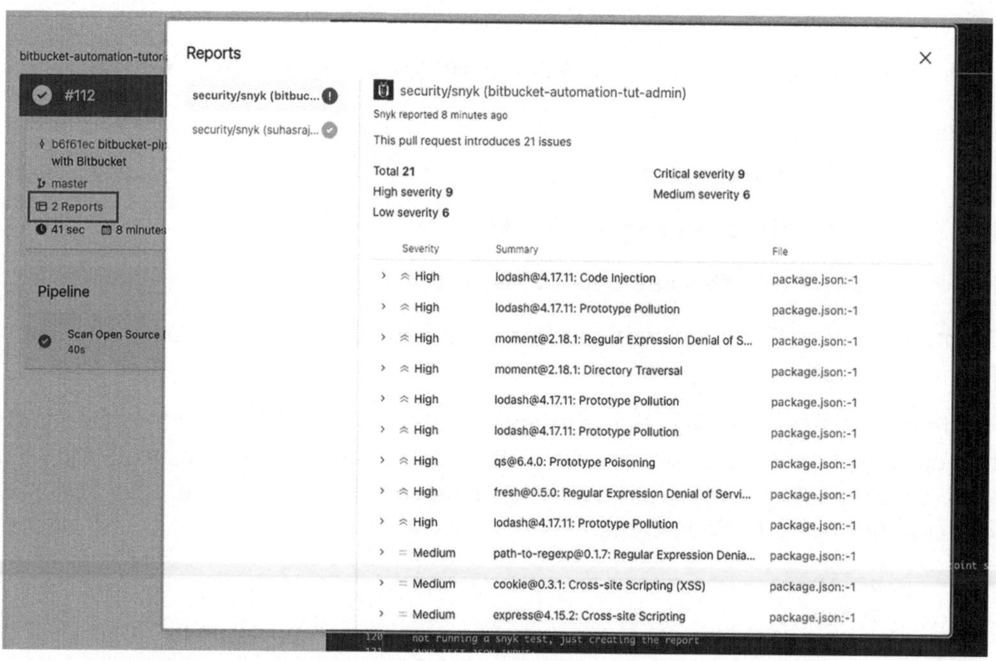


**Figure 8.8**: *Pipelines - Snyk Vulnerability Report for Node.js project*

We can also scan a Docker container image for security vulnerabilities using Snyk, ensuring that only high-severity or above vulnerabilities in open-source dependencies are flagged. Here is the sample pipeline:

```
pipelines:
  default:
    - step:
        name: "Build and Scan Container Image"
        services:
          - docker
        script:
          - docker build -t test .
          - docker tag test test:${BITBUCKET_COMMIT}
          - pipe: snyk/snyk-scan:0.4.3
            variables:
              SNYK_TOKEN: $SNYK_TOKEN
              LANGUAGE: "docker"
              IMAGE_NAME: test
              TARGET_FILE: "Dockerfile"
              CODE_INSIGHTS_RESULTS: "true"
              SEVERITY_THRESHOLD: "high"
              DONT_BREAK_BUILD: "true"
              MONITOR: "false"
```

# Integrating Jenkins with Bitbucket Cloud Using Webhooks

Bitbucket Cloud webhooks enable Jenkins to trigger jobs automatically whenever code changes occur in a repository, such as a push or pull request update. This integration helps streamline CI/CD workflows by ensuring builds and tests run automatically after every commit. Webhooks eliminate the need for manual job triggers, reducing development overhead and improving deployment efficiency. By setting up Jenkins to listen for webhook events from Bitbucket, teams can ensure a more automated and seamless software development lifecycle.

**Steps to Set Up:**

1. In Bitbucket Cloud, go to **`Repository settings`** > **`Webhooks`** and create a new webhook.
2. Set the URL to your Jenkins endpoint (for example, http://98.84.176.133:8080/bitbucket-hook/).

   **Note**: *We have selected Skip certificate verification as we are using an HTTP-based Jenkins URL for demo purposes. Additionally, we have selected Push* *webhook events, but we can choose different events based on actual requirements, such as triggering a build when a pull request is created.*

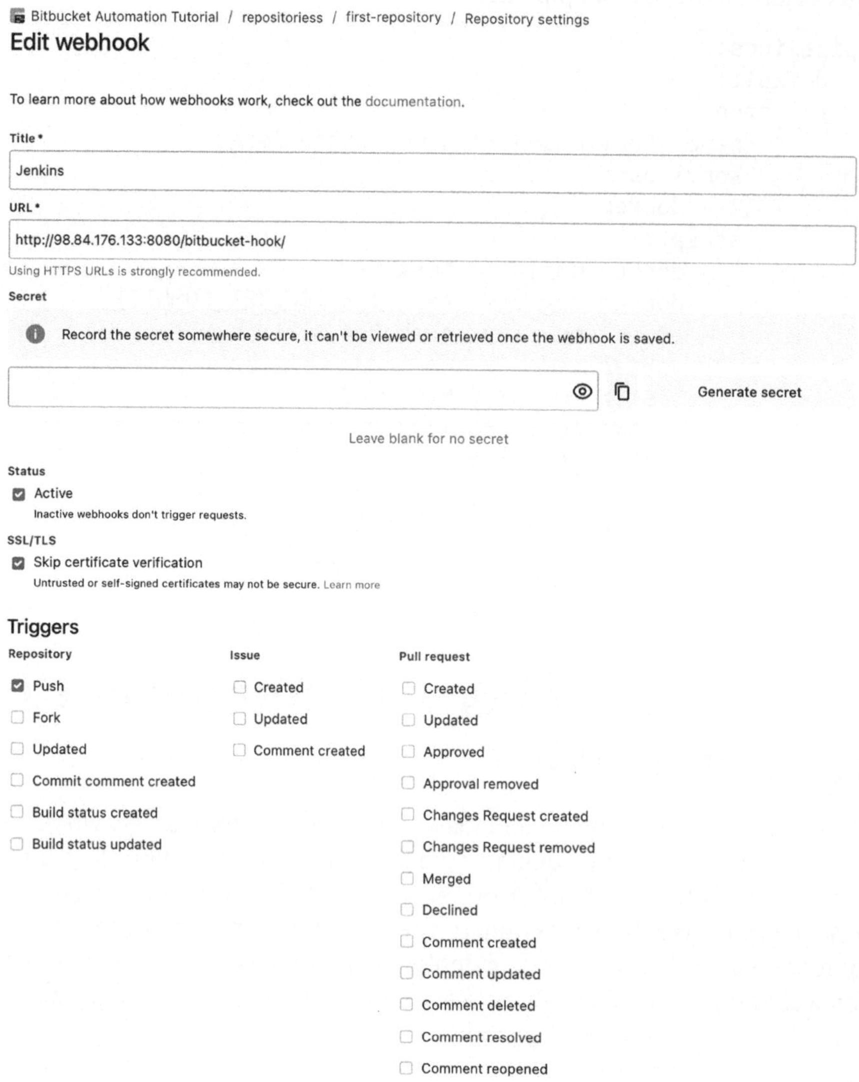


***Figure 8.9**: Jenkins integration using Webhooks*

3. In Jenkins, install the Bitbucket Plugin or Generic Webhook Trigger Plugin (if not already installed).

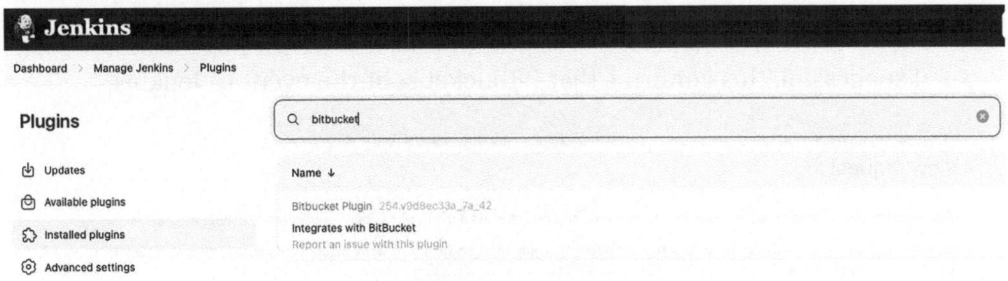


***Figure 8.10**: Jenkins Bitbucket plugin*

4. In Jenkins, create a Freestyle or Pipeline Job and configure it to pull code from Bitbucket using app password credentials or API tokens.

***Figure 8.11**: Jenkins job - git checkout*

Select build trigger "**`Build when a change is pushed to BitBucket`**"

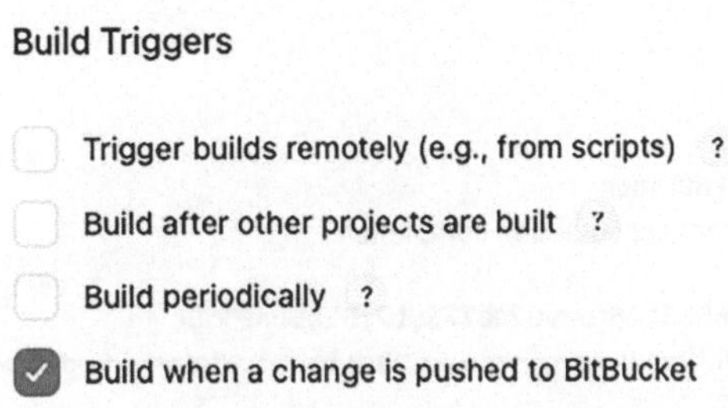


***Figure 8.12**: Jenkins job - Build Triggers*

Test the integration by pushing code to Bitbucket and verifying that Jenkins triggers the job successfully.

**Verify Webhook in Bitbucket**

1. Navigate to **`Repository Settings`** → **`Webhooks`**.

2. Check if the webhook received a 200 success response.
3. If successful, this confirms that Bitbucket sent the event to Jenkins.

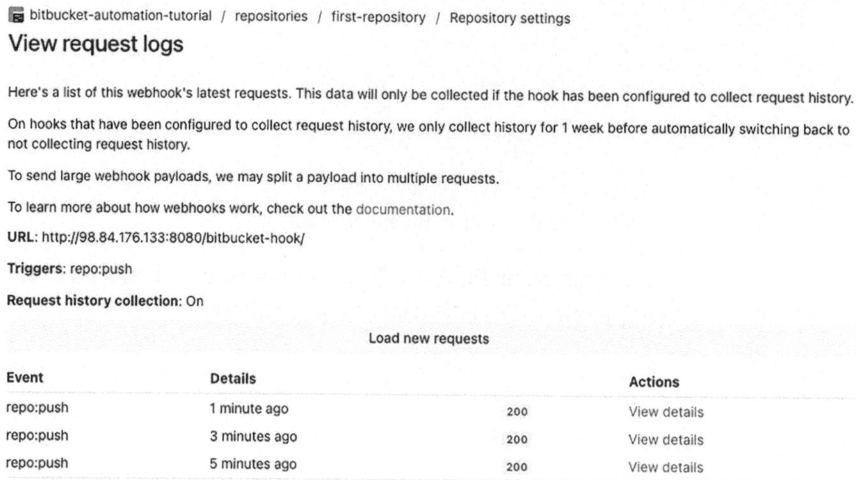


***Figure 8.13**: webhook push events*

Check Jenkins Console Log in Jenkins Dashboard, go to the triggered job.

Open "`Console Output`" and look for logs such as **`Started by BitBucket push by Suhas`**

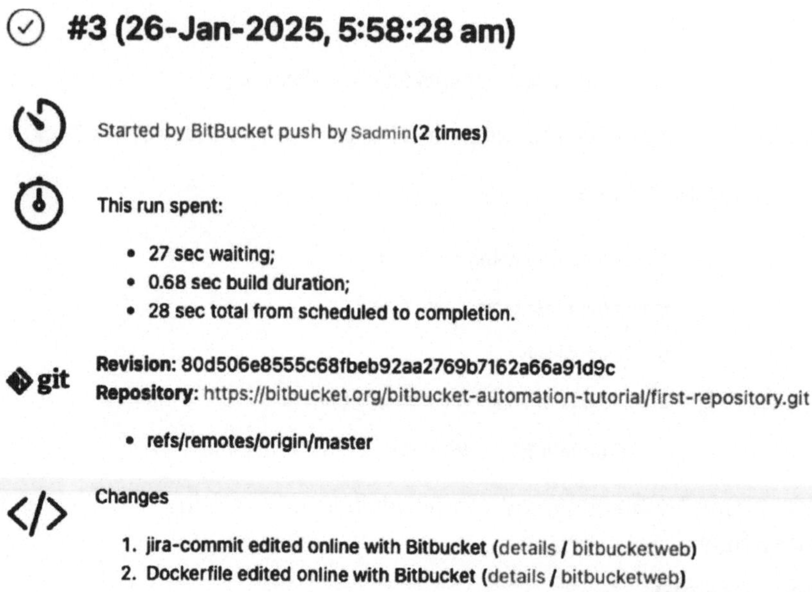


***Figure 8.14**: Jenkins Build logs*

This confirms that Jenkins detected the push event from Bitbucket Webhooks.

# Setting Up Notifications in Slack

Bitbucket Cloud allows teams to receive real-time notifications in Slack whenever there are updates to a repository, such as commits, pull requests, and build status changes. This integration improves collaboration by ensuring that developers are instantly informed of critical updates. By using Bitbucket's built-in Slack integration, teams can customize which events trigger notifications and to which channels they are sent. With Slack notifications enabled, developers can quickly review and respond to changes without constantly checking Bitbucket manually.

**Steps to Set Up:**

1. In **`Bitbucket Cloud`**, go to **`Repository settings`** > **`Integrations`** > **`Slack`**.
2. Click **`Add to Slack`** and authorize Bitbucket to access your Slack workspace.

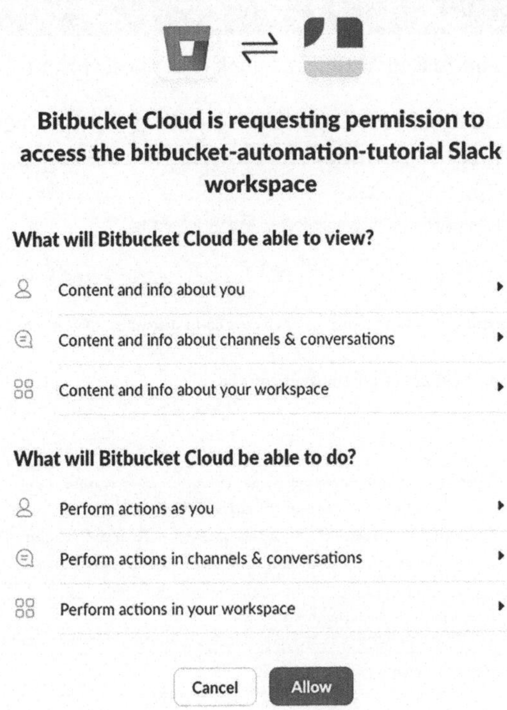


***Figure 8.15***: *Bitbucket slack integration*

3. Select a Slack **`Channel`** where notifications should be sent.

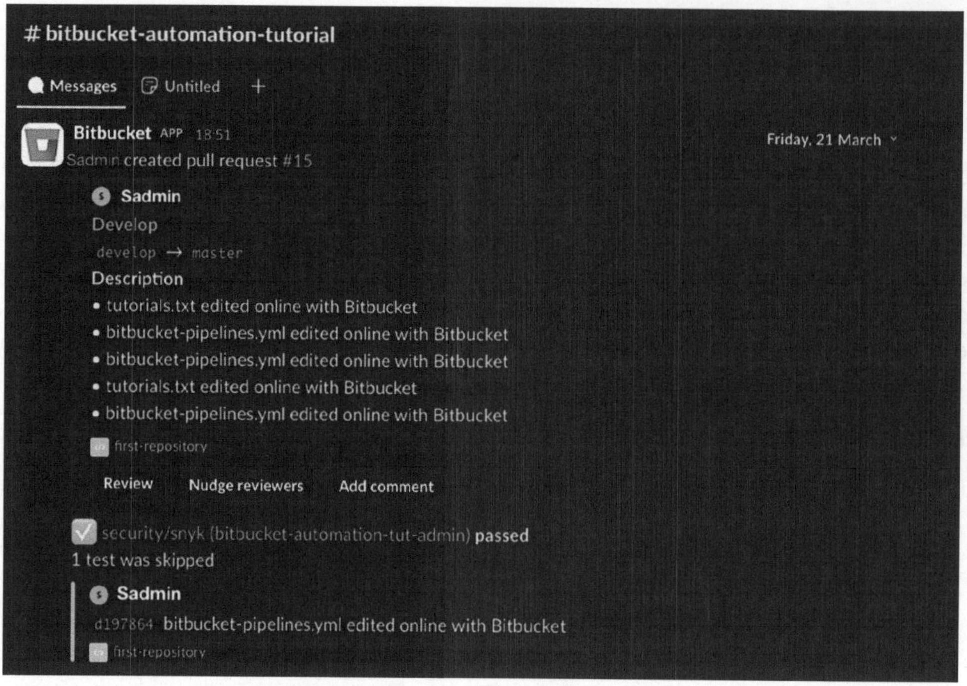


***Figure 8.16**: Bitbucket slack chat subscription*

4. Configure notification settings by selecting which repository events (for example, commits, PRs, builds) should trigger messages.

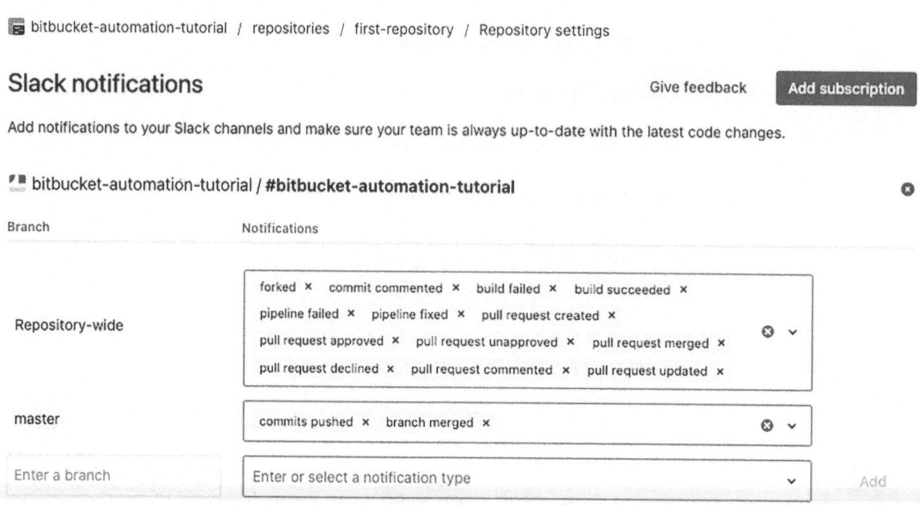


***Figure 8.17**: Bitbucket slack notifications Settings*

5. Save the settings and perform a test push or PR to verify Slack notifications.

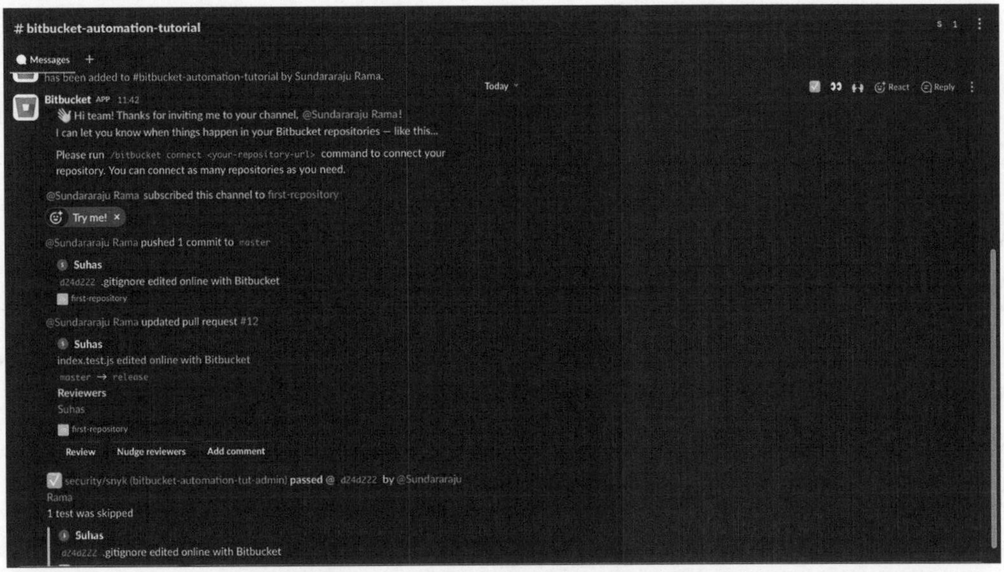


***Figure 8.18**: Bitbucket slack notifications*

# Integrating Microsoft Teams with Bitbucket

Microsoft Teams integration with Bitbucket Cloud helps development teams stay updated on repository activities, such as pull requests, commits, and pipeline builds. This setup allows Bitbucket to send automated messages directly to a Teams channel, improving collaboration and response times. Webhooks or native Microsoft Teams connectors can be used to configure these notifications based on specific repository events. By integrating Bitbucket with Teams, organizations can ensure smoother communication and faster issue resolution.

**Steps to Set Up:**

1. In **`Microsoft Teams`**, go to **`Apps > Connectors`** and search for **`Bitbucket Cloud`**.
2. Install the **`Bitbucket Cloud connector`** and authorize access to your **`Teams workspace`**.
3. In **`Bitbucket Cloud`**, go to **`Repository settings > Webhooks`** and create a new webhook.
4. Generate a **`webhook URL`** in Microsoft Teams and paste it into the webhook configuration in Bitbucket.

5. Select the repository events (for example, PR creation, merge, build success/ failure) that should trigger notifications.

6. Save the webhook and test by making a commit or opening a pull request in Bitbucket to verify notifications in Teams.

# Custom Notifications via Email in Bitbucket Pipelines

You can configure Bitbucket Pipelines to send build notifications via email using the Atlassian Email Notify Pipe. The following example shows how to integrate it.

**Step 1**. Configure SMTP Settings

Before setting up notifications in Bitbucket Pipelines, ensure you have:

- An SMTP provider (for example, Gmail, AWS SES, SendGrid, Outlook).
- SMTP login credentials (username and password).
- SMTP server details (host and port).

**Step 2**. Add **bitbucket-pipelines.yml**

Modify your **bitbucket-pipelines.yml** to include email notifications.

```
image: node:18
pipelines:
  default:
    - step:
        name: Build & Test
        script:
          - echo "Running build and tests..."
          - npm install
          - npm test
        after-script:
          - pipe: atlassian/email-notify:0.13.2
            variables:
              USERNAME: 'myemail@example.com'
              PASSWORD: $SMTP_PASSWORD
              FROM: 'myemail@example.com'
              TO: 'recipient@example.com'
              HOST: 'smtp.gmail.com'
              PORT: '587'
              TLS: 'true'
              SUBJECT: 'Bitbucket Pipeline Notification'
```

```
            BODY_PLAIN: 'The build on branch ${BITBUCK-
ET_BRANCH} has completed. Check logs here: https://bitbucket.
org/${BITBUCKET_WORKSPACE}/${BITBUCKET_REPO_SLUG}/addon/pipe-
lines/home#!/results/${BITBUCKET_BUILD_NUMBER}'
```

- **`USERNAME`**: Email address used for authentication.
- **`PASSWORD`**: SMTP password (store it as a repository variable $SMTP_PASSWORD).
- **`FROM`**: Sender email address.
- **`TO`**: Recipient email.
- **`HOST`**: SMTP server (for example, smtp.gmail.com, smtp.sendgrid.net, email-smtp.us-east-1.amazonaws.com for AWS SES).
- **`PORT`**: Use 587 for TLS (or 465 for SSL).
- **`TLS`**: Set to true to enable secure email transmission.
- **`SUBJECT`**: Custom subject for the notification email.
- **`BODY_PLAIN`**: Email body, including Bitbucket branch, repository, and build link.

**Step 4**. Secure Credentials

It is recommended to store sensitive information such as the SMTP password as a repository variable.

a. Go to **`Bitbucket`** → **`Repository settings`** → **`Repository variables`**.

b. Add a variable:

   - **`Key`**: **`SMTP_PASSWORD`**
   - **`Value`**: Your SMTP password.
   - Mark it as **`secured`** (hidden in logs).

**Step 5**. Test the Setup

a. **`Commit`** and push the changes.

b. Run a Bitbucket Pipeline.

c. Check the recipient inbox for build notifications.

**Email Notifications on Build Failures Only**

If you want to send emails only on build failures, modify the script:

```
script:
  - |
    if [ "$BITBUCKET_EXIT_CODE" -ne 0 ]; then
      pipe: atlassian/email-notify:0.13.2
      variables:
```

```
          USERNAME: 'myemail@example.com'
          PASSWORD: $SMTP_PASSWORD
          FROM: 'myemail@example.com'
          TO: 'recipient@example.com'
          HOST: 'smtp.gmail.com'
          PORT: '587'
          TLS: 'true'
          SUBJECT: 'Bitbucket Pipeline Failed'
          BODY_PLAIN: 'The build on branch ${BITBUCKET_BRANCH}
has FAILED. Check logs here: https://bitbucket.org/${BITBUCK-
ET_WORKSPACE}/${BITBUCKET_REPO_SLUG}/addon/pipelines/home#!/re-
sults/${BITBUCKET_BUILD_NUMBER}'
    Fi


This ensures emails are sent only if the build fails (BITBUCK-
ET_EXIT_CODE ≠ 0).
```

**Example: Using HTML Email Body**

To send formatted HTML emails, store an HTML file in the repository (for example, **`email-template.html`**) and update:

```
script:
  - pipe: atlassian/email-notify:0.13.2
    variables:
      USERNAME: 'myemail@example.com'
      PASSWORD: $SMTP_PASSWORD
      FROM: 'myemail@example.com'
      TO: 'recipient@example.com'
      HOST: 'smtp.sendgrid.net'
      PORT: '587'
      TLS: 'true'
      SUBJECT: 'Bitbucket Build Notification'
      BODY_HTML: 'email-template.html'
```

**Summary**

- Integrates with SMTP services such as Gmail, AWS SES, and SendGrid.
- Customizable email content for build success or failure.
- Secure handling of credentials using Bitbucket repository variables.
- Works with HTML templates for rich email formatting.

# Conclusion

In this chapter, we covered integrating code quality, security, and third-party tools in Bitbucket Cloud. We explored SonarCloud for automated code analysis, Snyk for security vulnerability checks, and Jenkins integration using webhooks. We also configured custom notifications for build events via Slack, Microsoft Teams, and email using Bitbucket Pipelines. These integrations enhance CI/CD workflows, ensuring high-quality and secure code while providing real-time alerts for better collaboration.

In the next chapter, we will dive into Bitbucket APIs, exploring how to automate repository actions, manage pull requests, and access pipeline builds programmatically.

# CHAPTER 9
# Bitbucket Cloud APIs

## Introduction

Bitbucket Cloud APIs provide powerful capabilities to automate, manage, and integrate various aspects of your repositories, workspaces, and projects. This chapter explores how to use Bitbucket Cloud APIs for workspace management, commit and pull request handling, pipelines automation, user management, reporting, and third-party integrations. By leveraging these APIs, teams can streamline workflows, enhance security, and improve productivity.

Before diving into specific Bitbucket API endpoints, we will first understand the basics of APIs, authentication methods, querying techniques, filtering, and pagination. Additionally, we will explore how to access APIs using tools, such as cURL, Postman, Python, and Bash.

## Structure

In this chapter, we will discuss the following topics:

- Understanding APIs and Authentication in Bitbucket Cloud
- Managing Workspaces, Repositories, and Projects with Bitbucket Cloud APIs
- Handling Commits and Pull Requests via API
- Automating Pipeline Operations with API
- User permissions through API
- Reporting, Auditing, and Analytics Using Bitbucket Cloud APIs

## Understanding APIs and Authentication in Bitbucket Cloud

An Application Programming Interface (API) allows applications to communicate with each other. Bitbucket Cloud APIs enable developers to interact programmatically with their repositories, pipelines, and teams.

**Bitbucket Cloud API Basics**

- **Base URL:** `https://api.bitbucket.org/2.0/`
- **Request Methods:** GET, POST, PUT, DELETE
- **Response Format:** JSON

# Authentication Methods

Bitbucket Cloud APIs support different authentication mechanisms:

# Basic Authentication

Uses Bitbucket username and an app password.

```
curl -u username:app_password https://api.bitbucket.org/2.0/repositories
```

**Note**: *To Find Your Bitbucket Username and App Password*

- ***Username***: *Your Bitbucket username is the same as your Bitbucket Cloud account ID. You can find it in the* ***`Bitbucket account`*** *settings under* ***`Personal settings`*** *→* ***`Bitbucket settings`*** *→* ***`Username`****.*
- ***App Password***:
    a. *Go to* ***`Bitbucket Settings`*** *(click on your profile picture →* ***`Personal Settings`****).*
    b. *Navigate to* ***`App passwords`*** *under* ***`Access Management`****.*
    c. *Click* ***`Create app`*** *password.*
    d. *Give it a label (for example, "****`Bitbucket API Access`****").*
    e. *Select required permissions based on what you need ((for example,* ***`Repository Read/Write`****,* ***`Pull Request Access`****).*
    f. *Copy the app password (it will not be shown again).*

# OAuth 2.0 Authentication

OAuth 2.0 allows secure access without exposing credentials, making it ideal for integrating with third-party applications.

**Steps to Authenticate Using OAuth 2.0:**

1. Navigate to **`Bitbucket Settings`** → **`OAuth consumers`**.
2. Click **`Add consumer`** and provide:
    a. Name (for example, "**`Bitbucket API App`**").

   b. Callback URL (required for web apps; can be http://localhost for testing).

   c. Permissions (for example, repository read/write).

3. Save and copy the **Key** and **Secret**.

**Obtain an access or bearer token:**

Use the following command to request an access token:

```
curl -X POST -u "client_id:client_secret" \
  https://bitbucket.org/site/oauth2/access_token \
  -d grant_type=client_credentials
```

Replace **client_id** and **client_secret** with values from your OAuth consumer.

Use the Access Token for API Requests:

```
curl -H "Authorization: Bearer access_token" https://api.bit
bucket.org/2.0/repositories/workspace
```

**Access Tokens**

Bitbucket provides long-lived Access Tokens that work like OAuth tokens used for non-user-specific authentication for API calls and integrations. Unlike app passwords, they are tied to a repository, project, or workspace and offer limited permissions (scopes) defined at the time of creation. Access Tokens do not expire unless manually revoked and cannot be used to log in to Bitbucket Cloud.

**Types of Access Tokens:**

1. **Repository Access Tokens:** Grants access to a single repository, commonly used for CI/CD pipelines.

2. **Project Access Tokens** (Premium feature): Provides access to all repositories within a specific project.

3. **Workspace Access Tokens** (Premium feature): Allows managing all repositories and projects within a **workspace**.

Access tokens authentication in API requests:

```
curl -H "Authorization: Bearer access_token" https://api.bit
bucket.org/2.0/respositories
```

# Queries, Filters, and Pagination

Bitbucket Cloud APIs support query parameters, filtering, and pagination to help refine API responses efficiently.

## Filtering API Results

Filters allow you to retrieve specific data based on conditions, such as dates, names, or statuses.

**Example**: Get repositories created after January 1, 2024

```
curl -u username:app_password "https://api.bitbucket.org/2.0/
repositories/workspace?q=created_on>2024-01-01"
```

- **`q=created_on>2024-01-01`**: Filters repositories created after the given date.

**Example**: Filter repositories where the name contains "**`demo`**"

```
curl -u username:app_password "https://api.bitbucket.org/2.0/re-
positories/workspace?q=name~\"demo\""
```

- **`q=name~"demo"`**: Fetches repositories with names containing "**`demo`**".

**Example**: Fetch only repositories that are public

```
curl -u username:app_password "https://api.bitbucket.org/2.0/re-
positories/workspace?q=is_private=false"
```

- **`q=is_private=false`**: Fetches only public repositories.

## Sorting API Results

Sorting lets you retrieve results in ascending or descending order.

**Example**: Fetch repositories sorted by creation date (newest first)

```
curl -u username:app_password "https://api.bitbucket.org/2.0/re-
positories/workspace?sort=-created_on"
```

- **`sort=-created_on`**: Returns repositories sorted by creation date (descending).

**Example**: Sort pull requests by the last update (oldest first).

```
curl -u username:app_password "https://api.bitbucket.org/2.0/re-
positories/workspace/repo_slug/pullrequests?sort=updated_on"
```

- **`sort=updated_on`**: Sorts pull requests in ascending order (oldest first).

## Pagination in Bitbucket API

By default, Bitbucket API responses are paginated. The default page length is 10 items per page, but you can increase it up to 100 using the **`pagelen`** parameter.

- **Example**: Retrieve 50 repositories per page

  ```
  curl -u username:app_password "https://api.bitbucket.org/2.0/re-
  positories?pagelen=50"
  ```

  **`pagelen=50`**: Increases the number of results returned per page.

- **Example**: Fetch the next page of results

  Each API response contains a "**next**" field with a URL to fetch the next set of results.

  ```
  curl -u username:app_password https://api.bitbucket.org/2.0/repositories?pagelen=50&page=2
  ```

  **page=2**: Fetches the second page of results.

- **Example**: Get all pull requests for a repository with pagination

  ```
  curl -u username:app_password https://api.bitbucket.org/2.0/repositories/workspace/repo_slug/pullrequests?pagelen=20&page=1
  ```

  This fetches 20 pull requests per page.

# Accessing Bitbucket APIs

Bitbucket APIs can be accessed via cURL, Postman, Python, or Bash scripts. We have already covered examples of accessing APIs using cURL, and now we will explore other options.

# Using Postman

Postman provides a user-friendly interface to make API requests.

**Steps to Use Bitbucket API in Postman:**

1. Open Postman and create a new request.
2. Select **Basic Auth** and enter:
   - **Username**: Your Bitbucket username.
   - **Password**: Your Bitbucket app password.
3. Use API endpoints such as:

   ```
   GET https://api.bitbucket.org/2.0/workspaces
   ```
4. Click **Send** to view the API response.

**For OAuth 2.0**:

- Add an Authorization Header with:

  Authorization: **Bearer <access_token>**

**Using Python:** Python's requests library can be used to interact with Bitbucket APIs.

**Example**: Fetch user details

```
import requests
from requests.auth import HTTPBasicAuth
url = "https://api.bitbucket.org/2.0/user"
response = requests.get(url, auth=HTTPBasicAuth("username", "app_
password"))
print(response.json())  # Print user data
```

**Example**: Create a new repository

```
import requests
from requests.auth import HTTPBasicAuth
url = "https://api.bitbucket.org/2.0/repositories/workspace/
new-repo"
data = {
    "scm": "git",
    "is_private": True,
    "description": "My new private repository"
}
response = requests.post(url, json=data, auth=HTTPBasicAuth
("username", "app_password"))
print(response.json())  # Print response
```

## Using Bash (Token-Based Authentication)

Bitbucket also supports token-based authentication, where API requests use OAuth tokens.

**Example**: Fetch user details using an OAuth Bearer Token

```
TOKEN="your_api_token"
curl -H "Authorization: Bearer $TOKEN" https://api.bitbucket.
org/2.0/user
```

**Example**: Fetch all repositories in a workspace

```
 TOKEN="your_api_token"
curl -H "Authorization: Bearer $TOKEN" "https://api.bitbucket.
org/2.0/repositories/workspace"
```

# Managing Workspaces, Repositories, and Projects with Bitbucket Cloud APIs

Bitbucket Cloud APIs allow seamless management of workspaces, repositories, and projects. The API endpoints enable users to create, update, and delete repositories, manage access permissions, and organize projects effectively.

# Understanding Key API Endpoints

This section explains some key API endpoints:

## /2.0/workspaces

This endpoint is used to retrieve information about workspaces. Workspaces group multiple repositories and define access levels for users.

**Example**: Retrieve "**bitbucket-automation-tutorial**" workspace details

```
curl -X GET -u username:app_password https://api.bitbucket.
org/2.0/workspaces | jq
```

This API call returns details about the workspaces associated with the authenticated user.


```
{
  "values": [
    {
      "type": "workspace",
      "uuid": "{43b9fc03-56a6-4d71-9cfb-90fcb83b9c4b}",
      "name": "bitbucket-automation-tutorial",
      "slug": "bitbucket-automation-tutorial",
      "is_private": true,
      "created_on": "2024-09-15T06:36:49.879349+00:00"
    }
  ],
  "pagelen": 10,
  "size": 1,
  "page": 1
}
```


***Figure 9.1**: List workspaces API*

## /2.0/repositories

This endpoint is used to manage repositories within a workspace. It supports operations, such as creating, updating, listing, and deleting repositories. Additionally, it enables actions such as forking a repository, managing webhooks, retrieving and updating repository inheritance settings, and handling group permissions, among many others. Listed here are a few examples:

### List all repositories in a workspace

Retrieve all repositories within a specific workspace using the API:

```
curl -X GET -u username:app_password https://api.bitbucket.
org/2.0/repositories/{workspace} | jq
```

This returns a JSON response containing repository details, such as name, slug, owner, and visibility.

```
{
  "type": "workspace",
  "uuid": "{43b9fc03-56a6-4d71-9cfb-90fcb83b9c4b}",
  "name": "bitbucket-automation-tutorial",
  "is_private": true,
  "links": {
    "html": { "href": "https://bitbucket.org/bitbucket-automation-tutorial/" }
  }
}
```

***Figure 9.2**: List repositories API*

**Create a new repository in a workspace**

We will create a repository with specific settings, such as repository privacy type and visibility:

```
curl -X POST -u username:app_password \
    -H "Content-Type: application/json" \
    -d '{"scm": "git", "is_private": true, "project": {"key":
"PROJ"}}' \
    https://api.bitbucket.org/2.0/repositories/bitbucket-
automation-tutorial/test-repo-api | jq
```

This command creates a private Git repository "**test-repo-api**" under the workspace "**bitbucket-automation-tutorial**"

```
{
  "type": "repository",
  "full_name": "bitbucket-automation-tutorial/test-repo-api",
  "links": {
    "self": { "href": "https://api.bitbucket.org/2.0/repositories/..." }
  },
  "name": "test-repo-api",
  "scm": "git",
  "owner": { "display_name": "bitbucket-automation-tutorial" }
}
```

***Figure 9.3**: Create repository API*

**Get repository webhooks**

List all webhooks configured for a specific repository:

```
curl -X GET -u username:app_password \
    https://api.bitbucket.org/2.0/repositories/bitbucket-auto
mation-tutorial/first-repository/hooks | jq
```

```
{
  "type": "webhook_subscription",
  "uuid": "{398b814d-5f49-4bd5-acce-728af0129d36}",
  "url": "https://api.snyk.io/webhook/...",
  "active": true,
  "skip_cert_verification": false,
  "events": [
    "pullrequest:created",
    "pullrequest:fulfilled",
    "repo:push",
    "pullrequest:rejected",
    "pullrequest:updated"
  ],
  "created_at": "2025-01-19T13:46:24.988097+00:00",
  "subject": { ... }
}
```


***Figure 9.4***: *List repository webhooks API*

This helps in retrieving details about webhooks set up for repository automation.

These are just a few examples; the Bitbucket API provides extensive functionality to manage repositories efficiently.

# Handling Commits and Pull Requests via API

Using the Bitbucket Cloud API, teams can automate commit tracking, pull request creation, merging, and other repository operations. This enables seamless workflow automation, efficient code management, and better collaboration among developers.

## Retrieving Commit History for a Repository

The commit history API allows you to fetch the list of commits made to a repository. This can be useful for tracking changes, reviewing contributions, and integrating commits into other tools.

**Example: Get Commit History**

```
curl -X GET -u username:app_password \
    https://api.bitbucket.org/2.0/repositories/bitbucket-auto
mation-tutorial/first-repository/commits | jq
```

```
{
  "values": [
    {
      "type": "commit",
      "hash": "d24d222723c4091b11b8f4986312effea04fd86a",
      "author": {
        "user": {
          "display_name": "Sadmin",
          "nickname": "Sadmin"
        }
      },
      "message": ".gitignore edited online with Bitbucket",
      "summary": { "raw": ".gitignore edited online with Bitbucket" }
    }
  ]
}
```


***Figure 9.5**: List commits API*

**JSON Output Structure:**

- `hash`: The commit ID.
- `date`: The timestamp of the commit.
- `author`: The user who made the commit.
- `message`: The commit message.
- `repository`: The repository name and workspace.

You can use pagination (`pagelen` and next fields) to navigate through multiple pages of commit history.

# Creating a Pull Request (PR)

This API enables developers to automate PR creation as part of their CI/CD pipeline.

**Example: Create a Pull Request**

```
curl -X POST -u username:app_password \
    -H "Content-Type: application/json" \
    -d '{
          "title": "New Feature PR",
          "description": "Adding a new feature for better
performance",
          "source": { "branch": { "name": "feature/ui" } },
          "destination": { "branch": { "name": "master" } }
        }' \
    https://api.bitbucket.org/2.0/repositories/bitbucket-auto
mation-tutorial/first-repository/pullrequests | jq
```

```
{
  "comment_count": 0,
  "task_count": 0,
  "type": "pullrequest",
  "id": 14,
  "title": "New Feature PR",
  "description": "Adding a new feature for better performance",
  "rendered": {
    "title": {
      "type": "rendered",
      "raw": "New Feature PR",
      "markup": "markdown",
      "html": "<p>New Feature PR</p>"
    },
    "description": {
      "type": "rendered",
      "raw": "Adding a new feature for better performance",
      "markup": "markdown",
      "html": "<p>Adding a new feature for better performance</p>"
    }
  },
```


***Figure 9.6**: Create pull request API*

**JSON Output Structure:**

- **`id`**: The unique ID of the pull request.
- **`title`**: The title of the pull request.
- **`state`**: Indicates whether the pull request is OPEN, MERGED, or DECLINED.
- **`source`**: The branch where the changes are coming from.
- **`destination`**: The branch where the changes will be merged.
- **`author`**: The user who created the PR.
- **`reviewers`**: The users assigned to review the PR.
- **`links`**: Provides a direct link to the PR.

Pull request created with ID 14:

***Figure 9.7**: Created pull request using API*

Similarly, we can perform pull request merges and list existing pull requests based on their statuses using the Bitbucket Cloud API. These APIs provide a powerful interface, allowing us to programmatically access and perform actions on Bitbucket resources.

# Automating Pipeline Operations with API

The Bitbucket Pipelines API enables teams to trigger, manage, and monitor pipeline builds programmatically, allowing greater automation in CI/CD workflows. Using the API, we can:

- Trigger pipeline builds on a branch, tag, or commit.
- Retrieve pipeline statuses to monitor execution.
- Cancel or stop running builds if needed.
- Fetch logs to debug failures.
- Rerun previous pipeline builds with the same or modified configurations.

## Trigger a Pipeline Build

A pipeline build can be triggered programmatically for a specific branch or commit. This is particularly useful for:

- Automating deployments on specific branches (for example, master, develop).
- Running tests against feature branches before merging.
- Executing scheduled jobs from external services.

**Example**: Trigger a Pipeline for the master Branch

```
curl -X POST -u username:app_password \
     -H "Content-Type: application/json" \
     -d '{
          "target": {
            "ref_type": "branch",
            "type": "pipeline_ref_target",
            "ref_name": "master"
          }
        }' \
     https://api.bitbucket.org/2.0/repositories/bitbucket-auto-
mation-tutorial/first-repository/pipelines/ | jq
```

API JSON output:


```
{
  "uuid": "{02696b24-cf3e-46ea-80c8-0c67a790e751}",
  "repository": {
    "full_name": "bitbucket-automation-tutorial/first-repository",
    "uuid": "{108ed6be-1ec7-4960-8cb8-76bb1f1909b1}"
  },
  "state": {
    "name": "PARSING",
    "type": "pipeline_state_parsing"
  },
  "stage": {
    "name": "PARSING",
    "type": "pipeline_state_parsing_parsing"
  },
  "build_number": 136,
  "creator": {
    "display_name": "Sadmin"
  }
}
```


***Figure 9.8:*** *Trigger pipelines API*

API Request body:

| Field | Description |
|---|---|
| `target` | Defines the pipeline execution target. |
| `ref_type` | Specifies whether the target is a branch or tag. Here, it is a branch. |
| `type` | The type of pipeline target. It should always be "**`pipeline_ref_target`**". |
| `ref_name` | The name of the branch or tag on which the pipeline should run. Here, it is "**`master`**". |

***Table 9.1:*** *API Request body*

Triggered Pipelines build with ID 136:

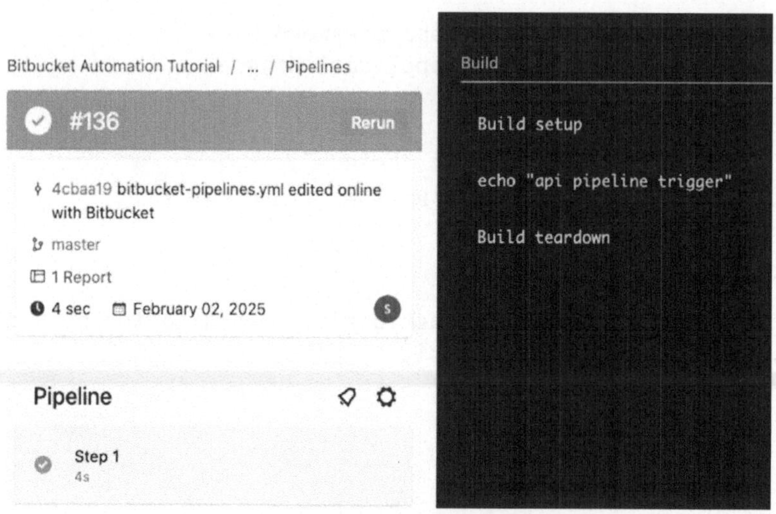


***Figure 9.9:*** *API triggered pipelines build*

There are multiple other operations that can be performed using the Bitbucket Pipelines API, such as fetching build logs, scheduling pipeline builds, creating repository variables, and more. The Bitbucket Pipelines API is powerful for automating CI/CD workflows, allowing seamless integration with external systems, deployment tools, and monitoring services.

# User Permissions Through API

Bitbucket Cloud APIs provide endpoints to retrieve user and repository permissions. These APIs help in auditing permissions for users and repositories.

**Retrieve Workspace-Level Permissions**

**Endpoint**: `GET /workspaces/{workspace}/permissions`

This API fetches a list of users and their permissions at the workspace level.

```
curl -X GET -u username:app_password https://api.bitbucket.
org/2.0/workspaces/bitbucket-automation-tutorial/permissions | jq
```


```
{
  "values": [
    {
      "type": "workspace_membership",
      "user": { "display_name": "Sadmin" },
      "workspace": { "name": "bitbucket-automation-tutorial" }
    }
  ]
}
```


***Figure 9.10**: workspace permissions API*

The preceding API response provides details about users in the **`bitbucket-automation-tutorial`** workspace and their assigned permissions.

**API Response JSON Structure**

1. **`values`** (List of Users in the Workspace): Contains multiple user objects representing members of the workspace.
2. **User Details**
   a. **`user.display_name`** → The full name of the user.
   b. **`user.nickname`** → The username used in Bitbucket Cloud.
   c. **`user.account_id`** → A unique identifier assigned to the Bitbucket account.
   d. **`user.uuid`** → A system-generated unique ID for the user.

   e. **user.links.html.href** → The Bitbucket profile URL for the user.
   f. **user.links.avatar.href** → The avatar image link for the user.

3. **Workspace Details**
   a. **workspace.name** → The name of the workspace (**bitbucket-automation-tutorial**).
   b. **workspace.slug** → A URL-friendly version of the workspace name.
   c. **workspace.links.html.href** → The public Bitbucket workspace URL.
   d. **workspace.links.self.href** → The API endpoint to retrieve workspace details.
4. **Permissions**
   a. **permission** → Defines what actions the user can perform in the workspace.
      i. "**create-project**" → This user can create new projects in the workspace.
      ii. "**owner**" → This user has full administrative control over the workspace.
5. **Pagination**
   a. **pagelen** → Maximum number of users listed per page (default is 50).
   b. **size** → Total number of users in the workspace.
   c. **page** → The current page of the paginated response.

**Retrieve Repository-Level Permissions**

**Endpoint**: `GET /workspaces/{workspace}/permissions/repositories`

This API retrieves repository-level permissions for all repositories in a given workspace.

```
curl -X GET -u username:app_password \
   https://api.bitbucket.org/2.0/workspaces/bitbucket-auto
mation-tutorial/permissions/repositories | jq
```

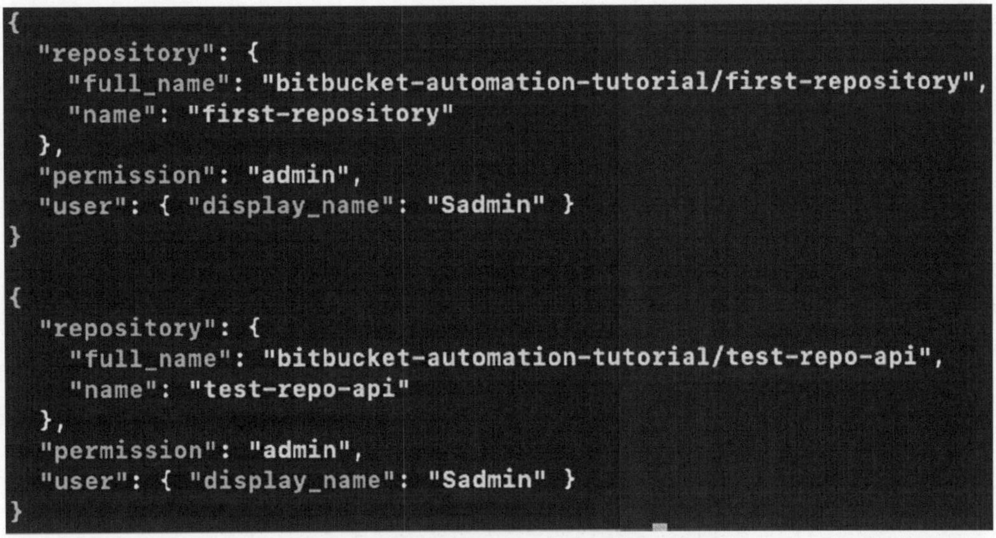


***Figure 9.11***: *Repository permissions API*

# Reporting, Auditing, and Analytics Using Bitbucket Cloud APIs

Bitbucket APIs can be used for auditing repository activities and generating custom reports for deeper insights. We have already covered accessing basic Bitbucket resources using APIs, including repositories and pull requests.

Now, let us automate listing the participants of each pull request in a given repository and export the data to a CSV file.

**Approach**

- We will use the Bitbucket Pull Requests API endpoint.
- Fetch the list of pull requests from a repository.
- Iterate over each pull request to extract participants (reviewers).
- Write the data into a CSV file for reporting purposes.

## Overview of the Script

The script pr-participants.py is hosted in https://bitbucket.org/bbcloud-support-scripts/pull-requests-with-participants-list/src/master/. It automates extracting pull request participant details and saving them into a CSV file.

```
import requests
from requests.auth import HTTPBasicAuth
import csv
```

```
from ndicts import NestedDict

try:
    import env
    username = env.username
    password = env.app_password
    repository = env.repository_slug

except [ImportError, AttributeError]:
    print('Could not locate one or more attributes within the
"env.py" file. '
          'Please follow the readme to ensure that all attributes
are present and try again.')
    exit()

def getPullRequestslist():
    pr_list = []
    next_page_url = 'https://api.bitbucket.org/2.0/reposito-
ries/%s/pullrequests?fields=next,values.id&&state=MERGED&&state=OP
EN&&state=DECLINED' % repository

    # Keep fetching pages while there's a page to fetch
    while next_page_url is not None:
        response = requests.get(next_page_url, auth=HTTPBasic
Auth(username, password))
        page_json = response.json()

        # Parse repositories from the JSON
        for repo in page_json['values']:
            PR_ID = str(repo['id'])
            pr_list.append(PR_ID)
        next_page_url = page_json.get('next', None)

    return pr_list

def getPullRequestStats(pr_list):
    with open("pr-stats.csv", "w") as file:
        writer = csv.writer(file)
        writer.writerow(["PR Number", "PR Author", "PR Title",
"Participants - Reviewers"])
        for pr_id in pr_list:
            next_page_url = 'https://api.bitbucket.org/2.0/
repositories/%s/pullrequests/%s?fields=next,id,author.display_
name,rendered.title.raw,participants.user.display_name' %
(repository, pr_id)
```

```
            # Keep fetching pages while there's a page to fetch
            while next_page_url is not None:
                response = requests.get(next_page_url, auth=HTTP-
BasicAuth(username, password))
                page_json = response.json()
                nd = NestedDict(page_json) #nested dictionaries
                PR_ID = str(nd['id'])
                PR_Author = nd['author']['display_name']
                PR_Title = nd['rendered']['title']['raw']
                list = []  #participants is a list nested with
dictionaries
                for participant in page_json["participants"]:
                    print(participant)
                    PR1 = participant['user']['display_name']
                    list.append(PR1) #append to empty list
                Participant_reviewers = ", ".join(list) #will
join a list of strings into a string with ", " as delimiters
                writer.writerow([PR_ID, PR_Author, PR_Title,
Participant_reviewers])
                next_page_url = page_json.get('next', None)

def main():
    pr_list = getPullRequestslist()
    getPullRequestStats(pr_list)

if __name__ == '__main__':
    main()

Script URL: https://bitbucket.org/bbcloud-support-scripts/
pull-requests-with-participants-list/src/master/
```

**Workflow Overview**

The script fetches all pull requests in a given repository, retrieves participants (reviewers) for each PR, and exports the data to **`pr-stats.csv`**.

1. Authenticate with the Bitbucket API using a username and app password.
2. Fetch a list of pull requests (Open, Merged, and Declined) using the API.
3. Retrieve PR details, such as ID, author, title, and participants.
4. Write extracted data to a CSV file for reporting.

**Main Functions**

- **`getPullRequestslist()`**
  - Fetches all pull requests from a repository.

  - Uses pagination to retrieve all results.
- **`getPullRequestStats()`**
  - Iterates through PRs and extracts details.
  - Retrieves participants (reviewers) and formats them.
  - Saves the data into **`pr-stats.csv`**.
- **`main()`**
  - Calls both functions to execute the workflow.

**Script repository structure**

```
├── .gitignore
├── README.md
├── env-template.py  # Sample config for credentials
├── pr-participants.py  # Main script
├── requirements.txt  # Dependencies
```

**Running the Script**

1. **Install dependencies**:

   ```
   pip install -r requirements.txt
   ```

2. **Set up authentication**:

   Create **`env.py`** and add:

   ```
   username = "your_bitbucket_username"
   app_password = "your_app_password"
   repository_slug = "your_repository"
   ```

3. **Run the script**:

   ```
   python pr-participants.py
   ```

4. **Output**: The CSV file **`pr-stats.csv`** will contain PR number, author, title, and reviewers.

| A | B | C | D |
|---|---|---|---|
| PR Number | PR Author | PR Title | Participants - Reviewers |
| 12 | Sadmin | index.test.js edited online with Bitbucket | Sadmin |
| 14 | Sadmin | New Feature PR | |
| 9 | Sadmin | tutorials.txt edited online with Bitbucket | |
| 13 | bitbucket-automation-tutorial | [Snyk] Fix for 21 vulnerabilities | |
| 11 | Sadmin | issue-jira-key created online with Bitbucket | Sadmin |
| 10 | Sadmin | bitbucket-pipelines.yml edited online with Bitbucket | |
| 8 | Sadmin | tutorials.txt edited online with Bitbucket | Sadmin, Sadmin |
| 7 | Sadmin | CODEOWNERS created online with Bitbucket | Sadmin, Sadmin |
| 6 | Sadmin | merge-conditions edited online with Bitbucket | Sadmin |
| 5 | Sadmin | merge-conditions created online with Bitbucket | Sadmin |
| 4 | Sadmin | merge-conditions created online with Bitbucket | |
| 3 | Sadmin | Develop | Sadmin |
| 2 | Sadmin | Develop | Sadmin, Sadmin |
| 1 | Sadmin | pull request tutorials | |

***Figure 9.12**: List Pull Request Participants using API Automation*

# Conclusion

In this chapter, we explored the power of Bitbucket Cloud APIs for managing workspaces, repositories, commits, and pull requests. We covered automating pipelines, managing users, generating reports, and integrating with third-party applications such as Jenkins.

In the next chapter, we will explore Forge apps, including dynamic pipeline configurations and connected apps in Bitbucket Cloud for extended automation and integrations. We will also address use cases that cannot be solved using conventional features.

# CHAPTER 10
# Integrating Forge in Bitbucket Cloud

## Introduction

In today's fast-paced development environments, extending and customizing your version control system is essential. Bitbucket Cloud not only manages code but also serves as a powerful hub for continuous integration/continuous deployment (CI/CD) and collaboration. This chapter explores how to extend Bitbucket Cloud through the Forge integration framework:

- **Atlassian Forge**: A cloud development platform that enables developers to create and deploy custom apps directly within Bitbucket Cloud. It provides a secure and scalable environment to extend Bitbucket functionalities using modern tools and frameworks.
- **Dynamic Pipelines in Forge**: A feature of Atlassian Forge that allows you to create flexible, event-driven CI/CD workflows. Dynamic Pipelines automatically adjust to changes in branches, commits, or user actions, ensuring that builds are efficient and context-aware. These pipelines are defined and managed through Forge apps, enhancing automation and customization.

We will begin by exploring Atlassian Forge and how it integrates seamlessly with Bitbucket Cloud to build pull request custom merge check functionalities. We will then delve into Dynamic Pipelines, demonstrating their flexibility and power in automating CI/CD workflows.

## Structure

In this section, we will cover the following topics:

- Overview of the Atlassian Forge Framework
- Forge Tunneling
- Pull Request Custom Merge Checks in Forge

- Manifest File
- Forge Dynamic Pipelines
- Installing Dynamic Pipelines in Bitbucket Workspace

# Overview of the Atlassian Forge Framework

Atlassian Forge is a cloud-based development platform designed to simplify app development within the Atlassian ecosystem. With Forge, developers can build secure, scalable apps that run natively in Atlassian products, such as Bitbucket Cloud, Jira, and Confluence.

**Key benefits include:**

- **Security by Default:** Apps run in a secure sandboxed environment.
- **Seamless Integration:** Native access to Atlassian APIs and UI components.
- **Simplified Deployment:** One-click deployment and automatic scaling.

**Architecture and Components**

Forge applications are structured around a few core components:

- **Manifest File:** Defines modules, permissions, and triggers.
- **Functions:** Serverless functions written in JavaScript that handle backend logic.
- **UI Modules:** Components that allow you to add custom user interfaces (panels, dialogs, and so on) within Bitbucket.

Following is the sample Forge manifest. This YAML configuration file serves as the blueprint for Forge app, defining its identity, permissions, and functional modules. Each section in the manifest plays a critical role in shaping how app interacts with Bitbucket Cloud.

**Sample Forge Manifest (YAML):**

```
modules:
  bitbucket:repoCodeOverviewCard:
    - key: hello-world-app-hello-world-repository-code-overview-
card
      resource: main
      resolver:
        function: resolver
      render: native
      title: Forge app for Mia
  function:
```

```
      - key: resolver
        handler: index.handler
resources:
  - key: main
    path: src/frontend/index.jsx
app:
  id: ari:cloud:ecosystem::app/your-app-id
  name: "My Bitbucket Forge App"
```

In this manifest, the app block defines the application's identity. The modules block contains two key modules: a Bitbucket repository code overview card that integrates a custom UI component into the repository view and a function module that provides dynamic data resolution for that UI component. Finally, the resources block ties the UI module to its front-end implementation file. We will explore each of these components in detail in the coming sections.

**To Begin Developing with Forge**

1. **Install the Forge CLI:**

```
npm install -g @forge/cli
```

**Verify the installation by checking the version:**

```
forge --version
```

2. **Perform Forge Login:**

**Generate an Atlassian API token** using the following link:

https://id.atlassian.com/manage/api-tokens

The CLI uses your token when running Forge commands to authenticate with Atlassian's cloud services.

```
forge login
```

3. **Create a Sample Bitbucket Cloud App:**

We will create the app in our **Bitbucket Automation Tutorial** workspace.

**To create a new app:**

```
forge create
```

**Enter the App Name:** Bitbucket Automation Sample App

**Available Categories:**

- **`Show All`:** Lists all available categories.
- **`Rovo Agent and action`:** Used for automation and background tasks using Atlassian Intelligence.
- **`UI Kit`:** Predefined UI components for rapid development.

- **`Custom UI`:** Allows custom front-end development using React.
- **`Triggers and Validators`:** Event-driven apps for automation and custom validation.

**Select a category:** "**`UI Kit`**"

4. **Choose the App Type:**

   **`Bitbucket -> bitbucket-repository-main-menu-page`**

- **Bitbucket:** To create an app specific to Bitbucket Cloud.
- **Repository Main Menu Page:** Adds a menu item at the bottom of the left navigation on repository pages, rendering content on a new page.

5. **Deploy and Test:**

After creating the Forge app, based on the category and module selections, Forge generates a default sample app. The generated project structure is organized to support efficient development and deployment. Here is an explanation of the generated file structure and its components:

**Project Structure:**

```
├── README.md
├── manifest.yml
├── package-lock.json
├── package.json
└── src
    ├── frontend
    │   └── index.jsx
    ├── index.js
    └── resolvers
        └── index.js
```

- **`README.md`:** Contains basic information about the app, including setup instructions, usage, and any other relevant details for developers.
- **`manifest.yml`:** The most important file in Forge apps. It defines the app's configuration, including modules, resources, permissions, and runtime settings.
- **`package.json` and `package-lock.json`:**

  These files manage dependencies and scripts for the app.

  - **`package.json`** specifies the dependencies, version, and scripts needed to run the app.
  - **`package-lock.json`** locks the dependency versions to ensure consistent installations.

- **`src`:**

  This directory contains all source code for the Forge app, organized as follows:

  - `frontend/index.jsx`:
    - This is the front-end component built using **UI Kit** with React-like syntax.
    - It renders the UI for the app and communicates with the back-end resolver using invoke.
  - **`index.js`:** The entry point for the app's back-end logic. It exports the handler defined in the **`resolvers/index.js`** file.
  - **`resolvers/index.js`:**
    - Contains the back-end logic using **`@forge/resolver`**.
    - Defines how the app responds to the front-end's requests using the invoke method.

**Code Breakdown:**

**`src/frontend/index.jsx`:**

```
import React, { useEffect, useState } from 'react';
import ForgeReconciler, { Text } from '@forge/react';
import { invoke } from '@forge/bridge';

const App = () => {
  const [data, setData] = useState(null);

  useEffect(() => {
    invoke('getText', { example: 'my-invoke-variable'
}).then(setData);
  }, []);

  return (
    <>
      <Text>Hello world!</Text>
      <Text>{data ? data : 'Loading...'}</Text>
    </>
  );
};

ForgeReconciler.render(
  <React.StrictMode>
    <App />
  </React.StrictMode>
);
```

- **Purpose:** This component:
  - Displays a "**`Hello world!`**" message.
  - Calls the **`getText`** function from the resolver and displays the returned data.
  - Shows "**`Loading...`**" until the data is fetched.

**`src/index.js:`**

```
export { handler } from './resolvers';
```

- **Purpose:** Exports the handler function from the resolver module, linking the back-end logic with the front-end.

**`src/resolvers/index.js:`**

```
import Resolver from '@forge/resolver';

const resolver = new Resolver();

resolver.define('getText', (req) => {
  console.log(req);
  return 'Hello, world!';
});

export const handler = resolver.getDefinitions();
```

- **Purpose:**
  - Defines the getText function, which returns "**`Hello, world!`**" when called by the front-end.
  - This is how the back-end communicates with the front-end using invoke.

# `manifest.yml`

The **`manifest.yml`** defines how the app is structured, its modules, and resources:

```
modules:
  bitbucket:repoMainMenuPage:
    - key: bitbucket-automation-sample-app-hello-world-reposito-
ry-main-menu-page
      resource: main
      resolver:
        function: resolver
      render: native
      title: Bitbucket Automation Sample App

  function:
```

```
    - key: resolver
      handler: index.handler

resources:
  - key: main
    path: src/frontend/index.jsx

app:
  runtime:
    name: nodejs22.x
  id: ari:cloud:ecosystem::app/your-app-id
```

**modules:** Defines the app's modules. In this example:

- **bitbucket:repoMainMenuPage:**
  - Adds a custom menu item in the repository's main navigation.
  - Uses UI Kit for rendering a native Bitbucket page.
  - Specifies a resolver function for back-end logic.
- function:
  - Defines the back-end resolver function.
  - Links to the handler in src/index.js.

**resources:** Specifies the front-end component (index.jsx) as the main resource.

**app:** Configures the runtime environment (nodejs22.x) and app ID.

**Deploying the App:**

1. **Deploy to Atlassian Cloud:**

   ```
   forge deploy
   ```

   - Deploys the app to Atlassian's cloud environment.
   - Initially deploys to the development environment for testing.
   - Once verified, you can promote the app to staging and production.

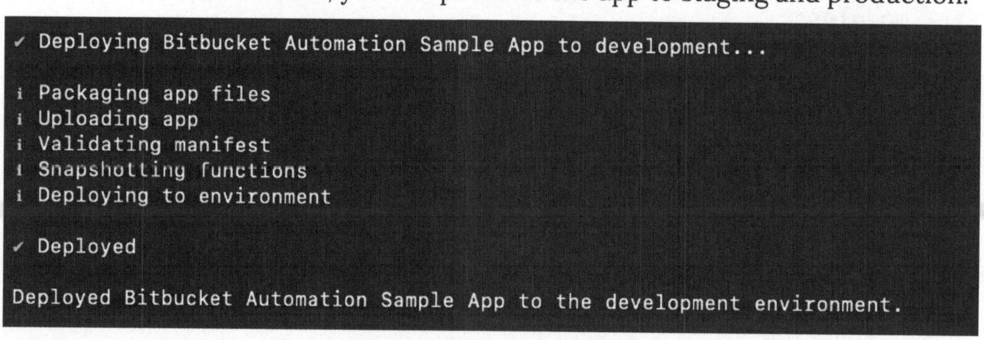


***Figure 10.1:*** *Forge deploy*

2. **Install the App in Bitbucket Workspace:**

   ```
   forge install
   ```

   It prompts for the Bitbucket workspace where you want to install the app. We choose "**`Bitbucket Automation Tutorial`**" workspace for deploying the app.

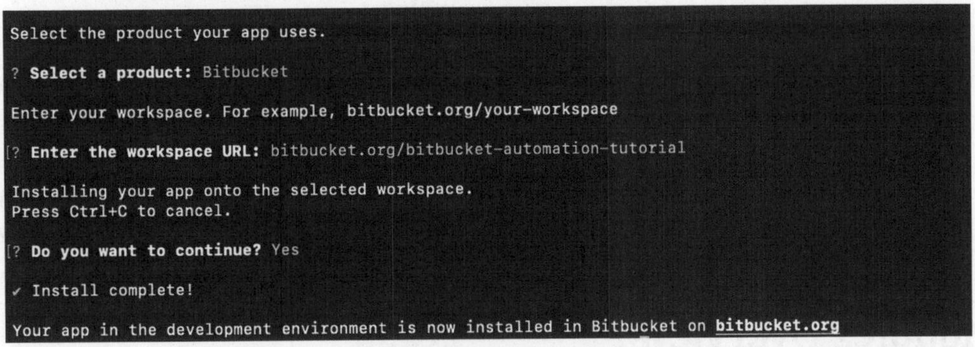


***Figure 10.2**: Forge deploy*

Once installed in the workspace, go to the main page view of any repository. In the bottom corner, you will notice the Forge app installed. Click on it, and you will see a "**`Hello World`**" message printed.

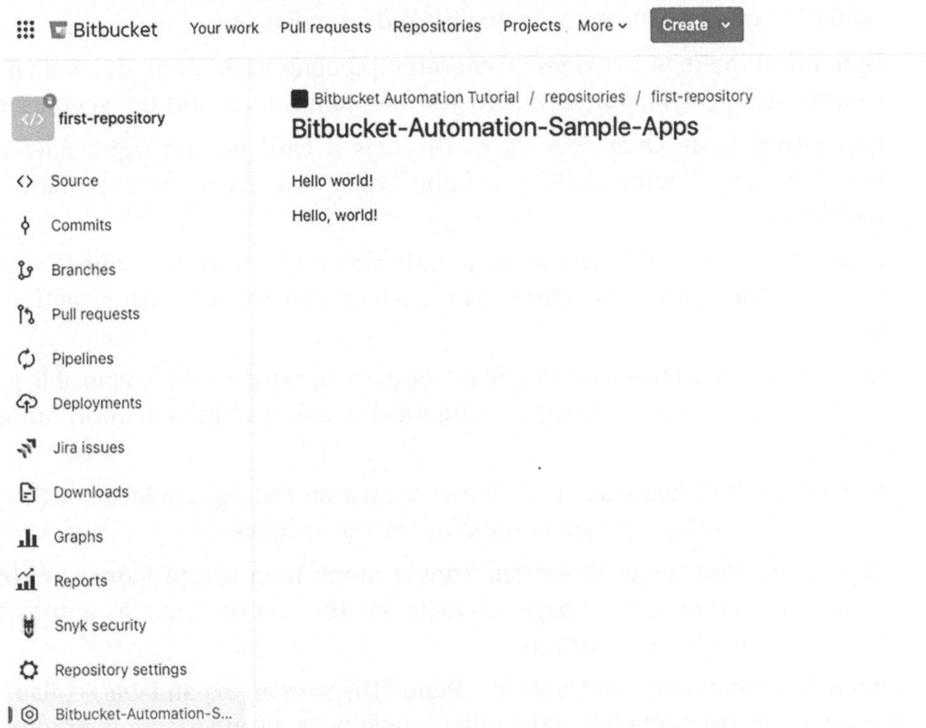


***Figure 10.3**: Forge Repository Main Menu Page App*

# Forge Tunneling

Tunneling runs your app code locally on your machine via the Forge CLI and Cloudflare.

```
forge tunnel
```

Tunneling helps debug the Forge app in two ways:

- **Real-time Logging:** By inserting `console.log()` statements in your code, you can see the output in the Forge CLI as the code executes, making it easier to track and fix issues.
- **Fast Turnaround for Changes:** The tunnel watches for code changes and automatically rebuilds your app. This means you do not need to deploy your app after every change, allowing you to test fixes faster and iterate efficiently.

# Modules Overview

Forge offers a variety of modules that are specifically designed for Bitbucket Cloud, allowing developers to enhance repository management, pull request workflows, and overall user experience. Here is a breakdown of the available modules:

- **Custom Merge Check:** Prevents pull requests from merging based on custom validation rules, ensuring code quality and compliance.
- **Dynamic Pipelines Provider:** Generates pipeline definitions dynamically at runtime, allowing flexible CI/CD workflows tailored to different scenarios.
- **Repository Code Overview Card:** Displays a card on the right sidebar of the repository Source page, providing quick insights or metrics about the codebase.
- **Repository Code Overview Action:** Adds a menu item in the "`more actions`" menu on the repository Source page, which can trigger custom actions or dialogs.
- **Repository Code Overview Panel:** Introduces an expandable/collapsible panel on the repository Source page, useful for displaying additional information or tools.
- **Repository Pull Request Card:** Shows a card on the right sidebar of the pull request page, offering extra context or review insights.
- **Repository Pull Request Action:** Adds a menu item in the "`more actions`" menu on the pull request page, enabling custom actions such as automation triggers or feedback collection.
- **Repository Pull Request Overview Panel:** Displays an expandable/collapsible panel on the overview tab of the pull request page, useful for summarizing key details.

- **Repository Main Menu Page:** Adds a new menu item at the bottom of the left navigation on repository pages, rendering custom content on a new dedicated page.
- **Repository Settings Menu Page:** Integrates an item in the Forge Apps section of the left navigation in the repository settings, providing a space for configuration options or advanced settings.
- **Workspace Settings Menu Page:** Adds an item in the Forge Apps section of the left navigation in the workspace settings, enabling workspace-wide configurations or tools.

These modules provide powerful customization options for Bitbucket Cloud, making it easier to extend functionality and improve user workflows.

# Pull Request Custom Merge Checks in Forge

In Bitbucket Cloud, custom merge checks ensure that pull requests meet specific conditions before merging. Using Forge, you can create custom rules that validate pull requests, improving code quality and compliance with organizational standards.

**Creating a Custom Merge Check with Forge**

To create a custom merge check using Forge, follow these steps:

**Create the App**: Run the following command to initiate a new Forge app:

```
forge create
```

**Select the Template**: During the creation process, select the following options:

```
Select a category: Triggers and Validators
Select a product: Bitbucket
Select a template: bitbucket-merge-check
```

This sets up a template designed to validate pull requests.

**Update the `src/index.js` File**: Replace the contents of src/index.js with the custom logic explained here.

```
import api, { route } from "@forge/api";

export const run = async (event, context) => {
  console.log(JSON.stringify(event, null, 2));

  const workspaceUuid = event.workspace.uuid;
  const repoUuid = event.repository.uuid;
  const prId = event.pullrequest.id;
```

```
  // Fetch the pull request details to get source and destination
branches
  const prDetailsUrl = route`/2.0/repositories/${workspa-
ceUuid}/${repoUuid}/pullrequests/${prId}`;
  const prDetailsResponse = await api.asApp().requestBitbucket
(prDetailsUrl);
  const prDetails = await prDetailsResponse.json();

  const sourceBranch = prDetails.source?.branch?.name;
  const destinationBranch = prDetails.destination?.branch?.name;

  if (!sourceBranch || !destinationBranch) {
    return { success: false, message: "Could not determine source
or destination branch" };
  }

  const commits = await fetchCommits(workspaceUuid, repoUuid,
sourceBranch, destinationBranch);

  let success = true;
  let message = "All commit authors have an email domain of
'gmail.com'";

  for (const commit of commits) {
    const email = commit.author.raw.split('<')[1].split('>')[0];
    if (!email.endsWith('@gmail.com')) {
      success = false;
      message = `Commit by ${commit.author.raw} has an invalid
email domain`;
      console.log(`Invalid commit found: ${commit.hash}, Author:
${commit.author.raw}`);
      break;
    }
  }

  return { success, message };
};

const fetchCommits = async (workspaceUuid, repoUuid, source-
Branch, destinationBranch) => {
  let nextPageUrl = route`/2.0/repositories/${workspa-
ceUuid}/${repoUuid}/commits?include=${sourceBranch}&ex-
clude=${destinationBranch}&fields=values.hash,values.author.
raw,next&pagelen=100`;
  const commits = [];

  while (nextPageUrl) {
```

```
    const res = await api.asApp().requestBitbucket(nextPageUrl);
    const pageJson = await res.json();
    commits.push(...pageJson.values);
    nextPageUrl = pageJson.next ? route`${pageJson.next}` : null;
  }

  return commits;
};
```

source code repository link: https://bitbucket.org/bitbucket-forge-apps/forge-app-commit-email-author-validator/src/main/

**Explanation of the Code: Importing Required Modules**

```
import api, { route } from "@forge/api";
```

- **api**: Used to make API requests to Bitbucket Cloud.
- **route**: Utilizes Forge's built-in URL routing to safely construct API endpoint URLs.

**Fetching Pull Request Details**

```
const prDetailsUrl = route`/2.0/repositories/${workspa-
ceUuid}/${repoUuid}/pullrequests/${prId}`;
const prDetailsResponse = await api.asApp().requestBitbucket
(prDetailsUrl);
const prDetails = await prDetailsResponse.json();
```

- Constructs a URL to fetch details of the pull request.
- Retrieves the source and destination branches for the PR.

**Validating Commit Authors' Email Domains**

```
for (const commit of commits) {
  const email = commit.author.raw.split('<')[1].split('>')[0];
  if (!email.endsWith('@gmail.com')) {
    success = false;
    message = `Commit by ${commit.author.raw} has an invalid
email domain`;
    console.log(`Invalid commit found: ${commit.hash}, Author:
${commit.author.raw}`);
    break;
  }
}
```

- Loops through all the commits in the pull request.
- Extracts the email of each author and checks if it ends with **`@gmail.com`**.
- If an invalid domain is found, the check fails, and a message is returned.

**Fetching Commits with Pagination**

```
let nextPageUrl = route`/2.0/repositories/${workspaceUuid}/$
{repoUuid}/commits?include=${sourceBranch}&exclude=${destination-
Branch}&fields=values.hash,values.author.raw,next&pagelen=100`;
const commits = [];
while (nextPageUrl) {
  const res = await api.asApp().requestBitbucket(nextPageUrl);
  const pageJson = await res.json();
  commits.push(...pageJson.values);
  nextPageUrl = pageJson.next ? route`${pageJson.next}` : null;
}
```

- Fetches all commits from the source branch that are not present in the destination branch.
- Handles pagination to retrieve all commits in batches of 100.
- Aggregates all commits into a single array for validation.

# Manifest File

This manifest file is specifically configured to create a Custom Merge Check using Atlassian Forge for Bitbucket Cloud. It defines the app's permissions, modules, and runtime environment, ensuring the app has the required access and functionality to perform the email domain validation check.

```
permissions:
  scopes:
    - read:pullrequest:bitbucket
    - read:repository:bitbucket
modules:
  bitbucket:mergeCheck:
    - key: check-email-domain
      function: main
      name: Check commit author email domain
      description: Ensure all commit authors have an email domain
of 'test.com'
      triggers:
        - on-merge
  function:
    - key: main
      handler: index.run
app:
  runtime:
    name: nodejs18.x
```

**Permissions**

```
permissions:
  scopes:
    - read:pullrequest:bitbucket
    - read:repository:bitbucket
```

- **Purpose:** This section defines the access permissions required for the app to function correctly.
- **Scopes:**
  - **`read:pullrequest:bitbucket`:**

    Grants read access to pull requests, allowing the app to:
    - Fetch pull request details.
    - Retrieve source and destination branches.
  - **`read:repository:bitbucket`:**

    Allows the app to:
    - Access repository metadata.
    - Read commit histories and author information.
- **Why Needed:**

  These permissions are crucial because the app:
  - Validates email domains by analyzing commit histories in pull requests.
  - Needs to access branches and repository details to perform checks.

**Deploy the app to your Bitbucket Cloud instance:**

```
forge deploy
```

# Enabling the Custom Merge Check

1. Go to **`Workspace Settings`** → **`Workflow`** → **`Custom Merge Checks`** → **`Enable`**

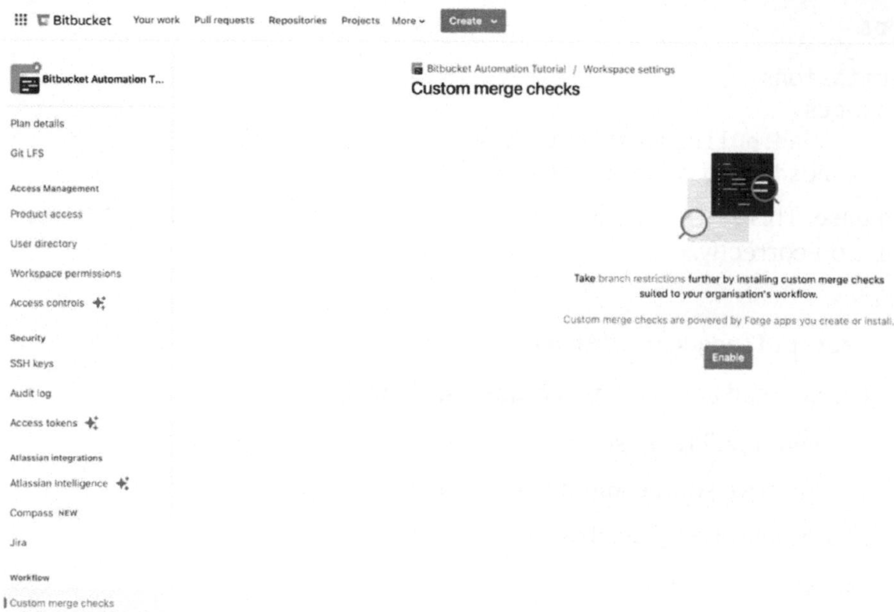


***Figure 10.4**: Forge Custom Merge Checks Workspace Settings*

2. Further enable the custom merge check for the branches you want to protect. In this example, the merge check is being applied to all branches under "**`first-repository`**".

Navigate to:

1. **`Repository settings`** → **`Workflow`** → **`Custom Merge Checks`**
2. Click **`Add check`**, then select the custom merge check from the list.
3. In the **`Add check`** dialog:
    a. **`Check App`**: Displays the unique identifier of the custom merge check.
    b. **`Name`**: A descriptive name for the merge check (for example, **`Bitbucket-Automation-PR-Merge-Check`**).
    c. **`Type`**: Displays as **`PRE-MERGE`**, indicating the check is triggered on pull request merge attempts.
    d. **`Branches`**: Set to **`All branches`** in this example, ensuring the check applies to every branch in the repository.
    e. **`Required`**: The checkbox is selected, making this merge check mandatory for all pull requests on the selected branches.

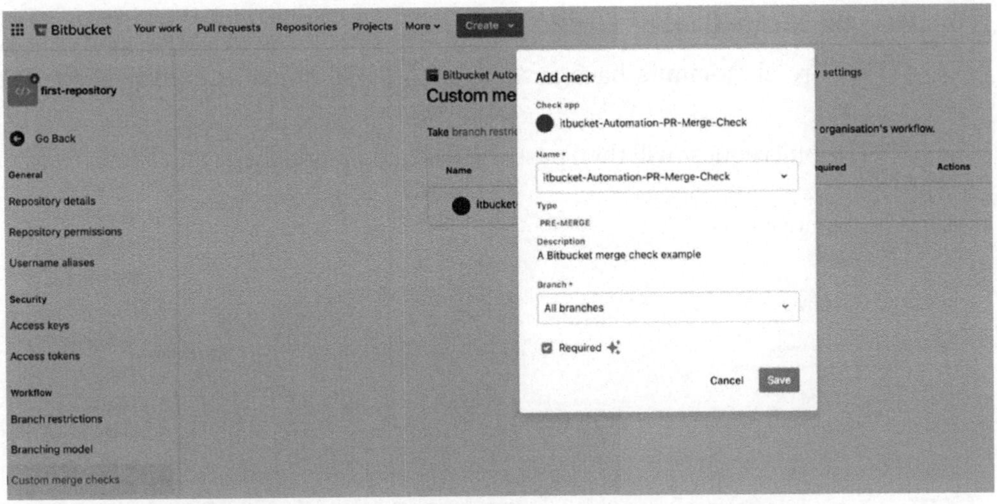


***Figure 10.5**: Forge Custom Merge Checks Repository Settings*

### Testing the Custom Merge Check

1. Open a **`Pull Request`**
   - Open a pull request in the repository where the merge check will be installed.
   - Ensure the pull request contains commits with email addresses that do end with **`@test.com`**.
2. Check the **`Merge Check in Action`**
   - The pull request will be blocked from merging.
   - A message will appear indicating that a commit has an invalid email domain.

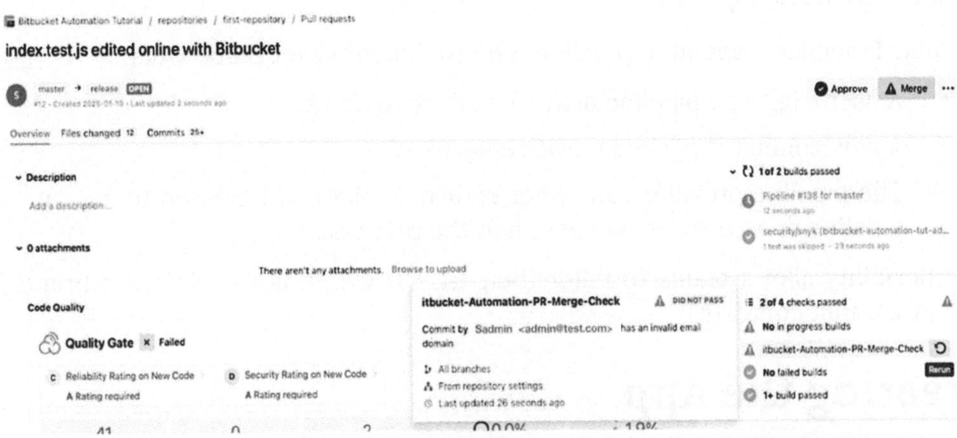


***Figure 10.6**: Failed Custom Merge Checks for Commit Author Email Domain*

3. **Pass the Merge Check**
   - Ensure all commits have authors with email domains ending in **`@gmail.com`**.
   - The pull request will then pass the custom merge check and allow merging.

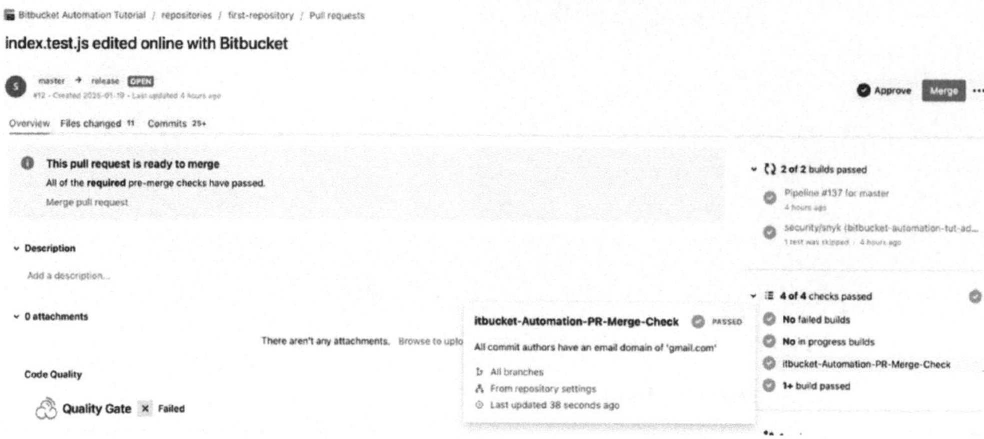


***Figure 10.7**: Passed Custom Merge Checks for Commit Author Email Domain*

# Forge Dynamic Pipelines

Dynamic Pipelines in Bitbucket Cloud allow you to create adaptable and event-driven CI/CD workflows. By using the **`bitbucket:dynamicPipelinesProvider`** module with Forge, you can generate pipeline configurations on the fly. This enables conditional execution of build steps based on branch, commit details, or user triggers, optimizing resources and reducing build times.

### What are Dynamic Pipelines?

Dynamic Pipelines respond to pipeline requests in Bitbucket Cloud when:

- A user triggers a pipeline manually or schedules it.
- A new commit is pushed to the repository.
- The pipeline provider can either return a valid configuration to execute the pipeline or an error message to halt the process.

This flexibility allows teams to tailor their CI/CD workflows to different branches, tags, or commit contexts.

# Creating the App

Generate a new app using the **Dynamic Pipelines Provider** template:

```
forge create
```

- **App Name**: Enter a name such as **`bitbucket-automation-dynamic-pipeline`**
- **Category**: Triggers and Validators
- **Product**: Bitbucket
- **Template: `bitbucket-dynamic-pipelines-provider`**

This creates the basic structure needed for the dynamic pipelines app.

# Setting Permissions

Dynamic Pipelines may need to access repository information such as commits or branches. To enable this, configure the necessary permissions.

Open **`manifest.yml`** and include:

```
permissions:
  scopes:
    - read:repository:bitbucket
```

This grants read access to:

- Commit details
- Branch information
- Repository metadata

These permissions are crucial for the app to analyze the context of the pipeline trigger.

# Adding a Dynamic Step in Dynamic Pipelines

To add a new step to the pipeline configuration dynamically, you need to update the src/index.js file. This modification checks if the default pipeline is selected and then injects a custom step at the beginning of the pipeline. This approach allows you to conditionally adjust pipeline behavior without modifying the static **`bitbucket-pipelines.yml`** file.

## Files to Update

**`src/index.js`:**

- This is the main file containing the pipeline logic.
- You will add a new function to modify the pipeline configuration dynamically.
- You will also update the main function to include the new dynamic step logic.

**Updating `src/index.js`**

**Step 1**: Adding a Dynamic Step Function

Add the following function to **`src/index.js`**:

```
const addDynamicStep = (request) => {
  // Check if the default pipeline configuration is present
  if (!request.pipelines_configuration?.pipelines?.default) {
    return { pipelines_configuration: request.pipelines_
configuration };
  }

  // Add a new step to the start of the default pipeline
  request.pipelines_configuration.pipelines.default = [
    {
      step: {
        name: "Dynamic Step",
        script: ["echo 'This step was added dynamically'"],
      },
    },
    ...request.pipelines_configuration.pipelines.default,
  ];

  return request;
};
```

- **Purpose:**
  - This function checks if the pipeline configuration contains a default definition.
  - If present, it prepends a new step named "Dynamic Step" to the start of the pipeline.
  - This new step runs a simple shell command to print a message.
  - If no default pipeline is defined, the configuration is returned unchanged.
  - This allows you to conditionally modify the pipeline at runtime.
  - It keeps the static bitbucket-pipelines.yml file unchanged while enhancing the workflow.

**Updating the Main Function**

Modify the main function in **`src/index.js`** to call the new **`addDynamicStep()`** function:

```
export const main = (request, context) => {
  // Apply the dynamic step logic to the pipeline configuration
  const updatedRequest = addDynamicStep(request);
```

```
  // Log the updated configuration for debugging
  console.log(`Updated Request: ${JSON.stringify(updatedRequest,
null, 4)}`);

  // Return the modified pipeline configuration to Bitbucket
Pipelines
  return { pipelines_configuration: updatedRequest.pipelines_
configuration };
};
```

- The main function now uses **`addDynamicStep()`** to modify the pipeline request.
- It logs the updated configuration, which helps in debugging when using Forge tunnel.
- It returns the modified configuration to Bitbucket Pipelines, which then runs the dynamic step.

**Deploy the app:**

```
forge deploy
```

# Installing Dynamic Pipelines in Bitbucket Workspace

After deploying, install the app in your Bitbucket workspace:

```
forge install
```

- **Product**: Bitbucket
- **Workspace URL**: `bitbucket.org/{your-workspace-id}` (eg: `bitbucket-automation-tutorial`)

This connects the app to your workspace, allowing it to respond to pipeline requests.

**Configuring Dynamic Pipelines in the Repository**

1. Go to **`Repository Settings`** → **`Pipelines`** → **`Dynamic Pipelines`**
2. Select the dynamic pipelines provider "**`bitbucket-automation-dynamic-pipeline`**".
3. Click **`Save`**.

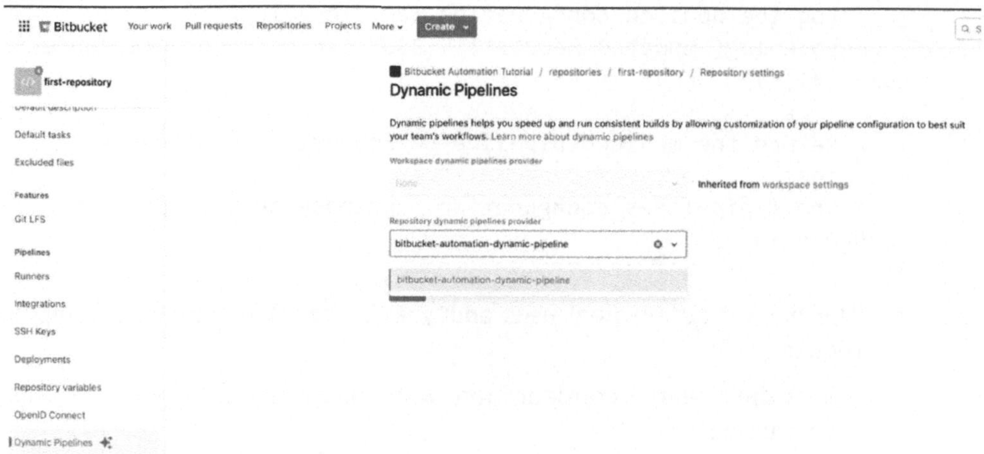


***Figure 10.8***: *Dynamic Pipelines Repository Settings*

This sets the repository to request dynamic pipeline configurations from the Forge app.

**Trigger a pipeline by:**

- Pushing a commit to the configured branch.
- Manually running a pipeline from the Bitbucket UI.

In the pipeline build output, we can observe that the first step of the pipeline is executed dynamically. The step is labeled as "**`Dynamic Step`**" and it displays the message:

echo '**`This step was added dynamically`**'.

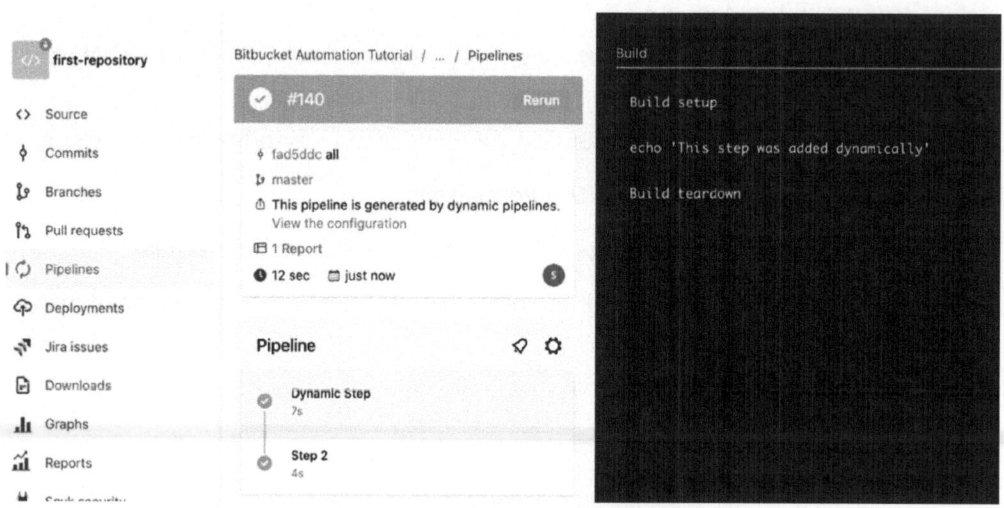


***Figure 10.9***: *Dynamic Pipelines Step*

This indicates that the step was injected into the pipeline configuration at runtime, demonstrating the power of Forge's dynamic pipelines feature.

**Viewing the Dynamic Pipeline Configuration**

We can view the complete configuration by selecting "**`View the configuration`**" in the Bitbucket UI. This displays the dynamically generated pipeline YAML, which includes:

Dynamic pipeline configuration

```
pipelines:
  default:
  - step:
      script:
      - "echo 'This step was added dynamically'"
      type: "inline"
      name: "Dynamic Step"
  - step:
      script:
      - "echo \"api pipeline trigger\""
      type: "inline"

```

***Figure 10.10**: Dynamic Pipelines Step Configuration*

**Testing with Forge Tunnel**

Use Forge tunnel to test the app locally while running the pipelines build:

```
forge tunnel
```

- The tunnel allows real-time logging and immediate feedback.
- You can see the incoming request payload and how the app responds.

**You should see output like:**

```
invocation: 8619083740ae460ca0fa97a6dc4ae5ba index.main
INFO    18:38:41.738  2ba7c167-d02d-4a5d-a805-dc3ce2298aa3
Updated Request: {
    "target": {
        "commit": {
            "hash": "master"
        },
        "type": "pipeline_commit_target"
    },
    "trigger": "definitions",
    "pipelines_configuration": {
```

```
        "pipelines": {
            "default": [
                {
                    "step": {
                        "name": "Dynamic Step",
                        "script": [
                            "echo 'This step was added
dynamically'"
                        ]
                    }
                },
                {
                    "step": {
                        "script": [
                            "echo \"api pipeline trigger\""
                        ],
                        "type": "inline"
                    }
                }
            ]
        }
    },
```

# Conclusion

In this chapter, we explored how to leverage Atlassian Forge and Dynamic Pipelines to automate and enhance CI/CD workflows within Bitbucket Cloud. As modern development environments demand agility and efficiency, automation becomes a key factor in maintaining productivity and consistency. Forge and Dynamic Pipelines provide powerful tools to achieve this through event-driven actions, real-time customizations, and seamless integrations.

# Index

## Symbols



## A

## B

## K



## L



## M



## N



## O



## P